The MU5 Computer System

**Macmillan Computer Science Series**

*Consulting Editor*
Professor F. H. Sumner, University of Manchester

G. M. Birtwistle, *Discrete Event Modelling on Simula*

J. K. Buckle, *The ICL 2900 Series*

Derek Coleman, *A Structured Programming Approach to Data\**

Andrew J. T. Colin, *Programming and Problem-solving in Algol 68\**

S. M. Deen, *Fundamentals of Data Base Systems\**

David Hopkin and Barbara Moss, *Automata\**

A. Learner and A. J. Powell, *An Introduction to Algol 68 through Problems\**

A. M. Lister, *Fundamentals of Operating Systems\**

Brian Meek, *Fortran, PL/I and the Algols*

Derrick Morris and Roland N. Ibbett, *The MU5 Computer System*

I. R. Wilson and A. M. Addyman, *A Practical Introduction to Pascal*

*The titles marked with an asterisk were prepared during the Consulting Editorship of Professor J. S. Rohl, University of Western Australia.

# The MU5 Computer System

Derrick Morris
Roland N. Ibbett

*Department of Computer Science,
University of Manchester*

*First published 1979 by*
THE MACMILLAN PRESS LTD
*London and Basingstoke*
*Associated companies in Delhi Dublin*
*Hong Kong Johannesburg Lagos Melbourne*
*New York Singapore and Tokyo*

Printed in Great Britain by Bell and Bain Ltd.,
Glasgow

**British Library Cataloguing in Publication Data**

Morris, Derrick
    The MU5 computer system.—(Macmillan
    computer science series).
    1. MU5 (Computer system)
    I. Title II. Ibbett, Roland N
    001.6′4044        QA76.5

    ISBN 0–333–25749–9
    ISBN 0–333–25750–2 Pbk

# Contents

This book is dedicated to all those
who contributed to the MU5 Project

# 1 Introduction

MU5 is the fifth computer system to be designed and built at the University of Manchester. The development of the systems leading up to MU5 is described by Lavington [1]. This book is concerned with the design, implementation and performance of MU5. It covers both hardware and software as these have been designed as an integrated system by a closely knit group of 'Engineers' and 'Programmers'. No attempt is made to assign individual credit.

A precise starting date for the project is difficult to pinpoint. Many of the ideas it embodies grew out of the previous Atlas Project. The records show that talks with ICT (later to become ICL) aimed at obtaining their assistance and support began in 1966. An application for a research grant was submitted to the Science Research Council in mid-1967, and a sum of £630 446 spread over 5 years became available in January 1968. In 1968 an outline proposal for the system was presented at the IFIP 68 conference [2]. The feasibility of constructing a big computer system for the amount of the grant relied upon the availability of production facilities, at works cost price, at the nearby ICT West Gorton Works. Even so, the finance was a limiting factor, and it was accepted that the hardware produced would only be a small version of the potentially large system that was to be designed.

The level of staffing may be of some interest. In 1968 a group of 20 people was involved in the design, made up as follows

    11 Department of Computer Science staff
    5 Seconded ICT staff
    4 SRC Supported staff

The peak level of staffing was in 1971 when the numbers, including research students, rose to 60. This fell during the commissioning period to 40. In the evaluation stage, from 1973, only 25 people were involved.

Motivation for the project was twofold. First there was the desire to continue the tradition of designing and building

1

advanced systems, pioneering ideas which could be exploited by the computer industry. In addition there was a requirement for a system to support the research school of the Department of Computer Science. Significant expansion of this research school was planned beginning with the first year of the Computer Science graduates in 1968. Experience had shown that research into hardware/system software could not be carried out on a computing service machine. It is excluded by both the nature of the work and by the excessive computing requirements of the simulation studies, and the automation of hardware and software design which dominate the research.

The design objectives are best covered by the following quotations from the grant application to the Science Research Council dated May 1967. It was felt that a computer should be provided 'off the shelf' to initiate the project.

'The computer required is an ICT 1905E specially fitted with a 750 ns store ... The 1905E will be transformed into a multi (initially 2) computer system by the addition of a completely new high-performance computer with a target throughput of 20 times that of Atlas ... It will be constructed by ICT (their agreement has been obtained) and will be charged at works cost price ... The 1905E, with the proposed modifications in view, will provide a vehicle which permits an immediate start on software developments aimed at the full system programs of the multi-computer system. The system programs will be written in a modular way to facilitate changes and extensions when these are required as the hardware develops.'

Thus the emphasis was on a multi-computer system containing at least one new high-performance machine having a target throughput 20 times that of Atlas.

'This factor will be achieved as follows

(1) Integrated circuits and interconnection techniques will give a basic computing speed of seven times Atlas.

(2) A 250 ns core store will be used, this is eight times the speed of the Atlas store.

(3) The design will include

Fast operand registers
Register to register arithmetic
Multiple arithmetic units

2

Items (1) to (3) will give a factor of about ten, indeed the time for the inner loop of a scalar product is expected to be 1 μs as compared with 12 μs on Atlas.

(4) An instruction set will be provided which will permit the generation of more efficient object code by the compilers. Particular attention will be given to the techniques for computing the addresses of array elements. Array bound checking will be provided as a hardware feature.

(5) The efficiency of the Atlas supervisor is approximately 60%. The provision of special hardware and the information obtained from a detailed study of the Atlas system over the past two years will permit this efficiency to be significantly increased.

Items (4) and (5) will give at least a further factor of two.'

Clearly, performance was to be measured in terms of system throughput rather than raw machine speed. Significant factors were to be sought from optimising the hardware to meet the software requirements and an available production technology was to be used. Indeed the chosen technology was that to be used in the construction of ICT 1906As. However, it was anticipated that associative storage would play a significant role in the system design [3] and that suitable integrated circuit elements would be developed for this purpose.

On the hardware side this book is mainly concerned with the design and implementation of the MU5 processor. However, the design was intended for a range of machines and the actual processor built is one example, which is towards the top of the range, with a scientific bias. The range was intended to go from machines of about PDP-11 cost to a multi-computer system incorporating several MU5s with differing biases at the top of the range. Thus the MU5 built has an 'Exchange' to which reference is made in several places. This is the hardware unit which connects the various computers of the total system. The software description takes into account both the range and the multi-computer aspects.

Although the design team had set themselves the task of designing a range of machines which could be marketed, it had no formal commitment to the computer industry. The ICT involvement was through the secondment of individual members of ICT to the University Team. Nevertheless, it could hardly

3

be fortuitous that the design of the ICL 2900 is so similar to MU5 that in 1969 the possibility of MU5 being marketed as an early member of the 2900 range was seriously considered. After a three-month 'convergence' exercise in early 1970, when the designs were drawn even closer together, the idea was abandoned because of ICL's fear that the cost of maintaining compatibility would outweigh any advantage of early availability. During this period some changes were made to the detailed design of MU5 in the name of compromise, not all of which have been beneficial. Although there has been no attempt to maintain compatibility since that time the MU5 operating system and compilers can be transferred to 2900 with ease. The converse is not true.

Software plans for the project were geared as much to the MU5 multi-computer system and the range concept as to the MU5 processor.

'The initial operating system will be for a single computer system but it will be extended to accommodate additional computers whose structures and order codes are different from those of the 1905E. It will be modular and easily changed in order to accommodate future hardware and software developments. The detailed design of the operating system has not been completed. However, it will have the following features

(1) Some form of file storage and on-line access

(2) Job queueing and scheduling for base load jobs

(3) Priority routes through the system for urgent jobs

(4) The basic supervisor will be kept to a minimum and most of the operating system facilities will run as non-privileged programs.'

Compilers were to be produced using ideas developed from the Atlas Compiler Compiler. The emphasis was to be on efficiency, compactness and machine independence.

These initial objectives remained as the project developed and the reader will judge the extent to which they have been achieved.

4

# 2 The Architecture of the MU5 Processor

The design of the MU5 processor was approached through its order code, this being the natural interface between software requirements and hardware organisation. Full interplay between the two aspects was considered vital throughout the design. Efficient processing of high-level language programs was the prime target. In 'number crunching' applications, this meant a fast execution rate for the high-level language programs. However, the system envisaged would be interactive, and to combat the system overheads this entails, it was considered important to produce small compilers and compiled programs. Thus, an order code was sought which satisfied the following conditions

(1) Generation of efficient code by compilers must be easy

(2) Programs must be compact

(3) The instruction set must allow a pipeline organisation of the CPU leading to a fast execution rate

(4) Information on the nature of operands (scalar or array element, for example) should be available to allow optimal buffering of operands.

In this chapter the order code of MU5 is examined from the point of view of its use and implementation. However, a large part of the order code of such a highly structured system is concerned with address generation, and before discussing this it is appropriate to establish the policy relating to address validation, the mechanism which protects one user from another.

## 2.1 INTERPRETATION OF ADDRESSES

The most far reaching decision in the design of an order code is whether the addresses it generates are real or virtual. If real addresses are generated they will be used directly to access the store. Therefore the address must have been previously validated, as it was being computed, say. The alternative offered by the IBM system, of tagging store blocks

5

to indicate ownership, was not considered flexible enough for a multi-access system in which the core allocation would be constantly changing. In effect, the real address based systems considered require that all address words contain an origin and a limit, and hence relate to bounded contiguous sections of store. Also the CPU must know which words in the store are address words. It then checks that each operand address is calculated from an address word, and that it falls within the specified limits. Since all address words are known to the system, out-of-use information can be moved out of main store until next required, provided the address words involved are appropriately marked and updated. A classic example of this type of machine is the Basic Language Machine [4], although it has never progressed beyond the prototype stage. Also the Burroughs machines since the 5000 series have had a similar type of controlled address formation, and currently the 'capability machines' promote a similar idea. Alternatively, if the order code generates virtual addresses, then special hardware is needed between the CPU and the store to validate the address and translate it into a real address. Sometimes the address will relate to information not in the main store, and the hardware will detect this and initiate its transfer, usually with software assistance. This special hardware may be a single datum and limit as for example in ICL's 1900, or multiple datum and limit as for example in the PDP-11, or a paging system as in Atlas.

The real address based systems have several attractions. Perhaps foremost from the performance point of view is the fact that the address generated by the CPU can be presented directly to the store, thus avoiding the time delay inherent in paging systems. Also the units of information delimited by address words, which would be the units the system might automatically move from one level of store to another, would be complete logical entities (procedures or arrays, for example). It can be argued that this is more efficient than moving fixed-size pages which represent arbitrary fragments of a program and its workspace [5]. The other side of this argument is that the problems of allocating and retrieving store in variable sized areas lead to some store not being utilised, for example because the empty areas may be too small. This has to be offset against the paging problem in which, even when all pages are in use, some will be partially occupied by unwanted information. It is by no means clear where the balance lies.

Two additional considerations led to the choice of virtual addressing for MU5. First it was felt that the most significant task of the operating system was store management, the dominant part of which is concerned with the automatic movement of information between levels of store. Such movement requires that the real addresses of the information moved be changed. If these real addresses are allowed to scatter through each program's private store, this task becomes complex. For example, the address words that require changing because of movement of information between levels of store are themselves subject to moving. Also, the same address might appear in several places. It was felt to be a cleaner solution to hold all information relating to the way a program maps into real store in a separate data structure outside the program and entirely under operating system control.

The second consideration was that a program should not be constrained in the way it might build a data structure within its own workspace by the mechanism for address validation. Close examination of, for example, the system proposed by Iliffe [4] will reveal the awkward constraint that arrays must be homogeneous.

Once the decision to base the system on virtual addressing had been taken, it was not difficult to reject the single datum and limit approach. Although such a system leads to an extremely simple organisation within the operating system, the entire program must be placed in a contiguous area of store each time the CPU is assigned to it. In contrast, one of the main attractions of Atlas had been the large virtual address space available to every user job, which could be used sparsely without significant penalty. For example, the compilers and operating system used the top half of the virtual store, user code was compiled into the bottom quarter, and the next quarter was used for the stack work space. Other smaller entities such as input and output buffers were fitted into the gaps in between. From this informal partitioning of the store on Atlas grew the idea of formalising the division into a segmented virtual store, which is also exploited in the Multics system [6].

In MU5 the final decision was to use a large virtual address, and to subdivide it into a segment number and a displacement within the segment. It was anticipated that large systems would be paged, but that small ones might employ multiple datum and limit registers (one per segment).

2.2 THE ORDER CODE

2.2.1 Choice of Instruction Format

The first step in choosing an instruction format is to decide how many operand addresses an instruction will have. Obviously this is influenced by the size of an operand address. If the

instruction contains only register addresses, so that main
store is addressed indirectly through registers, several
addresses can be accommodated. If full store addresses are to
be used, then one is usually the limit, although some
machines, for example the PDP-11, have variable sized
instructions and allow up to two full store addresses to occur
in the long instructions.

It was decided from the start of the MU5 design that in
order to comply with condition (1) above, there would be an
address form corresponding to each form of operand permitted
by high-level languages. Furthermore it was felt that to have
more than one such operand per instruction would conflict with
conditions (2) and (3). Only one facet of high-level language
programs caused concern on account of this decision. This was
the known high rate of usage of simple instructions such as

$$I := I + 1$$

Clearly, three instructions would be required to implement
this in a one address code. However, the high execution rate
expected of these simple orders and the possibility of them
overlapping with adjacent orders was thought to compensate.
For other reasons the possibility of using addressable fast
registers for frequently used operands or addresses was
rejected in favour of hardware optimisation using associative
memory. First there was the desire to simplify the software by
eliminating the need for optimising compilers. Equally
important though was the desire to have fast procedure entry
and exit, unfettered by the need to dump and restore
registers. Thus through general design considerations the
choice of format was restricted to the zero address (stacking
machine) type or some form of one address code.

From a compiler point of view the stacking machine is
attractive. The simple algorithm for translating from Algol to
Reverse Polish (and hence to stacking machine code) which
forms the basis of the 'Burroughs Compilogram' is a convincing
demonstration of this. Its simplicity stems from the fact that
operands carry directly over to Reverse Polish without any
relative change of position and a simple push down stack is
all that is required to sort the operators into correct
sequence. Consider for example

$$(A + B) * ((C + D) / (E + F))$$

which in Reverse Polish becomes

$$AB + CD + EF + / *$$

There were two arguments which steered the MU5 design away from the stacking machine form. The first is related to efficiency of hand-coding, which is something of a paradox since MU5 is a high-level language machine. However, observations on Atlas indicated that while high-level language programs were running, the CPU typically spent half its time executing in a small set of library procedures concerned with I/O handling, mathematical functions, etc. This basic library would be hand-coded. Thus from the performance point of view, this small amount of hand-coded software was just as important as all the compiler generated code. Unfortunately most of the hand-coded sequences worked out worse in stacking machine code than in single address code. This was because the main calculation, the address calculations and the control counting, tended to interfere with each other on the stack. The problems are illustrated by the following example of a simple move sequence, although either machine could have a single function for this purpose.

Single Address Code                    Stacking Machine Code

LOAD MODIFIER                           STACK MODIFIER
X: ACC = SOURCE[MODIFIER]               X: DUPLICATE
ACC => DEST[MODIFIER]                   DUPLICATE
INC AND TEST MODIFIER                   STACK SOURCE[TOP OF STACK]
IF NOT END BRANCH X                     SWOP
                                        STORE DEST[TOP OF STACK]
                                        STACK 1
                                        SUBTRACT
                                        IF NOT END BRANCH X

The point being made is that a single stack is under pressure when it has to support all the functions involved in counting, address calculation and main calculation. In any given context, detailed changes to the specification of instructions would ease the problem, but only at the expense of it recurring in a different context. A machine with several stacks would have worked better, for example

              a control stack
              an index stack
              an address stack
              the main stack

This sort of arrangement would also fit the pipeline requirement better since the stacks could be distributed along the pipeline.

The second argument against the stacking machine would apply equally to a multi-stack organisation. Consider the

9

example

$$A := B + C$$

For the two types of instruction format under consideration it would be coded as follows

```
ACC = B                    STACK B
ACC + C                    STACK C
                           ADD
ACC => A                   STORE A
```

If the operands normally come from main store the execution times of each of the above sequences would be about the same, since they will be controlled by the access times for A, B and C. However, if an operand buffering scheme is utilised, giving a high hit-rate (say > 90%) for operands such as A, B and C, the access time to the stack becomes important. On MU5 the stack and the operand buffers would be the same speed, and the above example would have caused six stack accesses in addition to the three operand accesses. Some, but not all, of the accesses could have been overlapped.

The instruction format eventually chosen for MU5 represented a merger of single address and stacking machine concepts. All the arithmetic and logical functions take one operand from an accumulator and the other operand is specified in the instruction address. Thus a sequence such as

```
ACC = B
ACC + C
ACC => A
```

typifies the style of simple calculations. However, there is a stack, and a variant of the load order (*=) causes the accumulator to be stacked before being re-loaded. Also a special address form exists (STACK) which unstacks the last stacked quantity. Thus, the above example could be written in MU5 code in a form approximating to Reverse Polish, as follows

```
ACC = B
ACC *= C
ACC + STACK
ACC => A
```

A more realistic use of the stack is in conjunction with parenthesised subexpressions. For example, the expression

$$(A + B) * ((C + D) / (E + F))$$

would compile into

```
ACC = A
ACC + B
ACC *= C
ACC + D
ACC *= E
ACC + F
ACC /: STACK
ACC * STACK
```

It is interesting to observe that if the operand to the left of an operator is stacked, it subsequently appears as the right hand side of a machine function. Therefore, for the non-commutative operations '-' and '/', the reverse operations denoted '-:' and '/:' have to be provided. In the notation used throughout this book

```
ACC / OPERAND    means    ACC = ACC / OPERAND
ACC /: OPERAND   means    ACC = OPERAND / ACC
                 etc.
```

Only one stack is provided in MU5, but there are five 'accumulators' or 'computational registers'. Each may stack its contents, and hence the effect is the same as having five stacks, provided the order of unstacking corresponds to the way the stacked quantities are interleaved. This condition is usually met. If it were not, the conventional stacking machine would not be acceptable. The significant difference in MU5 is that the top words of each of the five stacks are simultaneously available in the computational registers. Each of the registers serves a dedicated function and they are distributed along the pipeline in close proximity to the arithmetic unit associated with that function. These arithmetic units are

The B-unit - used for index arithmetic and control counting

The D-unit - used for address modification and bound checking

The A-unit - the main arithmetic unit providing fixed-point, floating-point and decimal facilities

The registers are

```
B       - a 32-bit modifier register
DR      - a 64-bit register for vector 'descriptors'
XDR     - similar to DR and used by the string move orders
X       - a 32-bit fixed-point register in the A-unit
A(ACC)  - a 64-bit register in the A-unit.
```

11

The existence of two registers X and A in the main arithmetic unit is largely historical, although there is some advantage in being able to perform control calculations in X without disturbing a partial result in A. Originally the system had two registers in the B-unit. These were notionally thought of as a modifier (BM) and an integer accumulator (BA) to be used for control calculations. However, the order code was symmetrical allowing both to be used as modifiers, and this could be usefully exploited in some of the hand-coded library procedures. During the 'convergence' exercise with ICL, the BA register was forfeited and replaced by the X register in the A-unit. However, the success of the pipeline approach described later is dependent upon the control and address calculations proceeding independently of the queue of orders waiting for the A-unit. Thus as well as being used as a modifier, B may also be used for simple integer calculations such as

$$I := I - J + 2$$

The X register is only used when the operands of the calculation require B to be used as a modifier, or when the operation is not provided by the B-unit (divide, for example).

The instruction format provided for operating on these registers is

| CR | F | ADDRESS |
|----|---|---------|
| 3  | 4 | 9       |

One combination of the CR (computation register) bits distinguishes a second format for the 'Organisational Instructions' concerned with control branching and manipulation of 'addressing' registers. The remaining seven combinations qualify the function (F) as follows

1 fixed-point operations on B
2 fixed-point operations on X
3 floating-point operations on A
4 decimal operation on A
5 unsigned fixed-point operations on A
  (used for multi-length working)
6 manipulation of DR and XDR
7 string processing functions (mainly for Cobol)

Even with these seven groups of functions, the existence of only four function (F) bits is restrictive, but the operators necessary for high-level language translation can be accommodated. It is the orders more commonly associated with hand-coding, such as shift operators, that have to be curtailed. This was not felt to be a serious omission because

12

such orders are used mainly for the selection of packed operands which in MU5 is carried out automatically by the D-unit. Groups 6 and 7 are discussed later.

There is close similarity in the functions provided in groups 1-5, the following being typical

|  |  |
|---|---|
| = | load (32-bit operand) |
| =' | load (64-bit operand) |
| *= | stack and load |
| => | store |
| + | add |
| - | subtract |
| * | multiply |
| / | divide |
| -= | logical non-equivalence (exclusive or) |
| V | logical or (inclusive or) |
| <- | shift |
| & | logical and |
| -: | reverse subtract |
| COMP | compare |
| CINC | compare and increment |
| /: | reverse divide |

In the case of organisational instructions it was felt that more functions were needed, so the address field was shortened to give the format

$$CR = 0 \quad F' \quad ADDRESS$$
$$3 \qquad 6 \qquad 7$$

These F' functions are summarised in Appendix 1. It can be seen that they fall into four main groups, namely

    Control transfers including procedure entry and exit
    addressing register manipulation
    conditional control transfers
    boolean

Some of the procedure entry functions (XC0, XC1, ..., XC6) provide entry to seven groups of Operating System procedures. Their action is to stack the operand, which defines the Operating System procedure required; then after setting the executive mode bit (section 2.3.1) they force control to fixed addresses in the Operating System. This controlled entry to Operating System is vital in maintaining the security of the system. Another form of entry to the Operating System occurs as a result of an 'interrupt' (section 2.3.1).

The addressing register manipulating functions are

13

self-explanatory. They are used mainly at procedure entry and exit time to achieve the effects described in section 2.2.2.

Conditional control transfers usually only branch a short distance. Therefore to help keep instruction sizes down their operands are interpreted as relative addresses to be added into the Control Register. As a further minor convenience to the software writers, provision is made for the complementary form of each standard condition to be specified (both '>' and '≤' are provided, for example). The shortage of functions precludes the possibility of the tests applying to the registers. Instead, they apply to condition bits which are set by the compare (COMP) and compare and increment (CINC) functions.

There are two kinds of boolean function included in the order code to facilitate the implementation of boolean statements in Algol-like languages. Both allow the standard logical operations to be applied to the Boolean Register BN and a boolean operand. In one set the least significant bit of the instruction operand is taken as the boolean operand, while in the other the operand part of the instruction is used to extend the function, and it defines the operation. The function itself specifies a conditional test to be applied to the condition bits. The result of this test is taken as the boolean operand.

The use of these boolean functions is demonstrated by the translation of the Algol conditional statement

        IF (a = b OR x > y) AND t THEN 'ST1' ELSE 'ST2';

where a and b are type INTEGER, x and y are type REAL and t is type BOOLEAN. With only straightforward local optimisation it is

```
                    B = a
                    B COMP b
                    BN = IF=
                    ACC = x
                    ACC COMP y
                    BN V IF >
                    BN & t
                    BN -= 1
                    IF BN, -> L1
                    'ST1'
                    -> L2
                    L1:
                    'ST2'
                    L2:
```

14

Unfortunately it was realised too late that the function
'IF~BN' should have been provided, hence BN sometimes has to
be inverted before the test as in the above example. It could
be eliminated if the compilers were clever enough to compile
code to compute the 'not' of the condition.

Until the mechanics of address generation have been
described, the example below may not be completely understood.
It is given at this point to emphasise the close
correspondence between the high-level language form of
arithmetic assignments and the machine code. Each line except
the JUMP order would be a 16-bit instruction if the example
was taken from an average Algol program.

$$W := Z[I - 1] * F + C(P,Q) / Y[J * 3 + K];$$

becomes

```
                    B = I
                    B - 1
                    ACC = Z[B]
                    ACC * F
                    STACK ACC
                    STACK LINK L1
                    STACK P
                    STACK Q
                    JUMP C
            L1:     B = J
                    B * 3
                    B + K
                    ACC / Y[B]
                    ACC + STACK
                    ACC => W
```

The total size is 32 bytes and this includes automatic
bound checks on Z and Y. The reader is invited to compare this
with the size of the corresponding sequence on other machines.

2.2.2 Address Generation

The aims of having an address form for each kind of high-level
language operand, and having compact instructions conflict. It
was therefore decided to allow different sizes of address and
to choose an encoding which represented the most common
operand forms in the shortest addresses. It was also decided
to have dedicated addressing registers whose functions relate
to the layout of the data space of high-level languages,
rather than general purpose modifiers. This helps to satisfy
conditions (3) and (4) as well as keeping the address size
down.

15

An examination of the operands in high-level languages indicates that provision should be made for

        SCALARS
        ELEMENTS FROM ARRAYS OR OTHER STRUCTURES
        STRINGS
        LITERALS
        FUNCTIONS (PROCEDURE CALLS)

Also the procedure organisation of languages allows operands to be

        LOCAL (to the current procedure)
        NON-LOCAL (or COMMON)
        GLOBAL
        STACKED

Clearly the scalar variables have names and provision is made in the order code to accommodate these names together with an indication of whether they are local or non-local, etc. This identification of names becomes very important when considering the hardware design of the processor. Studies of programs run on Atlas indicated that over a large range of programs, 80% of all operand accesses were to the named operands, and that only a small number of these named operands was in frequent use at any one time. Thus a system which kept these operands in fast registers would be able to achieve high performance, but for the reasons already discussed, the use of addressable fast registers was rejected. The alternative solution adopted in MU5 involves the use of an associatively addressed 'Name Store' which forms part of a 'one-level store' with the main store of the processor, and in which the allocation of named operands to registers is performed solely by the hardware.

It has already been mentioned that the design of MU5 incorporates a special functional unit (the D-unit) for providing access to arrays, strings and other structures. The route into these structures is via 'descriptors' which are themselves accessed like scalars. Thus the operand accesses for the named operands consist of a 'primary' access for an operand which could be a SCALAR or an ARRAY DESCRIPTOR, and in the latter case the operand is passed to the D-unit for it to make a 'secondary' access. This detachment of secondary address from the instruction fulfils two purposes. Not only is it the means whereby instructions are kept short, but it also facilitates the implementation of dynamic allocation of space to arrays and the handling of array parameters in procedures. For convenience at compile time, provision is made for literals of up to 64 bits to be coded explicitly into the

16

instruction. Also, to provide the generality required for the Algol-like languages, a mechanism for procedure calling is integrated into the stack concept.

Before considering the address generation in detail it is necessary to describe the intended store layout and the function of the dedicated addressing registers. These are

NB     a pointer to the scalars and descriptors of the current procedure

XNB    a pointer used to access any non-local or common scalars and descriptors

SF     a pointer to the stack

0      this is a pseudo-register always giving zero for access to global scalars and descriptors

The overall storage organisation provides each program with a segmented virtual store. One segment (or more in the case of languages which allow parallelism) is used for the named operands and the stack (the scalars and descriptors), while the rest are used for code and the secondary operands (elements of arrays and other structures). The segment holding the named operands is called the Name Segment or Procedure Stack. Its layout is given below.

```
! DISPLAY ! GLOBALS ! 1st PROC ! ---- ! CURRENT PROC !
                       ↑                ↑
                      NB               SF
```

There is a 'level of stack' in the Name Segment associated with each activated procedure, which is released when the procedure ends. Each level starts with a 'Link' to be used to exit from the procedure. The parameters and the local named variables of the procedure follow. Thus on entry to a new procedure, the Link (containing the return control address and NB) is stacked, next the parameters are stacked, and finally the procedure is entered. Inside the procedure NB is set to the address of the Link, and SF is advanced over the space required by the local names. SF may be further incremented, as operands are stacked, by means of the *= function and decremented, as they are unstacked, by means of the special operand STACK. In the case of languages which allow non-local access to the names of other procedures, an entry is also made in the Display.

The Display has one entry for each textual level in the program. Each time a procedure is called the NB value for the procedure is recorded in the entry corresponding to its textual level. Any non-local references to the variables of the procedure from nested subblocks are implemented by loading

17

XNB from the Display and then accessing relative to XNB. In recursive situations it is necessary to stack the old Display value on procedure entry, so that it may be re-set on exit. This mechanism is obviously geared to the dynamic storage allocation of Algol-like languages. If the allocation scheme is static, as in Fortran, the Display does not exist and XNB is used to address 'common' variables. The global variables at the beginning of the stack segment are conceptually 'own' variables. They are permanently allocated, and hence can remember information between different calls of a procedure. Exit from a procedure requires that the Display be re-set if it was stacked on entry, then SF is re-set to NB, and NB and control are re-set by unstacking the Link.

Thus the standard procedure call is a minimum of two instructions

        STACK LINK      L1
        JUMP            procedure name
        L1:

If the procedure has parameters, additional instructions are needed between these two to stack each parameter. Inside a procedure which has no nested procedures making non-local access to its names there will be three more instructions concerned with the 'red tape' of procedure calling.

        NB = SF - space accepted by LINK and PARAMETERS
        SF = SF + space required for local names
        .
        .
        .
        EXIT

The more general case involves manipulation of the Display as already described.

For reasons which will become clear after the buffering strategies are described, the Name Segment is not used for arrays. Therefore the software must run its own 'secondary stack' for dynamically declared arrays.

A point of detail to which reference is made later is that NB and SF are 16-bit registers. They always address into the Name Segment whose number is specified by a separate register (SN) usually zero and rarely changed. XNB is a 32-bit register containing segment and position within segment. Thus XNB based names can be in any segment. Full 32-bit addresses are also used in the Display, hence the Cactus Stack of Algol 68 can be implemented.

18

## 2.2.3 Address Encoding

The machine is designed to recognise that high-level language operands are referenced by name (or are constants). Hence the instruction addresses correspond to names (or literal constants).

In the 16-bit instruction format the encoding chosen is

$$CR(3) \qquad F(4) \qquad k(3) \qquad N(6)$$

or in the case of organisational functions

$$CR=0 \qquad F'(6) \qquad k'(1) \qquad N(6)$$

The N field corresponds to the operand name; thus the first declared name has $N = 0$ the second $N = 1$, etc. Of the eight combinations of k, which notionally specifies the kind of name, one is reserved to distinguish an extended address, and the rest are

| | |
|---|---|
| $k = 0$ | use N as a 6-bit signed literal |
| $k = 1$ | use N as a register name (B, DR, etc.) |
| $k = 2$ | use N as the name of a 32-bit local scalar |
| | i.e. operand is 32-bit store line (NB+N) |
| $k = 3$ | use N as the name of a 64-bit local scalar |
| | i.e. operand is 64-bit store line (NB+2N) |
| $k = 4$ | use N as above but pass operand to the D-unit |
| | for a modified secondary access (name[B]) |
| $k = 5$ | spare |
| $k = 6$ | as $k = 4$ but secondary access is unmodified |
| | i.e. name[0] |

Obviously only two of the above forms can be associated with k' and these are

| | |
|---|---|
| $k' = 0$ | use N as a signed literal |
| $k' = 1$ | extended address |

There are three other requirements not met by the above which have to be provided by the extended address of longer instructions. First, there are the names relative to the other addressing registers, XNB, 0, SF (the non-locals, the globals and the stacked operands, respectively). Second, there are the local variables in procedures where more names are declared than can be encoded in the 6-bit N. Third, there are the literals bigger than six bits. Thus both the k field and the N field have to be extended, and the general form of extended instruction has the 32-bit format

19

```
          CR(3)        F(4)       7(3)       K(6)
          N'(16)
```

From the detailed encoding of K (given in Appendix 1) it can be seen that in some cases the N' is omitted and the instruction again reduces to 16 bits. Also, in the case of literals, more 16-bit pieces may be added up to a maximum instruction size of 80 bits.

## 2.2.4 Secondary Operands

In order to access data structure elements, descriptors are passed to the D-unit, together with an indication of whether or not modification is required. The unmodified descriptor is retained in the DR register and can be used again. If modification is specified the modifier is taken from B.

Two main types of descriptor are provided. They are

| String Descriptors | Ts | LENGTH | ORIGIN |
|---|---|---|---|
| | 8 | 24 | 32 |
| Vector Descriptors | Tv | BOUND | ORIGIN |
| | 8 | 24 | 32 |

String descriptors describe strings of bytes. If the string is short enough it can be accessed as a normal operand. Short strings are always right justified and filled out to the register size with zeros. A more usual use of the string descriptor is in conjunction with the string processing functions.

In the vector descriptors the type bits (Tv) control the modification, and give the size of element in the array. This may be 1, 2, 4, 8, 16, 32, 64 or 128 bits, but the present MU5 hardware does not implement the sizes 2 and 128. As with strings, short operands are right justified and zero filled. Normally the modifier is checked against the bound (and that it is $\geq$ 0), and an interrupt is caused if the check fails. Before addition of the modifier and origin occurs, the modifier is scaled. This means that the displacement caused by modification is in units of element size. Special bits within the type allow both the bound check and the scaling to be inhibited.

The introduction of arithmetic type into descriptors was considered, but its extension to the named operands, which could not be dynamically typed except at the individual word level, seemed less attractive. Since the benefits were not tangible in a machine intended for high-speed execution of the

20

standard programming languages, the idea was dropped. For the few occasions where the operand type is not known at compile time, a software escape is provided through a special descriptor type which forces a procedure call whenever it is used. The main use of this mechanism though, is in the implementation of Algol 'thunks'.

It has been a constant source of regret that only one bound could be fitted into the final descriptor format. Until the 'convergence' exercise the design was based on the following descriptor format containing two bounds

| LOWER BOUND | UPPER BOUND | TYPE/ORIGIN |
|:-:|:-:|:-:|
| 16 | 16 | 32 |

This had the additional advantage that programs which forfeited the bound checking could use 32-bit descriptors. The main argument in favour of the alternative format was based on the need for a very large virtual address. In the original MU5 descriptor the address size changed with element size, being 24 bits for 32-bit elements, 25 bits for 16-bit elements and so on. Experience with the MU5 system to date indicates that the above address, giving 256 segments each of 1/4 Mbyte size, would have been more than adequate. Of course the 16-bit bounds were marginally restrictive and the hardware bound check had to be forfeited in some very large programs. To compensate for the loss of double bound checking, facilities are provided for the XDR register to point to a 'dope vector' while the address of an element in a multi-dimensional array is built up in DR. This dope vector contains triples, which are the two bounds and the multiplier (or stride), for each dimension. Each subscript is computed in B and a special function is then used which checks against both bounds and computes the displacement before adding it into DR.

Another deficiency of the present format is that string descriptors apply only to byte strings. In an earlier design strings could be of any size of element from single bits up to words. This, combined with the ability to manipulate complete strings (provided they were not too big) in the registers, was a powerful means of handling the 'structures' of more modern languages such as Algol 68. Perhaps too much emphasis was placed on Cobol and Fortran, and the growing importance of the Algol 68 type of data structures in, for example, system programming languages not fully appreciated. Even so, the descriptor system, which is common to both MU5 and ICL 2900, offers more facilities in support of Algol 68 than most machines.

## 2.2.5 Array Operations

The instructions and operand forms available for vector operations in a conventional language are now examined in more detail. Data structures, and fields within such structures, are described using vector descriptors of the form

$$Tv \qquad BOUND \qquad ORIGIN$$

The type bits (Tv) include the size of each element of the vector, which may be between 1 and 64 bits. The Bound Field contains the number of elements in the vector, while the Origin Field comprises the address of the start of the vector. The instructions required to access element i of a vector z are

        B = i           Load the B (modifier) register
                                    with the subscript i
    ACC = z[B]      accumulator = the Bth element of z

The instruction ACC = z[B] first loads the descriptor z into the DR register. Then B is scaled according to element size, added to the origin of DR and the required element is accessed. Simultaneously, a check is made that B is in the range $0 \leq B < Bound$, and an interrupt occurs if this check fails. This coding, and that in subsequent examples, assumes that the lower bound of the array is zero. If this is not the case, an additional instruction is needed to subtract the lower bound from B. On conventional machines, even omitting the bound check, several orders are used to access a dynamic array element. This is the principal reason why many compilers attempt to optimise subscript calculations.

A simple example of the use of vector accessing orders is the scalar product loop

        FOR i := 1 STEP 1 UNTIL n DO
        sum := sum + x[i] * y[i];

which becomes

                B = 1
        LOOP: B => i
                ACC = x[B]
                ACC * y[B]
                ACC + sum
                ACC => sum
                B CINC n
                IF /=, ->LOOP

22

This assumes that the compiler optimises out three unnecessary B = i orders but that it does not optimise to the extent of moving the B => order to outside the loop. Hence the loop comprises seven 16-bit instructions. The performance of this loop is discussed in Chapter 11.

The group 6 functions mentioned above are concerned with manipulating descriptors and the registers of the D-unit. Some of these functions, namely DR=, SUB1, SUB2 appear in the examples below. A full list is contained in Appendix 1.

A descriptor z may describe a vector of descriptors so that the sequence

```
B  = i
DR  = z[B]
B  = j
ACC = DR[B]
```

could be used to access an element z[i,j] of a two dimensional array. Use of a multiplication technique with the subscript arithmetic taking place in B has the advantage that the subscript calculation is independent of operations queued for the main accumulator. It does, however, require a fast multiply function in the B-unit. In this case z[i,j] becomes

```
B = i
B * n
B + j
ACC = z[B]
```

In this case only the final access, not individual subscripts, is bound checked.

A further, more elaborate, hardware facility is provided to deal with the full generality of array accessing in Algol. This is convenient for arrays with dynamic upper and lower bounds, or cross-sections of arrays. It uses a dope vector containing three 32-bit elements for each dimension, namely, a lower bound which is subtracted from the subscript, an upper bound against which the subscript value is checked, and a stride by which the subscript is multiplied. The hardware instructions SUB1 and SUB2 use this dope vector for such subscript calculations. Thus z[i,j] with full bound checking becomes

```
B = i
SUB1 z1      process first subscript using dope vector z1
B = j
SUB2         process next subscript
```

23

```
B = DO        move composite subscript to B
ACC = z[B]    access element
```

The SUB1 order causes the XDR register to be loaded with the descriptor of the dope vector and, after bound checking B, it sets the origin of the DR register (DO) to the product of (B - lower bound) and the stride of the first triple. Each subsequent application of the SUB2 order steps DO on to the next triple, and after bound checking the value in B, it adds the product (B - lower bound) * (stride) into DO.

## 2.2.6  String and Vector Operations

Special purpose orders are provided for the string processing functions which occur in Cobol and PL/1. These fall into two classes string-to-string and byte-to-string. The string-to-string orders operate on two fields, or strings, each described by a descriptor. The descriptor of the destination string is held in the DR register while that for the source string is held in a second descriptor register, XDR. As the operation of the instruction proceeds, the descriptors in DR and XDR move along the strings. No visible register is used by the strings themselves. The operand of the order is an 8-bit mask, that determines which bits within each byte are to be operated on, together with an 8-bit filler and in some cases four 'function' digits used as described below. Provision is made in the hardware for these orders to be interrupted (section 7.4.3). Examples of the orders are

SMVB  Move one byte from the source to the destination string, or use the filler byte if the source is exhausted.

SMVF  Move the whole source string to the destination string followed by filler bytes if the source is shorter than the destination.

SCMP  Compare the source and destination strings byte by byte ending when inequality is found, or the destination string is exhausted.

SLGC  Logically combine the source and destination strings into the destination. The form of combination (logical OR, for example) is selected by the 'function' bits in the operand.

Consider the use of these orders in the implementation of the MOVE verb in Cobol. Suppose that two fields C and D are specified

24

```
            02      C      PIC      X(7)
            02      D      PIC      X(7)
```

In MU5 descriptors would be created at compile time for C and D, each describing a 7-byte field starting at the required byte address. The Cobol sentence

```
                    MOVE C TO D
```

would then become in MU5 instructions

```
        XDR = C       set source descriptor for C
        DR  = D       set destination descriptor for D
        SMVF          move the field described by XDR to that
                      described by DR
```

If D is specified as

```
            02      D      PIC      X(9)
```

then the final two bytes of D must be spaces. The filler option of SMVF allows this to be carried out automatically. The sequence becomes

```
                    XDR = C
                    DR  = D
                    SMVF 'space'
```

If the source field is too long, then the SMVF order terminates when the destination field is full, and an optional interrupt enables this condition to be monitored if required.

   Extension of the above technique to vector operations of a mathematical form was considered. For example a vector add of the form

$$F := F + E$$

would become

```
                    DR  = F
                    XDR = E
                    VECTOR ADD
```

However, in the standard high-level languages for which MU5 was intended, operations of this type would be programmed out into loops. Thus the idea was dropped in favour of a pipeline approach which would lead to execution rates for such loops approaching the peak rate at which the store could deliver the vector operands.

## 2.3 ORGANISATION OF THE HARDWARE

The design of the hardware of the MU5 Processor initially centred around the Name Store and the descriptor mechanism. Simulation studies of the Name Store indicated that a hit-rate of around 99% could be obtained with 32 words of store. The special associative circuits designed for this store were expected to be capable of operation in 70 (later to become 40) ns, but an additional 70 ns was necessary to read the value from the conventional field. However, a fixed-point arithmetic unit could be constructed to perform simple functions such as addition and subtraction in under 50 ns, using the MECL 2.5 technology from which MU5 was to be built, and clearly the two activities in the Name Store would have to be overlapped if the store speed was to approach the arithmetic speed. Furthermore, the addition, of name to base register, required a comparable amount of time, and so the design was based on an instruction pipeline (with 5 stages) eventually called the Primary Operand Unit (or PROP). PROP would receive instructions at its input and supply at its output functions and primary operands ready for execution or further interpretation by the descriptor system.

The descriptor system was seen to require two logically distinct pieces of hardware, one to form addresses (the Descriptor Addressing Unit) and one to select the operand from within the corresponding store word (the Descriptor Operand Processing Unit). These two parts, known individually as Dr and Dop, formed the D-unit. The A-unit (containing principally the floating-point execution hardware) clearly had to be placed after Dop in the overall design of the Processor, since it would be processing the array elements accessed by the D-unit. In contrast the B-unit was better placed in parallel with the Descriptor Addressing Unit, since it was to supply modifier values, and would, therefore, operate mostly on named quantities rather than array elements. Thus the final configuration of the Processor became that shown in figure 2.1. PROP is supplied with instructions by the Instruction Buffer Unit (IBU), and the virtual to real address translation takes place within the Store Access Control Unit (SAC), which coordinates requests to the Local Store. SAC also developed into a pipeline structure, to keep pace with the demands of the other units.

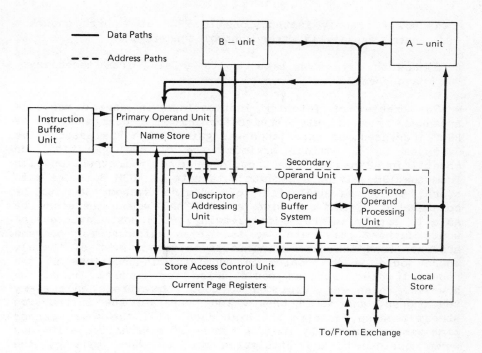

Figure 2.1 The MU5 Processor

A number of consequences flowed from the adoption of this
configuration, particularly in relation to the positioning of
the Control Point (the position an instruction must reach
before the Control Register, or Program Counter, is
incremented). On the one hand the Control Point should be as
far along the pipeline as possible so that any interrupts
caused by an instruction can occur before the Control Register
is altered, while on the other hand it should be as early in
the pipeline as possible, since fewer instructions must then
be discarded (and hence replaced) if the wrong sequence of
instructions is proceeding behind a control transfer
instruction. The need to preserve the state of the Processor
at an interrupt is also important, so the fact that
instructions alter registers at different points along the
pipeline has to be considered carefully. In MU5 it was decided
that the Control Point should be placed at the end of PROP,
which itself executes all the organisational orders, and from
which point orders proceeding to the B-unit can be guaranteed
to complete. Furthermore, each instruction reaching the end of
PROP will have obtained its primary operand or given a page
fault interrupt due to its unavailability. Having made the
Control Point decision, there remained two problems

27

(1) how to supply instructions to PROP at a high enough rate, especially after control transfers,

(2) how to deal with page faults arising from secondary accesses.

The problem of fetching instructions in normal sequence appeared comparatively straightforward. The design speed of PROP increased, as experience was gained with the associative circuits, to a nominal maximum rate of one operation, or 'beat', in 40 ns. Each beat could require 16 instruction bits from the IBU, giving a maximum data rate of 400M Bps. The main store, a 250 ns cycle-time plated-wire system, was to be constructed of 128-bit wide stacks, and would therefore be able to supply, without interleaving, 500M Bps. Interleaving would improve this rate, so that even allowing for operand accesses (and the Name Store would intercept most of these), there would be no problem in supplying instructions at the required rate. Problems would arise for control transfers, however. These were expected to occur on average once every ten orders, and would create long gaps in the instruction stream because, despite the high data rate, the store access time was comparatively long. A number of alternative solutions were considered, and simulation studies were made of the different possibilities. The solution chosen is based on a 'Jump Trace' mechanism (section 4.1), which attempts to predict the result of an impending control transfer instruction. Consideration of measurements taken from Atlas, and simulation studies of this system, showed that it was possible to predict correctly the sequence of instructions following control transfers in about 65% of cases, and that only eight lines of Jump Trace store would be necessary to obtain this efficiency.

The problem of page fault interrupts caused by secondary operand accesses is also tied in with the access time/data rate problem. Considering this latter problem first, the time gap between the generation of a secondary operand address, and the receipt of the corresponding store word, was expected to be over 600 ns. Since floating-point addition and subtraction would take only around 100 ns, this figure was unacceptably high. However, the difference between the access patterns for named variables and data structure elements precluded the use of a system corresponding directly to the Name Store for secondary operands. In effect, a small group of named variables is generally used repeatedly, while a large group of data structure elements is generally selected sequentially. Therefore the technique adopted was a 'Function Queue'. As each address is generated by Dr, the corresponding function, together with control information, is entered into the Queue.

28

A function leaves the Queue when the word containing its operand is received from store. Since the store accessing system is itself a form of pipeline, the effective access time is reduced by a factor corresponding to the number of positions in the Queue. In a synchronous system, no extra operand buffering would be required, but because the MU5 Processor operates asynchronously, it is essential that as many buffers as Queue positions be available to receive the returning store words. Thus an Operand Buffering System (OBS) became an essential part of the Processor design. This system, together with the D-unit, forms the Secondary Operand Unit (SEOP). Simulation studies of this system showed that by fetching 128-bit store words containing the required operand, and retaining these words in associatively addressed buffers, many operands are thereby automatically pre-fetched, and the corresponding store requests avoided.

A significant fraction of the access time for secondary operands is taken up with generating a virtual address and obtaining either a real address or a page fault interrupt. In the case where such an interrupt arises, however, the Control Register will have been incremented on beyond the address of the corresponding instruction. Therefore in order to be able to re-execute the instruction after the interrupt has been serviced, the Queue is designed to contain all functions for which store requests are outstanding. The Page Registers can then be manipulated by the Operating System using orders which do not involve the Queue, or, if a process change is required, the whole of the Queue and its associated buffer registers can be preserved (for subsequent restoration) in the store, thereby unblocking the Queue and allowing other processes to be run.

The inclusion of a Queue in the design generates additional problems because of the different types of operand to be sent to the A-unit. ACC orders using named variables are ready for execution at the end of PROP, but since orders must be obeyed in correct program sequence, they cannot be allowed to overtake ACC orders awaiting secondary operands. Various solutions to this problem are possible, but the one adopted in MU5 is to send all ACC orders through SEOP, by providing a bypass to the descriptor mechanism for named variables. A second problem is the long separation of the A-unit from the Name Store in PROP. Thus if a name held in the PROP Name Store were to be used to accumulate a total calculated by ACC orders in a small program loop, the order reading the total from the Name Store would have to be held up until the value calculated by the previous pass through the loop had been returned. The solution adopted to overcome this problem is the provision of some buffering for named variables used by ACC orders close to

29

the A-unit, the logical place for which is within the Operand Buffer System. Thus OBS actually contains 8 lines x 128 bits of Vector Store, 24 lines x 64 bits of Name Store together with 8 lines x 64 bits for literals supplied by PROP. The hardware automatically ensures that names used with ACC functions are normally kept in OBS, and names used with non-ACC functions in PROP, and also deals with any necessary interactions.

## 2.3.1 Interrupts

In the previous section we were mainly concerned with the normal execution of instructions, but the design must also provide for exception conditions which give rise to interrupts. Already mentioned is the page fault, or non-equivalence, interrupt which is discussed more fully in section 9.3. There are other interrupts, and they can be broadly classified into

> program based interrupts
> external event based interrupts
> system error interrupts

Examples of the first kind are

> the CPR non-equivalence interrupt
> illegal store access interrupts
> descriptor faults (e.g. bound check fail)
> arithmetic overflow

of the second kind

> transfer complete interrupts
> timer interrupt

and of the third kind

> parity error
> power failure warning

From the point of view of hardware organisation, the first group are the most difficult to deal with, because ideally they require the pipeline to stop precisely on or before the instruction causing the interrupt. In the case of arithmetic faults in the A-unit, for example, a precise interrupt can only be obtained if there is no overlapping of instructions between the A-unit and the Control Point, a situation quite at variance with the hardware design. Imprecision of arithmetic interrupts can generally be tolerated, however, and in cases where precise interrupts are essential, the overlapping of orders in the pipeline can be inhibited by program. In fact, by using a register-register order which stores the content of the ACC into an imaginary 'Z' register in the B-unit, no further orders can leave PROP until the A-unit has completed all outstanding orders (section 4.2.4). Normally this order is not used, but the compilers allow the user to choose to have it inserted in cases where the source of error is difficult to trace. One option is to have 'ACC => Z' compiled after the last machine instruction in the translation of each source statement. This enables the error condition to be related to a particular source instruction. Another extreme option would be after every machine instruction.

Some descriptor faults (illegal type/size combinations, for example) occur precisely in MU5, but the bound checking occurs too late in the cycle of events in the D-unit to allow a precise interrupt. The reasons for this are discussed in Chapter 5. This imprecision restricts the usefulness of the bound checking facility, and a different organisation of the hardware would be used in a redesigned machine. As it stands the program knows of the interrupt, but cannot in general rectify the condition and continue, because a few orders overrun might have occurred. In the case of CPR non-equivalence, the interrupt must at least be made to appear precise, since the order causing it cannot complete until the interrupt is serviced. Hence the special arrangements involving the Function Queue in OBS, described above.

With the second and third groups it is enough to inject the interrupt into the pipeline and allow preceding orders to complete.

From the software point of view, interrupts are best classified according to the action they require. Thus in MU5 there are eight types of interrupt, divided into two groups of four, the System Interrupts and the Process Interrupts. These interrupts are

|                    |                               |
|--------------------|-------------------------------|
| System<br>Interrupts | System Error<br>CPR Non-equivalence<br>Exchange Transfer Complete<br>Peripheral Window and Timer |
| Process<br>Interrupts | Instruction Count Zero<br>Illegal Order<br>Program Fault<br>Software Interrupt |

Some protection and privileged facilities are needed by the procedures which service these interrupts. These are obtained

31

by the setting of bits in the Machine Status register, such as the 'Level 0' and 'Level 1' digits. The Level 1 digit is normally set during the running of a Process Interrupt procedure, and, as well as allowing access to the privileged V-store operands, it inhibits any other Process Interrupts. System Interrupts can still occur, however, since these are only inhibited by the setting of the Level 0 digit. The Machine Status register also contains an Executive Mode digit which allows fully interruptable but privileged code to run, digits which inhibit the types of Process Interrupt a program may wish to deal with itself, the Test bits used by control transfers, and other miscellaneous digits.

Associated with each type of interrupt are two words of protected core resident information, known as the Old Link and New Link. When an interrupt occurs, the existing instructions in the PROP pipeline are abandoned, and the contents of the Control Register, Name Base and Machine Status registers are preserved in the Old Link. These registers are then overwritten, by a control transfer instruction, with the information held in the New Link. Thus it is the setting of bits in the Machine Status part of a New Link that determines the interrupt inhibit status of the procedure which services an interrupt. At the end of the interrupt procedure, the information preserved in the Old Link is normally used to restore the Processor to its original state.

## 2.4 THE STORE HIERARCHY

The decisions concerning the stores for MU5 were taken in 1968. This was before large capacity high speed semiconductor stores had become feasible, and the most promising development among the analogue store technologies was plated-wire. Plessey had a plated-wire store under development with an expected cycle time of 250 ns. Unfortunately the price of £16 750 per 2K stack of 128-bit words was restrictive.

MU5 was being designed as a machine to run very large programs, and support the order of hundreds of interactive terminals. Although the terminal activities would be very variable, their store requirements were not be expected to be less than thousands of words. Thus a total store requirement of several million words was anticipated. Clearly it could not be by plated-wire store only. In fact, for this size of store, even medium speed (2.5 µs) core store available from Philips at £41 500 per 128K stack of 32-bit words was too expensive. A store hierarchy with some plated-wire store to obtain performance, and drum or fixed-head disc to obtain capacity was the only solution.

Ideally the store at the fast end of the hierarchy should be large enough to accommodate the active parts of several interactive jobs, and a background job. If an Atlas type of 'one-level' store with demand paging is to be used, the transfer time for pages must be matched to the machine speed. Consider an MU5 with a 10 MIPS instruction rate and a modest sized main store backed up by a drum with a 20 ms revolution time. Even with very high packing density on the drum, page transfers would cost on average 10 ms. This time would be equivalent to 100 000 instruction times. If a page size of 1K bytes was used, then for 75% CPU utilisation to be achieved, a program must obey 300 instructions for every byte of each new page brought in to store before requiring further new pages. Clearly, this intensity of CPU usage would not apply to the pages that might be considered to be the active part of a program such as those containing

(1) the frequently used facilities and working space of a compiler

(2) an array to which a simple cyclic algorithm applies

unless, of course, they could simultaneously fit into store. Therefore, the conclusion was that if the plated-wire store is not big enough to accommodate the active parts of several jobs, an intermediate store, very much faster than the drum (for demand paging), is needed between the two.

This line of thought has resulted in MU5 having a 'one-level' store which maps on to a hierarchy of three levels as shown in figure 2.2. The CPU operates on the Local Store and pages are brought on demand from either Drum or Mass Stores. They are rejected first to Mass and later to Drum. In practice this means that bulk of the paging traffic is between Mass and Local and residual traffic to Drum is at a bearable level. The actual implementation uses fixed-head disc but it is convenient to refer to it as a Drum to avoid confusion with the other discs in the system which are used for file storage.

The 'one-level' store of MU5 contains all the working space and files needed by the current terminal users and the active background jobs. Most of the files are stored on further large capacity discs, or archive discs or tapes. Thus the full storage hierarchy has at least two more levels than are shown in figure 2.2.

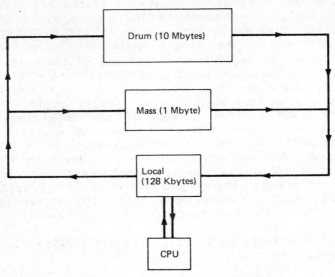

Figure 2.2 The Store Hierarchy

2.5 THE EXCHANGE

The data routes needed to implement the store hierarchy and
the multi-computer connections are extensive. To increase the
flexibility and allow scope for future development it was
decided to generalise these connections into a highway system
known as the 'Exchange' into which all the storage devices and
computers of the MU5 complex are connected. This Exchange has
been built as an integral part of the MU5 Project using
basically the same technology as that used for the MU5
Processor. Logically it is a multiple-width OR gate operated
as a packet switching system at the star point of the
interconnections. This configuration involves only a very
short common path for transfers between the various units and
was chosen in preference to a distributed highway or 'bus'
system in order to accommodate the high data rate associated
with paging transfers. Thus transfers can occur at a rate of
one every 100 ns, and each can involve a 64-bit data word
together with address and control bits.

As an example of the use of the exchange consider the
paging transfers between the Mass and Local stores which are
organised by a Block Transfer Unit (BTU) attached to the
Exchange. When MU5 requires a block of data to be transferred
from the Mass Store to the Local Store, it writes into the
BTU, via the exchange, the starting addresses for the transfer
in each store, together with the block size and start command.
The Processor is then free to continue computation, while the

34

BTU generates the necessary requests, via the Exchange, to the Mass and Local Stores to carry out the transfers. Reading from a store involves two Exchange transfers, one in which the address is sent to the store, and one in which data is returned. In between these two transfers, however, the Exchange is free to carry out transfers between other units in the system.

The addressing scheme used for the Exchange allows up to 16 units to be accommodated, although technological considerations have limited the actual number of units to a maximum of 12. The units actually connected are shown in figure 2.3 The mu5 machine has not been previously mentioned. It is a machine designed as the bottom end of the range. In the MU5 complex its role is to provide a graphics work station.

The overall system organisation shown below is discussed again in Chapter 9. First the technology used and the detail design of the MU5 processor are described.

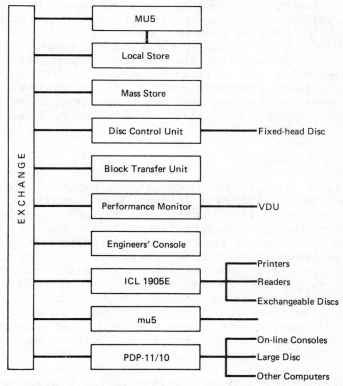

Figure 2.3 The MU5 Multi-computer System

35

# 3   Technological Implementation

The implementation of any computer system design in hardware
requires the use of a number of different technologies. These
may be roughly divided into the areas of circuit technology,
including the techniques used for interconnection, and storage
technology. Some overlapping of these areas is inevitable,
however, since the fastest levels of storage are normally
compatible with the circuit technology. The circuit technology
used in MU5 is basically that developed by ICL for their 1906A
computers, but in order to accommodate the different
architecture òf MU5, a number of additions and extensions have
been made. Furthermore, because there was to be no prototype
for MU5, and the ICL automated interconnection technique was
to be used, it was very important to verify the logical design
by simulation. A logic simulator was therefore developed as an
additional design aid. The storage technologies used in the
MU5 complex cover a wide range of speeds and capacities. At
the fastest level integrated circuit stores are used, backed
up by progressively slower but larger devices. These include
plated-wire stores, bulk core stores and fixed-head disc
stores.

## 3.1 CIRCUIT TECHNOLOGY

The ICL 1906A circuit technology used in the MU5 Processor is
based on Emitter Coupled Logic (ECL) integrated logic
circuits, mounted, with appropriate discrete resistors, on
printed circuit boards to form 'modules'. A number of factors,
particularly the use of associatively addressed fast stores in
the MU5 Processor, has required the extension of the range of
1906A modules, and some of these involved new circuits
developed during the project. Modules are interconnected by
insertion into connectors mounted on multi-layer platters,
each with a capacity of up to 200 modules (figure 3.1). The
platters themselves are housed in bays, each capable of
holding 33 platters in five groups, and two such bays make up
the MU5 Processor (figure 3.2).

Interconnections between platters within a group are made
by means of pressure connectors along adjacent edges, while
connections between groups of platters and between bays are

made through co-axial cables. The co-axial cables are terminated on printed circuit boards which are themselves connected to the platter by pressure connectors along the outer edges of each group. The Exchange is also constructed from this technology, but the large number of signals involved in data transfers between units cannot be accommodated by the available edge connectors. The platters forming the Exchange OR gate are therefore unique in having co-axial cables connected directly on to their surface.

Figure 3.1 MU5 Modules

Figure 3.2 MU5 Logic Bays

### 3.1.1 The ECL Logic Family

The circuit of the basic ECL 2.5 gate is shown in figure 3.3(a). A logic swing of less than 1 V is used, the logic 0 level being -0.8 V and the logic 1 level -1.76 V. The circuit operates by switching current in the reference transistor, which has its base held at -1.3 V by the voltage reference source contained within each integrated circuit. Thus, if one or more of the inputs A, B, C is held at the 0 level, the corresponding input transistor is turned ON, and the reference transistor is turned OFF. This in turn results in a 0 level at the output F. If all the inputs are held at logic 1, the reference transistor conducts and a logic 1 level appears at output F. The function obtained from the circuit is therefore

$$F = A.B$$

with the complementary phase also being available.

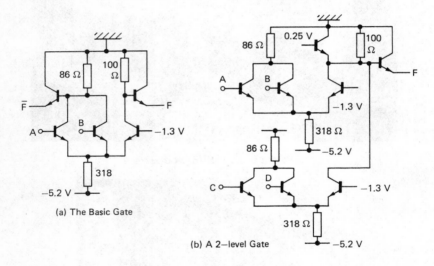

(a) The Basic Gate

(b) A 2—level Gate

Figure 3.3 ECL Circuits

More complex functions are obtained by joining the collectors of the reference transistors of two or more basic gate circuits together and inserting an additional transistor as a diode across the common load resistor to limit the voltage drop. Thus the function performed by the circuit shown in figure 3.3(b) is

$$F = A.B \text{ v } C.D$$

A range of integrated circuits is available containing various

38

combinations of these gates packaged together as shown in figures 3.4(a)-(d).

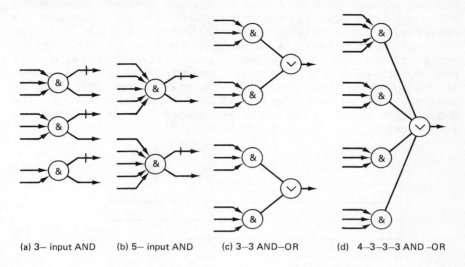

(a) 3— input AND    (b) 5— input AND    (c) 3—3 AND—OR    (d) 4—3—3—3 AND —OR

Figure 3.4 Basic Logic Elements used in MU5

Another, more complex integrated circuit contains two flip-flops of the type shown in figure 3.5. If the CLOCK and GATE signals are both held at logic 1, then the SET/RE-SET inputs are locked out and the output follows the DATA input. When CLOCK and GATE become 0, the output remains static, independent of DATA, but can be changed by application of SET or RE-SET. The propagation delay through the flip-flop for a CLOCK/GATE change is similar to that for a logic gate (around 2 ns), but a longer delay (of around 4 ns) is incurred by a SET/RE-SET change.

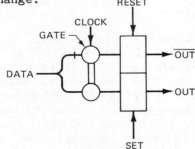

Figure 3.5 Logical Representation of a Flip-Flop

These integrated circuits are mounted on modules to give a range of gate and flip-flop types, and some modules contain

39

passive delay elements and hybrid networks to effect active delays and pulse forming circuits. Figure 3.6 summarises the numbers of each type of module (and other devices) used in ·the MU5 Processor. The pipeline structure of the Processor is reflected in the relatively large number of dual flip-flop modules, mainly used as storage registers in the various stages of the pipeline. Between pipeline stages gating of data and decoding, etc. is mainly performed by multiple-input AND/OR gates of the type shown in row 2. The most complex devices used are in the 16-bit random access memory, the associative circuits and their associated level translators. A fuller description is given in [7].

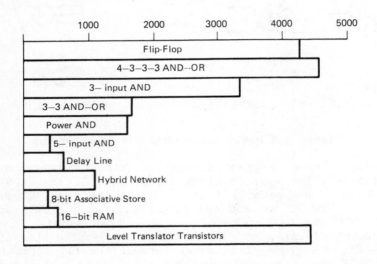

Figure 3.6 Numbers of Devices in MU5

## 3.1.2 Associative Storage

In a conventionally accessed store, each of N physical locations within the store is specified by an address, and every address corresponds to an actual location. In applications such as the MU5 Name Store, however, only a subset of the range covered by operand addresses is actually required in high-speed storage at any time and these addresses are sparsely distributed throughout the total range. To avoid extravagant use of high-speed storage, an associatively accessed store may be used in this situation. Such a store is made up of two fields, an associatively accessed field and a conventionally accessed field. The associative field contains, in random order, M currently required operand addresses, while the conventional field contains the corresponding values. Although the associative field may be loaded and examined by

40

conventional techniques (figure 3.7), it is used during a
store access in a different manner. In this case the required
operand address is presented to the associative field as an
'interrogate address'. If a word in the associative field is
exactly equivalent to the interrogate address, one of the
addressing lines to the conventional field is activated,
allowing access to the desired operand either for 'read out'
or 'write in'. If no word gives equivalence, an NEQ
(non-equivalence) signal is generated to inform the store
control mechanism that attention is required, normally to load
a new line. Multiple equivalence is usually regarded as an
error condition. Thus the associative field is accessed by
examination of its contents rather than by specification of a
location, and is also known as a Content Addressable Memory.

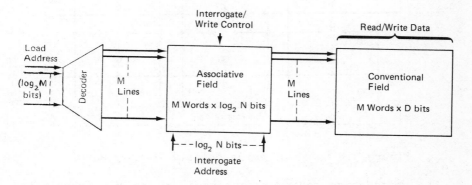

Figure 3.7 An Associatively Addressed Store

In order to carry out an associative search of the store,
each of the memory elements in the associative field must
perform not only the storage function, but also the logical
equivalence operation between the interrogate digit value and
the stored digit value. The principles involved are
illustrated by the model in figure 3.8. The storage function
is represented by two-way switches, and words 0, 1 and 2 are
shown containing 011, 101, 111 respectively. The Word Lines
are all held at some fixed voltage Vx, and each bit in the
interrogate word controls the voltage levels of the pair of
Digit Lines associated with its digit position. A logic 1
causes Da to be raised from the quiescent level Vq to the
higher level V1, where

$$Vq < Vx < V1$$

while a logic 0 causes Db to be raised instead. Thus current
flows from a raised Digit Line into all words where the switch
is selecting the raised Digit Line. For the interrogate

41

pattern 101 shown in figure 3.8, word 0 has two such units of current flowing from the two non-equivalent digits. Word 1, which is identical to the interrogate word, has no current flowing, and word 2 has one unit of current flowing. Equivalence is therefore recognised by the absence of current in a Word Line.

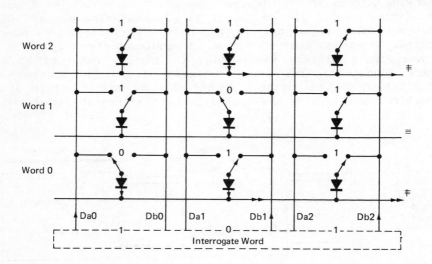

Figure 3.8 Model of an Associative Memory Matrix

The associative memory matrix used in the MU5 associative stores is described in detail in [8]. Each matrix consists of eight elements arranged as four words of two bits within one integrated circuit, and four such circuits are mounted on one module to form an 8-word by 4-bit array. The speed of operation within each element of the matrix is such that association or reading requires typically 5 ns, whereas writing requires 30 ns. In order to form a complete associative store, however, additional modules are required such as Word and Digit Drivers, Equivalence Receivers, Non-equivalence Detectors, etc., all of which involve level translators, and the total associate or read time depends on the delays introduced by these circuits and on the size of store. Additional modules are also needed to form the conventional field of the store. The latter is made up of 16 x 1-bit memory circuits mounted eight to a module to form a 32-word by 4-bit random access store, and additional Decode Driver and Write Driver modules are also required.

3.1.3 Interconnections

The majority of the integrated circuits used in MU5 are

42

mounted on 1.6 in. x 2.1 in. plug-in printed circuit modules
with 20 pins as shown in figure 3.1. Up to 200 of these
modules can be interconnected by means of a single 12-layer
printed circuit platter. The packing density of circuits on
these modules is relatively poor, however, and commonly used
complex logical entities such as adders and the associative
stores have been designed on 40-pin macro boards measuring 1.6
in. x 4.4 in. and 3.0 in. x 4.4 in. (these are also shown in
figure 3.1). The platters measure approximately 13 in. x 16
in. and are mounted in eleven columns of three within a logic
bay. Eight columns are mounted on movable double doors to
allow access for commissioning and maintenance, while the
remaining three columns are mounted in a fixed central plane
(figure 3.9). Figure 3.10 identifies the platters in the two
Processor Bays with the functional units to which they are
allocated (cf. figure 2.1). The Local Store is contained in
Bay 3 and the Exchange in Bay 4.

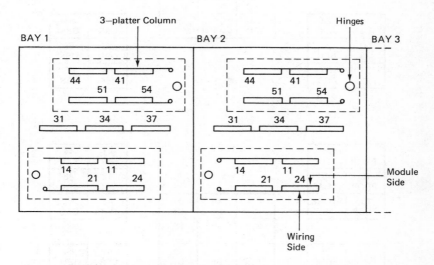

Figure 3.9 Plan View of Processor Layout

This arrangement of the circuits gives relatively short
lengths for interconnections whose source and destination are
situated on the same platter, but interconnections crossing
platter boundaries must travel an average of 12 in., and those
passing from a fixed plane to a door, or from one side of a
door to the other, travel an average of 8 ft along co-axial
cables. A histogram of the distribution of interconnection
lengths in the MU5 system, measured from the output pin of the
source circuit to the input pin of the destination circuit is
shown in figure 3.11. Since a maximum of three integrated
circuits can be mounted on a 20-pin module, or seven circuits

43

on a 40-pin module, relatively few interconnections are between circuits on the same module, and a typical connection involves a distance of about 1 in. to reach the platter, 4 in. on the platter and a further 1 in. from the platter to the destination on a second module. This gives a typical signal propagation delay of about 1 ns. Approximately 80% of all interconnections in MU5 are actually between integrated circuits on the same platter, 13% travel between adjacent platters, 5% go through cables to other platters in the same bay and 2% travel distances of up to 50 ft from bay to bay. In this last case the propagation delay is of the order of 80 ns.

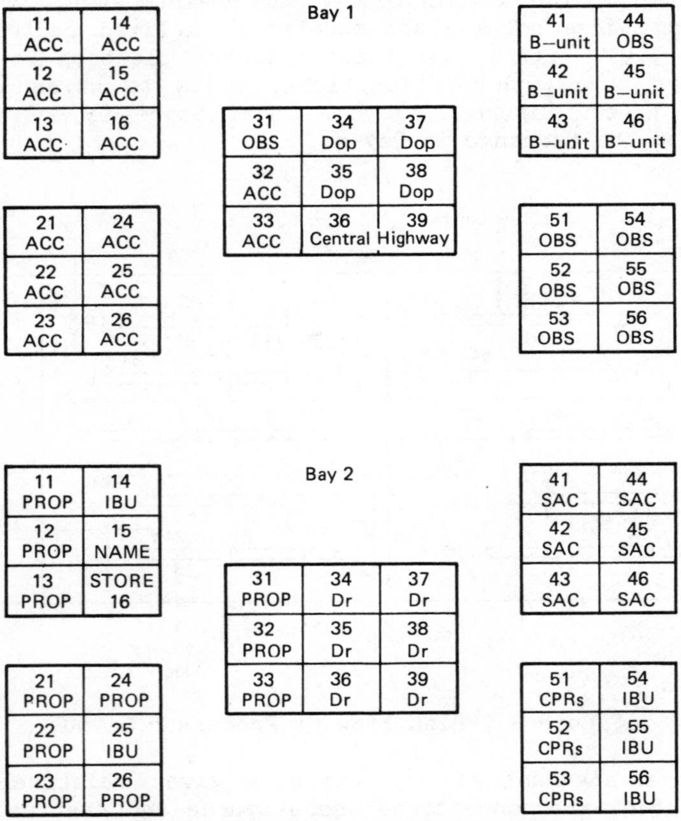

Bay 1

| 11 ACC | 14 ACC |
|---|---|
| 12 ACC | 15 ACC |
| 13 ACC | 16 ACC |

| 21 ACC | 24 ACC |
|---|---|
| 22 ACC | 25 ACC |
| 23 ACC | 26 ACC |

| 31 OBS | 34 Dop | 37 Dop |
|---|---|---|
| 32 ACC | 35 Dop | 38 Dop |
| 33 ACC | 36 Central | 39 Highway |

| 41 B—unit | 44 OBS |
|---|---|
| 42 B—unit | 45 B—unit |
| 43 B—unit | 46 B—unit |

| 51 OBS | 54 OBS |
|---|---|
| 52 OBS | 55 OBS |
| 53 OBS | 56 OBS |

Bay 2

| 11 PROP | 14 IBU |
|---|---|
| 12 PROP | 15 NAME |
| 13 PROP | STORE 16 |

| 21 PROP | 24 PROP |
|---|---|
| 22 PROP | 25 IBU |
| 23 PROP | 26 PROP |

| 31 PROP | 34 Dr | 37 Dr |
|---|---|---|
| 32 PROP | 35 Dr | 38 Dr |
| 33 PROP | 36 Dr | 39 Dr |

| 41 SAC | 44 SAC |
|---|---|
| 42 SAC | 45 SAC |
| 43 SAC | 46 SAC |

| 51 CPRs | 54 IBU |
|---|---|
| 52 CPRs | 55 IBU |
| 53 CPRs | 56 IBU |

Figure 3.10 Platter Allocation

The edge time of the ECL circuits is typically 2 ns, and to minimise the possibility of reflections due to the relatively long delays introduced by the interconnection distances, a matched transmission line approach is used. Thus each gate can drive two series matched 75 ohm lines from each output, and each line is capable of driving up to two input loads at the receiving end. Associated with each output is a group of

44

resistors, the output load resistor (excluded from the integrated circuit itself to reduce power dissipation within the package) and two series matching resistors. These are fabricated on a single ceramic chip in thick film technology and over 45 000 such chips are used in the MU5 system. The rise time at a gate input is degraded as a result of the capacitance which each input load represents and the series resistance of the line matching resistor, and an effective extra delay of 0.6 ns per input load is introduced. The rise time also increases as the distance between the two driven inputs increases. This has led to the adoption of a '3 Inch Rule' in the laying out of modules on platters, whereby module input pins connected to a common line are placed so as to be no more than 3 in. apart. An average gate thus introduces a delay of 2 ns due to propagation through the ECL circuit itself, 1 ns transmission time along the 6 in. interconnection path and a further 1 ns delay due to input loading, giving a typical delay per gate in the system of approximately 4 ns. By comparison, the circuit delay in CDC 7600 logic is about 2.5 ns, but the packaging is such that for large numbers of adjacent gates the additional transmission delay is very much less than 1 ns.

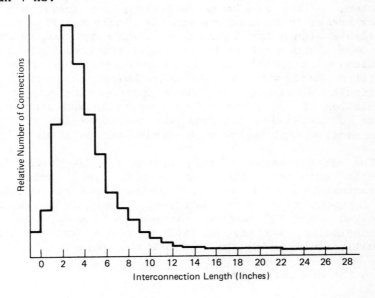

Figure 3.11 Interconnection Lengths

3.1.4 Platter Production

The multi-layer platters into which the modules are connected are made up of four logic layers, two outer layers containing

45

the pads for the edge connectors, and various power layers. Of
the logic layers, two 'X' layers contain horizontal tracks and
two 'Y' layers contain vertical tracks. Logic signal
interconnections are made between module pins by the selection
of a path composed of a sequence of X and Y segments joined by
means of plated-through holes. The selection of these paths is
made by a computer program which forms part of a Design
Automation system developed by ICL. This system requires as
input a specification of the types and placement of logic
elements and their logical interconnection. From this
specification the Design Automation system produces not only
logic drawings, module placement charts, 3 Inch Rule violation
lists, etc., but also data for a numerically controlled
plotter, which produces photographic plates for the
manufacture of the X and Y layers. Clearly it is essential
that the original logic specification should be as accurate as
possible, not only because the production process is itself
time consuming and expensive, but also because errors detected
afterwards involve breaking the existing connections and
adding 'hand-wires' on the platter surface. This problem of
itself is not too serious, in that all connections to module
pins are actually made via links on the surface of the
platter. In any case some hand-wires are inevitable due to
track breaks in manufacture and the finite tracking capability
available within the logic layers. More serious, however, is
the case where a change to the logic requires that additional
modules be inserted, and finding a convenient free module
position which will satisfy path length constraints may be
difficult. A solution to these problems was sought through
simulation of the logic before production was started, and a
suite of simulation programs was developed for this purpose
from earlier exploratory work carried out on Atlas [9].

The effectiveness of this system can be gauged from the
results obtained with the B-unit. This unit contains
approximately 2200 gates and flip-flops and during simulation
46 logical errors were detected. These faults would have
involved over 500 wiring changes on the platters during
commissioning, whereas in fact only one further fault was
actually found during the commissioning phase.

3.1.5 The MU5 Logic Simulator

Simulation of the MU5 logic was carried out on each functional
unit by means of a simulator program run on the 1905E
computer. The simulator accepts the same description of the
logic network as the ICL Design Automation system and
exercises it by applying sequences of input patterns. Three
basic types of information are required by the simulator; a
list of the logic gates in the network and their

46

interconnections, details of the input pattern to be applied to the network, and a precise description of the operation of each type of logic gate used. Networks may be synchronous or asynchronous. A synchronous network is one which is controlled by external clock signals and contains no internal timing circuits, so that the input patterns normally consist of an initial setting of the data signals followed by a series of clock pulses. In this case the simulator is simply required to propagate the signals through the logic levels, using truth-table models to represent the operation of the different types of logic gate, and to produce output in the form of a timing diagram showing the state of signals at the end of each clock phase. Fault monitoring may also be provided to indicate, for example, that the number of levels of gating in a clock phase is too large.

The MU5 logic simulator is considerably more complex than this, however, since it is designed to deal with asynchronous networks. Thus the language used for the specification of input patterns allows the sequencing of input data signals to be controlled by internal timing circuits as well as by external clock pulses. Furthermore, the models of the logic gates used by the simulator are more complex and reflect their true operation by taking into account such details as pulse widths and propagation delays. Output from the simulator takes the form of timing diagrams, fault monitoring which identifies timing errors such as short pulses, and detailed listings showing changes of state of network signals as they occur.

The central feature of the simulator itself is a time-ordered event list. Entries in this list indicate that, as a result of a change of state at the inputs to a gate, a new output state for that gate has been predicted. When an entry is removed from the top of the list, the predicted signal change can 'occur'. The simulator then examines the gates to which this signal is an input, thereby generating further predicted events which are entered into the event list. Although this technique is particularly well suited to the efficient simulation of asynchronous networks, it may also be used equally well for testing synchronous logic.

The internal data structures used to represent a logic network reflect the direct logical connection between a gate output and other gate inputs to which it is connected. Figure 3.12(a) shows a simple network and figure 3.12(b) the essential features of the internal representation of a part of that network. If, at simulated time t, either of the inputs to G1 changes, an 'AND-GATE' routine will predict a new state of the output signal A. This prediction will then be entered into the time ordered event list with an associated time of (t +

47

propagation delay). When the current simulation time reaches (t + propagation delay), this prediction appears at the top of the list and a test is made to see if it actually involves a change of state of A. If no state change occurs, the prediction is ignored. If a state change does occur, the appropriate inputs to gates G2 and G3 are changed and further predictions are made for signals B and C. Current simulated time is always set to the time associated with the entry at the top of the time-ordered event list. Thus if no signal changes are predicted for a long period, computer time is not wasted on the evaluation of signal states in the quiescent network.

The simulator uses individual routines to model the operation of AND gates, OR gates, AND-OR gates, flip-flops, pulse generators, etc. For each logic element, the corresponding routine assumes a suitable nominal propagation delay. The gates in figure 3.4, for example, are assumed to have a delay of 5 ns. The operation of more complex function macros is represented by appropriate combinations of the basic gates. This representation is then substituted in the network whenever a macro is encountered in the network description.

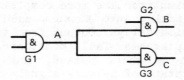

(a) A Simple AND—gate Network

| Gate Type | Output Name | Input States | Fan-out | Fan-out Details | |
|---|---|---|---|---|---|
| | | | | Input 1 to G2 | Input 0 to G3 |
| AND | A | | 2 | Input 1 to G2 | Input 0 to G3 |

(b) Internal Representation of Logic Networks

Figure 3.12 Representation of Logic Networks

The network description, used initially by the simulator and subsequently by the ICL Design Automation system, is encoded from original logic diagrams and entered into a logic source file via a simple editing system. Information is supplied about the grid reference of each gate on the logic drawing, the gate type, its physical placement within a logic bay, the names of its input waveforms and its unique output waveform name. This description is first checked, in order to ensure that the encoding is syntactically correct, by a 'compiler' which uses the specified waveform names to produce logic files. This compiler also substitutes the appropriate

48

combinations of basic gates for the complex function macros. After the logic files have been created or updated, the simulator extracts information about the gates and their interconnections and forms its own internal representation of the network. Simulation can then be initiated and controlled by a program of 'Driving Instructions' supplied by the user of the simulator.

Records kept during the simulation phase of the project show that during the period mid-1970 to mid-1971, 600 hours of 1905E Processor time (with the CPU operating at 5 μs per order) were used for the simulation of 84 platters. The amounts used for individual groups of platters varied considerably according to the nature of both the logic and its designers. Thus, some groups required less than 200 minutes of processor time per platter, several required around 600 minutes, and one group of six platters required over 1000 minutes per platter. One fact which became obvious was that, although the simulator was found by most users to be of great benefit, it did not turn poor designers into good ones. Some of the platters which soaked up large amounts of simulation time soaked up even more during commissioning.

### 3.1.6 Exchange Connections

As noted earlier, the Exchange involves more signals than can normally be accommodated by the platter edge connectors. Thus each pressure connector at the edge of a platter has 40 contacts, of which 20 are normally signal contacts and 20 are normally earths, giving a signal to earth ratio of 1:1. Varying this ratio to allow a greater number of signals reduces the noise immunity of the system, and 24 signals to 16 earths is the highest ratio which can be tolerated. Thus although 360 signals can normally be connected at the edges of an isolated platter, this number can, if necessary, be increased to 432, and an additional 80 or 96 connections can also be made via four vertical entry connectors mounted in pairs close to the ends of the platter. In the case of the Exchange, the logic necessary to implement the multiple-width OR gate which connects together the Units in the MU5 complex is contained on three adjacent platters. These platters are mounted in the centre column of the fixed centre plane in the Exchange Bay and have a maximum of 1104 external connections available. The OR gate is actually 120 bits wide, of which 113 are used and 7 are available for expansion or repair, thus requiring a total of 2880 input and output connections for twelve Units. Clearly this number of connections cannot be made by the normal technique, and a different method is employed whereby the co-axial cables which would normally be connected via printed circuit boards and pressure connectors

are soldered directly on to the platter surface (figure 3.13).
At their other ends the co-axial cables are terminated in
multi-pin connectors mounted on panels in the outer column
positions of the centre plane of the Exchange Bay. Connections
to the Units are then made via separate cable bundles and
connectors which mate with the fixed connectors on the panels.

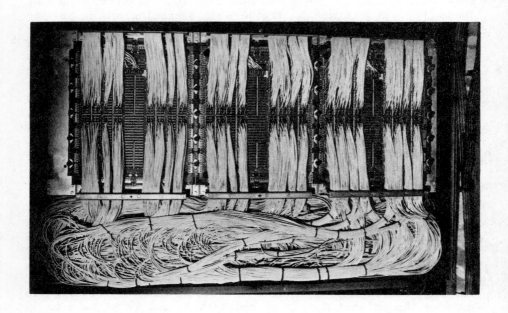

Figure 3.13 The Exchange OR Gate

3.1.7 Asynchronous Timing

The timing of operations within a central processor can either
be synchronous or asynchronous, and both systems have their
advantages and disadvantages. In the MU5 Processor it was
decided that an asynchronous system would be used for
interactions between functional units. Thus a 'handshake'
system is used such that functions and data are passed from
one unit to another when the sending unit has the data
available and when the receiving unit is not busy. It was felt
that this type of operation, in which data transfers take
place asynchronously, would allow the system to operate at a

50

greater speed than a completely synchronous system where transfers only take place at fixed times. This is particularly important when the units concerned are not heavily used. Where a number of communicating pipeline stages are heavily used, however, the time penalty incurred by the handshake becomes a dominant factor, and a synchronous system may be preferred. Thus the CDC 7600 central processor, for example, is completely synchronous, and some units of the MU5 Processor are internally synchronous. Asynchronous systems can also give rise to additional problems, particularly when a unit can accept requests from a number of sources.

This problem, which occurs in a number of places in the MU5 system, is illustrated by the paths through the Store Access Control (SAC) to the Local Store (section 6.4.2). Here three different functional units may request a store cycle at any time, and in the event of a clash, SAC must decide which request to accept. Each incoming request pulse is staticised on a flip-flop, and the outputs of these three flip-flops drive a combinational priority logic circuit. The outputs from this circuit, only one of which can be a 1, form the inputs to a set of decision flip-flops. These flip-flops are strobed when SAC is free to accept a request and sufficient time has elapsed for the priority circuit to have settled after receipt of the first request.

Because a second request may occur a short time after the first request, however, it is possible for the inputs to the decision flip-flops to change state just before the end of the strobe, leaving the outputs somewhere between a 0 and a 1 level. Under these conditions the time taken for the flip-flop outputs to reach proper logic levels may be long compared with the normal propagation delay, and it is possible for subsequent circuits to operate inconsistently.

Clearly sufficient time must be allowed for the decision flip-flops to settle to a constant level, or failure of the control circuits may occur. The settling time of the circuit used here is a function of its gain-bandwidth product, and the displacement of the output from the mid-level at the time the strobe is removed. In the case of an output starting from the exact mid-level, it is possible for an infinitely long settling time to be required, but the probability of such an occurrence is extremely low. It can be shown [10] that an ECL flip-flop with a propagation delay of 2.2 ns requires over 30 ns settling time for the failure rate to be reduced to 1 per month. Since the number of decision flip-flops required in a system is relatively small in most cases, however, considerable advantage can be gained by using a special circuit with a higher gain-bandwidth product than the standard device. Thus a flip-flop with 1.8 ns propagation delay requires around 20 ns settling time for the same reliability, and moving to an even faster device, such as a tunnel diode, reduces this time further. An ECL compatible flip-flop using tunnel diodes has therefore been developed for use in critical decision circuits in MU5. The measured delay through the flip-flop is still quite long (approximately 7 ns) because of the level conversion circuits, but the actual decision time is of the order of 100 ps. This gives an MTBF of 136 years for a settling time of 3 ns or a total delay through the flip-flop of 10 ns.

## 3.2 STORAGE TECHNOLOGY

As in any large computer system, a number of different storage technologies are used in MU5 in order to provide an economic balance between speed and capacity. Thus at the fastest level in the hierarchy (figure 3.14) associatively addressed integrated circuit stores are used, while the main storage unit associated with the MU5 Processor, the Local Store, uses plated-wire technology. At the next level in the hierachy is the Mass Store, a 2.5 μs cycle-time core store, and beyond that is the Fixed-head Disc Store, which incorporates a Disc Transfer System capable of organising data transfers through the Exchange between any one of up to four discs and the Mass or Local Stores. These are high-speed discs offering a limited capacity of about 10 Mbytes. Bulk file storage is therefore provided on other computers in the complex.

Transfers of information between the integrated circuit stores and the Local Store are controlled entirely by hardware under normal running conditions, while transfers between the Local Store and the rest of the hierachy are controlled by software (section 9.3).

### 3.2.1 The Local Store

The MU5 Local Store consists of four plated-wire memory stacks each containing 4096 72-bit words (64 data bits + 8 parity bits), and having a 260 ns cycle time. Plated-wire stores are essentially 2-D systems and each of the stacks of the MU5 Local Store is internally organised on a 2048 144-bit word basis as shown in figure 3.15. No parity checking is performed within the store and so no distinction is made between data and parity bits. The stacks are individually controlled by timing circuitry in the Local Store Interface logic (section 6.3) which connects the stacks with SAC and the Exchange, so that under normal running conditions the stacks are interleaved and successive accesses to separate stacks may be overlapped to give a higher overall access rate. In the event

52

of a hardware failure in one or more stacks, a Fail-soft capability allows the store to be re-configured, so that the best use can be made of the remaining stacks. Thus, for a read request to a given stack, the appropriate twelve address bits, as selected by the Fail-soft logic in the Local Store Interface, are copied into the Address Buffer, and the eleven least significant digits select a line in the stack for reading. The data from all 144 digit wires is copied into the Data Buffer and the least significant address digit then selects the even or odd half. The requested half is copied into the Output Buffer 130 ns after the Address Buffer was strobed. The reading process is destructive, as in a core store, so the outputs of the Data Buffer are fed back to the digit drivers and a write operation is performed in order to restore the contents of the line. The complete read/write cycle is completed after 260 ns.

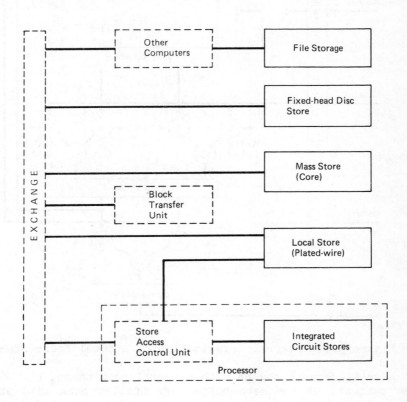

Figure 3.14 Storage Technologies in the MU5 Sysytem

The store is constructed in a 144-bit wide arrangement mainly in order to reduce the number of word drivers required for a given amount of storage (these circuits drive very much more current than the digit drivers, and are therefore much more expensive), but advantage can be taken of this fact when servicing 128-bit word requests from units within the Processor. By setting the appropriate control digit when a request for an even-addressed 64-bit word is made, the corresponding odd-addressed 64-bit word (which is of necessity available in the Data Buffer) is automatically copied into the Output Buffer 50 ns after the even-addressed 64-bit word, and the two halves of the 128-bit word can be returned to the requesting unit in rapid succession.

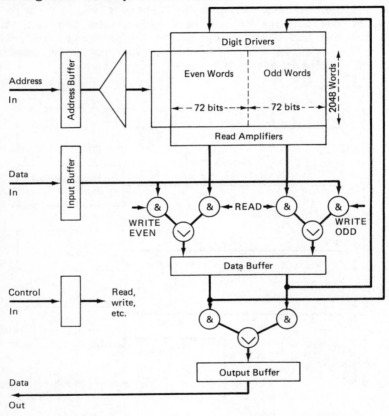

Figure 3.15 Internal Organisation of a Local Store Stack

A write request begins with a normal read phase, but before the contents of the data buffer are written back into store, the appropriate half is overwritten with new information. Although there is no reason in principle why 128-bit word write requests should not be organised on a similar basis, there seemed no justification for incorporating such a facility at the time when the specification of the stores was

54

agreed with the manufacturer. In the light of experience
gained during the subsequent design of the Processor,
particularly with regard to the implementation of the
store-to-store orders (section 7.4), there might have been
some justification for its inclusion.

### 3.2.2 The Mass Store

The Mass Store interface logic allows up to four individual
stores to be connected, but as a result of cost
considerations, only two are connected. These stores are
fairly straightforward 2.5-D core stores, each containing 128K
words of 36 bits (32 data bits + 4 parity bits). The interface
logic interleaves addresses to allow access to 64 data bits in
one cycle, and also contains fail-soft logic which re-orders
the addresses and allows the system to operate at reduced
efficiency in the event of a hardware malfunction in one of
the stores.

### 3.2.3 The Fixed-head Disc Store

The Fixed-head Disc Store developed for use as part of the MU5
complex is designed to accommodate four 'head per track' disc
units linked to the Exchange via a Disc Transfer System. The
first two disc units each contain eight 12 in. diameter
recording surfaces with 64 tracks per surface. Data bytes are
recorded in parallel on eight tracks in blocks of 1024, and
each 20.5 ms revolution gives access to 37 blocks. The total
capacity is thus 2.4 Mbytes per unit. The recording code is
Modified Non-Return to Zero (NRZI) recorded at a constant bit
frequency of 2.2 MHz. The maximum packing density is 1520 bits
per inch on the inner track and the data rate is 1 byte every
450 ns [11]. The 'programmers' would have been happy to accept
a system engineered to a less exacting standard, and to
sacrifice some capacity for the convenience of having 32
blocks per revolution. The task of computing addresses of
empty blocks, for example, is greatly simplified if the total
number of blocks is a power of 2. (The positions of empty
blocks are recorded in a bit list and the positions of bits in
this list are used in the computation.) The 'engineers' were
concerned to push the limits of performance, however, and to
maximise the storage capacity.

The limit on information packing density in any high-
performance recording system is usually imposed by the timing
variations which occur between writing and read-back, and
these are of two distinct types, 'skew' and 'peak shift'. Skew
is a long term phase variation on read-back between parallel
tracks which were initially recorded using the timing from a
common 'write clock'. The major contributions to skew in a

55

flying head system are the positioning accuracy of the retractable heads, variations in head inductance, differing cable lengths associated with individual heads, delays in the selection and read-back circuits, and gyro-precession of the rotating surface. On the disc used in the MU5 system, a figure of 250 ns was specified by the manufacturer for the maximum skew between heads using a common write and read amplifier.

Peak shift arises from the super-position of read-back pulses at high packing densities and the amount of shift is dependent upon the pattern. Thus, unless adaptive writing techniques are used, this shift must be considered as purely random. On the MU5 discs, the worst-case peak shift is 3% of one bit period (equivalent to approximately 14 ns) at 1500 flux reversals per inch, rising to 25% at 3000 flux reversals per inch. Further random timing variations occur due to noise in the read-back channel. These are usually circuit dependent and are of the order of 20 ns in the MU5 system.

Thus skew is the dominant effect and in most. systems leads to the adoption of self-clocking codes such as Phase Modulation, Frequency Modulation and Delay Modulation. The conventional NRZI detection system cannot deal with skew of this magnitude, but, by use of a 'Self-Phasing' technique, the effect of skew can be reduced to acceptable levels. In this situation the NRZI recording code yields a higher bit-packing density than any of the three self-clocking codes and was therefore adopted for use in the MU5 system. (More recent commercial disc systems employ different techniques, using block codes, which allow even higher densities to be achieved.)

The Self-Phasing system operates by measuring the skew on each data track at the start of every data block and holding its value constant throughout the reading of the block. Since the block is only a small proportion of a revolution, the gyro-precession effects can be neglected. The measurement is performed on a preamble pattern of 5 successive bits (00100) recorded in NRZI format on each track immediately prior to the normal data. This isolated 1 does not undergo any peak shift and can therefore be used for accurate skew measurement.

The measurement is carried out by digital techniques and permits a total skew of two bit periods, equivalent to 900 ns at 1500 bits per inch. The value of skew is held as a 3-bit binary number, thus dividing the two-bit period into eight separate skew values and allowing the skew to be measured to within 112 ns. When this is used to re-align the parallel data streams, a margin of 337.5 ns remains to accommodate peak shift and other dynamic timing variations.

# 4 The Primary Instruction Pipeline

In Chapter 2 we saw how the MU5 Processor developed into two pipeline systems, the Primary and Secondary Instruction Pipelines. In this chapter we shall follow the flow of instructions through the units which constitute the Primary Instruction Pipeline (figure 4.1). The Primary Instruction Pipeline operates at a maximum rate of one instruction per 50 ns. This performance is achieved by dividing each unit into a number of stages, each of which can complete its part of the instruction processing within the 50 ns period and then accept the next instruction [12]. The design is presented in some detail to illustrate how conceptual elegance sometimes has to be compromised in order to achieve practical solutions.

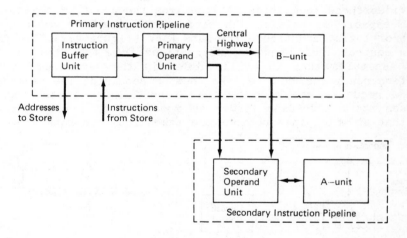

Figure 4.1 The Primary and Secondary Instruction Pipelines

Instructions enter the pipeline as 128-bit words supplied from store by the Store Access Control Unit, and the Instruction Buffer Unit arranges to send 16-bit instruction 'parcels' to the Primary Operand Unit (PROP) in the correct program sequence. PROP accesses the primary operand in each case so that instructions which enter PROP in the form of 'function/operand-specification' leave it five stages later in the form of 'function/operand'. B-orders and Organisational orders requiring only a primary operand are then ready for execution and can be sent via the Central Highway either to the B-unit or back to PROP. Orders requiring a secondary operand access, and all ACC orders, are sent to the Secondary Operand Unit. Operands are also returned across the Central Highway from the B-unit to PROP in the case of store orders, and via a private highway from the B-unit to the Descriptor Addressing Unit when the contents of the B-Register are required as the modifier in a data structure access.

## 4.1 THE INSTRUCTION BUFFER UNIT

In any computer system there is clearly a need to supply instructions to the processing section at a rate matching its execution rate. For sequential instructions in MU5 the required rate can be achieved quite easily since the maximum execution rate requires one 16-bit instruction every 50 ns and the Store Access Control Unit can supply successive 128-bit words from the Local Store at intervals of 65 ns. However, because the _access_ time is much longer than this, a system is required which can send out instruction requests well in advance of their being required by PROP, and which can also buffer the corresponding replies. The Instruction Buffer Unit provides these facilities. It contains three buffer registers, each capable of holding 128 bits, which together with their control logic, constitute the Data Flow (figure 4.2). The Data Flow control logic unpacks instructions from the first buffer and assembles them in cyclic order in the second and third buffers ready for PROP to take them as required. The necessary store requests are made by the Store Request System, which issues store addresses formed by a counter at a rate matched to that at which instructions are taken from the Data Flow.

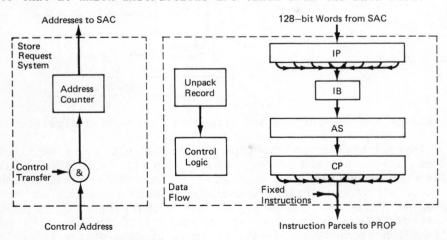

Figure 4.2 The IBU Store Request and Data Flow Systems

58

This system operates satisfactorily until a control transfer occurs as a result of either an unconditional control transfer instruction, or a conditional control transfer instruction for which the condition is met. Then all the pre-fetched instructions must be abandoned, and the correct new instruction cannot be sent to PROP until the store has been accessed, using the new control address, and the instruction has passed through the Data Flow. Thus a large gap occurs in the instruction stream, and the 50 ns rate is not maintained. The net effect of this on the performance of the Processor clearly depends on the frequency with which control transfer instructions occur, and the extent of this problem is well illustrated by performance measurements taken from the Atlas computer.

The average execution time of Atlas computational orders was 2 μs, but observations of the number of orders actually obeyed over long periods of time indicated an average order time of 3 μs. At the time it was thought that the discrepancy might be due to store clashes between instruction and operand accesses. However, statistics collected over a large sample of programs showed that 20% of all orders obeyed were control transfers, a much larger figure than had been expected, and high enough to explain the reduced instruction rate. Control transfers required 7 μs for their execution, giving an average instruction time of

$$2 * 80/100 + 7 * 20/100 = 3 \text{ us}$$

The expected times for execution of control transfer instructions and the fastest computational instructions in MU5 were 950 ns and 50 ns respectively. Thus, even if the frequency of control transfers could be reduced to one order in ten, the comparable average execution time would be

$$50 * 90/100 + 950 * 10/100 = 140 \text{ ns}$$

This represents a reduction by a factor of almost three from the peak rate.

A system similar to that used in the CDC 7600 computer [13], in which recently used instructions and their addresses are preserved in a high-speed loop-catching buffer, might be expected to improve this situation. However, this system is only satisfactory if the number of instructions being obeyed within the loop is less than the buffer size. For MU5 a system was sought which would operate satisfactorily without constraints on loop size. The first system considered had buffer registers containing the first few instructions at the destination or 'jump-to' addresses of recently obeyed control

59

transfers. Access to these instructions would be via an associative search on their addresses (figure 4.3). The pre-fetching mechanism would proceed normally until a control transfer occurred, and the destination address would then be presented to the associative store. If a match was found, the instructions in the corresponding buffer register would be read out and sent to the Primary Operand Unit. If no match was found, one of the set of associative and buffer registers would be updated when the instructions had been obtained from store.

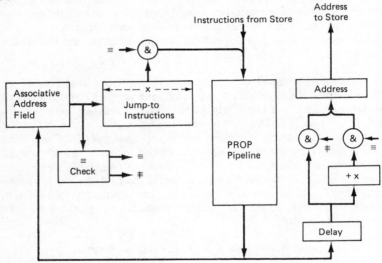

Figure 4.3 An Associatively-Addressed Instruction Buffer

Simulation studies of this technique [14] showed that only eight lines of store would be needed to trap 80% of jump instructions and that increasing the number of lines to sixteen would only produce an extra 1% improvement. The problem in implementing this scheme was the width of the buffer store. In order to allow the pre-fetching mechanism to catch up after a control transfer, each line of the buffer would need to hold up to 950 ns worth of instructions. At 50 ns per 16-bit instruction the number of bits needed in each line amounts to over 300.

In order to retain the advantage obtained by using an associatively addressed store, without incurring the cost of buffering large amounts of data, an alternative system is used in practice. This system uses an eight-line associatively addressed 'Jump Trace' store (figure 4.4) to predict the outcome of an impending control transfer [15]. Whenever a new instruction address is generated by the IBU it is presented to

60

the associative 'jump-from' address store before being sent to
SAC. If an equivalence is found, this address is replaced by
the corresponding 'jump-to' address, so that pre-fetching of
the new sequence takes place instead. When the control
transfer instruction which gave equivalence in the trace is
sent to PROP, it is accompanied by a bit indicating that the
instructions following it are 'out of sequence'. This bit is
used in PROP to determine the action after execution of the
control transfer. If the following instructions have been
correctly predicted, execution of instructions continues
uninterrupted. If the instructions are not out of sequence,
but should have been, a request is made to SAC for the
instructions at the 'jump-to' address, and at the same time a
line in the Jump Trace is loaded with the 'jump-from' and
'jump-to' addresses. Thus when the 'jump-from' address
re-occurs within the IBU, the instructions at the 'jump-to'
address are automatically pre-fetched.

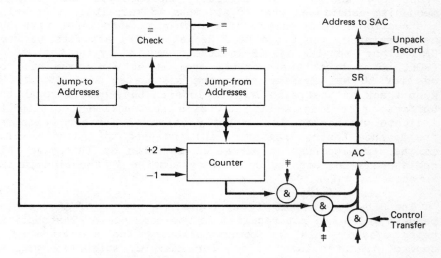

Figure 4.4 The Store Request and Jump Trace Systems

Simulation studies of this system indicated that about 75%
of control transfers could be trapped using an eight-line
store, and that, as before, increasing the number of lines in
the store did not significantly improve the performance. The
apparent drop in performance as compared with the system of
figure 4.3 occurs because the prediction mechanism sometimes
predicts a transfer which does not occur. No attempt is made
to correct the Jump Trace when a predicted branch does not
occur, however, since the drop in performance is more than
offset by the fact that the prediction mechanism allows useful
overlapping of instructions to continue in PROP when the
prediction is correct (section 4.2.7).

61

## 4.1.1 Data Flow within the IBU

The Data Flow section of the IBU is concerned with receiving the store words returned by the Store Access Control Unit and supplying a stream of 16-bit instruction parcels to PROP. Instructions are normally accessed in groups of 128 bits (equivalent to one full line of the Local Store) but for technological reasons all data highways in the system are limited to 64 bits. A 128-bit word is therefore returned to the IBU as two successive 64-bit words which are copied into the appropriate section of the input register IP (figure 4.2).

Instruction parcels are transferred from IP to the additional Storage Register AS, via the 16-bit Intermediate Buffer IB. (IB is incorporated to overcome skew timing problems associated with the sending of parallel data through several logic levels and then over long distances within the Processor, and is not logically necessary). The filling mechanism associated with AS attempts to keep it full of valid instructions, while the filling mechanism associated with the next register, the Close Pack Register (CP) attempts to keep CP full by emptying AS. CP is itself emptied by the actions of PROP, which takes instructions from it at a maximum rate of one per 50 ns. Monitor registers associated with AS and CP keep track of the valid instructions as they pass through the buffers, recording a bit for each instruction position to indicate whether it is currently valid. A further register, the Advance Control Register (AC), is used to indicate which is the next instruction parcel to be taken by PROP, and this register is incremented by 1 every time an instruction parcel is actually taken.

The 128-bit word in IP may contain a number of instruction parcels which are not required in the sequence of instructions being obeyed. This can occur following the execution of a control transfer instruction, for example, which may jump to any position within the 128-bit word. The three least significant digits of the requested address and the number of instruction parcels required from the 128-bit word are therefore contained in one of four registers in an Unpack Record. This Unpack Record is filled at one end by the Store Request System as requests are sent to SAC (figure 4.4), and emptied at the other end by the Data Flow control logic as data returns from SAC. The Unpack Record also contains a Sequence bit, a Same Word bit and a Control Overflow bit.

The Sequence bit is set to a 1 if the last instruction to be unpacked from the word is to be followed by an instruction which is out of sequence as a result of the actions of the Jump trace. This bit is used by PROP when obeying control

62

transfer instructions (section 4.2.7).

The Same Word bit indicates that loop catching is in operation. Although no additional buffers are incorporated into the IBU to allow for conventional loop-catching, the existing buffers can be used for this purpose in cases where the jump-from and jump-to addresses are in the same 128-bit word. When a jump-to address is read out of the Jump Trace, the presence of the Same Word bit indicates to the Store Request System that the required word is already available and that no further request need be made.

The Control Overflow bit indicates that the request is for an instruction beyond the end of the segment addressed by the Control Register, a fault condition which can arise as a result of pre-fetching. This bit is used by PROP to cause an interrupt if an attempt is made to execute the instruction (section 4.2.8).

4.1.2 The Store Request System

The Store Request System (figure 4.4) initiates requests for 128-bit words from SAC at the required intervals. Two different types of request may occur according to circumstances, ordinary requests and priority requests. Priority requests are made whenever PROP signals a discontinuity in the instruction stream, that is, that the instructions following the one currently being executed must be replaced by a different sequence. Following such an event, the instruction address received from PROP is loaded into both the Advanced Control Register, AC, and the Store Request Register, SR, and a priority request made to SAC. AC is then incremented at 40 ns intervals (it operates at a faster rate than PROP) and whenever a carry across the 128-bit word address boundary occurs, the new address is copied into SR and an ordinary request is made to SAC. In addition, each new address generated in AC is checked against the contents of the associative jump-from field of the Jump Trace. If an equivalence occurs the corresponding jump-to address is read out and used instead. The Store Request System then continues to make ordinary requests starting from this new address.

Ordinary requests normally continue to be made until an instruction sequence discontinuity arises. This happens whenever

(1) An Interrupt occurs

(2) An Escape Descriptor access is made (section 5.1.3)

63

(3) The IBU sends an incorrect sequence of instructions

In cases (1) and (2) the output of CP is inhibited and a pair of hard-wired instructions is sent to PROP instead (figure 4.2). When an Interrupt occurs, the current orders in the PROP pipeline are abandoned, and a special instruction is sent through the SEOP to SAC to ensure that all previous orders have completed their CPR equivalence checks (section 6.4.2). Once this action is complete, an eight-bit Interrupt Entry register is strobed, and the instructions

    SET LINK    System V-store Address
    EXIT        System V-store Address

are sent to PROP. The System V-store addresses refer to the core resident links (section 2.3.1), and in order to select the correct links, contain an encoding of the contents of the Interrupt Entry register. The encoding is such that if more than one interrupt is present, the address corresponds to the one with highest priority.

Escape Descriptors are detected by SEOP, which sends a special reply to PROP instead of its normal handshake signal. PROP abandons all current orders and signals the IBU, which sends the orders

    STACK LINK  Literal ( = 0)
    JUMP        D[0]

In either case the second instruction of the pair is a control transfer which causes a priority request for the newly addressed instructions and re-enables the output of CP. Case (3) occurs whenever an unpredicted control transfer instruction causes a jump or when a predicted control transfer does not cause a jump.

The operation of the Store Request System can also be temporarily halted as a result of interlocks incorporated into the IBU to ensure that no loss of information occurs as a result of asynchronous operation. These interlocks simply cause time delays before the next ordinary request can be sent. For example, the rate of issuing of requests from the IBU to SAC is normally geared to the maximum rate at which PROP can process instructions. When PROP executes an instruction which requires a long interval of time for its completion, however, a hold-up occurs and this hold-up propagates back through PROP to the IBU data-flow buffers. Since the IBU is obliged to accept data from SAC as soon as it becomes available, sufficient space must be maintained in these buffers to receive it. In order to meet this condition

64

and to be able to maintain the maximum throughput rate, IBU ordinary requests may be held up in SAC after the address translation stage (section 6.4.2), until the IBU can guarantee to accept the requested instructions.

### 4.1.3 The Jump Trace

Although the Jump Trace is in principle a fairly straightforward system, a number of factors complicated its implementation. For example, although most control transfers use a literal (and therefore invariant) operand, some do not, and in these cases the jump-to address will vary on some subsequent executions of the instruction. No attempt has been made in MU5 to take advantage of cases where this variation occurs infrequently, however, since it was felt that the extra hardware complication needed to check the correctness of the predicted jump-to address would not be cost-effective. Instead, the problem of variable jump-to addresses is avoided by only loading the Jump Trace for those control transfers which use a literal operand.

A further problem arises from the variable instruction length. The Control Register always addresses the first parcel of a multi-length instruction, but clearly jump-from addresses must always correspond to the last. This address must therefore be computed specially, since it is not otherwise required. Consider, however, the action of a conditional control transfer. The value in the Control Register after its execution will either be the address of the first parcel of the next instruction in sequence (the jump-from address + 1), or some quite different address (the jump-to address). The first alternative can be generated immediately, since it requires no operand, whereas the second must await the arrival of the operand and the result of the condition. The Control Adder associated with the Control Register in PROP can therefore perform two cycles with no loss of performance, and when an unpredicted control transfer using a literal operand occurs, both values are sent to the IBU. The first is loaded into register AC (figure 4.4) and then decremented by the address counter before being used to load a line in the jump-from field. The second is loaded into AC and thence into the jump-to field and also into SR to be sent to SAC as a priority request. The line used in the Jump Trace is selected by a Fill Pointer according to a cyclic replacement algorithm and as each line is overwritten a 'use' digit associated with it is set. These use digits are normally only re-set, and the Trace thereby cleared at a process change, when the Process Number Register in PROP is altered.

The technological problems which arise in the

65

implementation of the Jump Trace are mainly concerned with timing. All instruction addresses are presented to the jump-from field as they are generated by the Advance Control Register (AC), and the association proceeds in parallel with the operation of the counter. This allows the 40 ns address generation rate to be sustained. However, if an equivalence is found, the next address is not that generated by the counter but that read out of the jump-to field. This action requires an additional 40 ns. To sustain an average 40 ns rate, advantage is taken of the fact that the addresses generated in AC are sequential, and association is performed simultaneously on two addresses differing only in their least significant digit. Thus the associative field is actually 30 bits wide with the 31st bit of the full virtual instruction address being held in a separate non-associative flip-flop. This bit is then used to determine whether or not an equivalence is genuine. When a genuine equivalence does occur, the corresponding jump-to address is read out and copied into AC and into SR.

## 4.2 THE PRIMARY OPERAND UNIT

The provision of separate Primary and Secondary Operand Units in the MU5 Processor arose from the distinction made in the order code between different types of operand, particularly between named or literal operands and data structure elements. The basic idea was that the Primary Operand Unit (PROP) would be concerned with accessing the operand specified directly by the instruction and routing the instruction, together with its primary operand, to the appropriate following unit for execution or further processing. PROP would therefore contain the Name Store, and if the primary operand was a named variable or literal for example, the instruction would be ready for execution at the end of PROP. An instruction involving a descriptor would be sent to the Secondary Operand Unit (SEOP). As described in section 2.3, however, a Name Store was also incorporated into SEOP, and some instructions can therefore leave PROP without their primary operand.

Figure 4.5 shows the basic hardware in PROP and the various stages of operation involved in processing a typical instruction. Instructions are received from the IBU into registers DF (function) and DN (name). The first action is the decoding of the instruction to select the appropriate base (NB, XNB or SF) and the name part of the instruction. For access to a 32-bit variable, the name is shifted down one place relative to the base and the least significant digit is used later to select the appropriate half of the 64-bit word obtained from the Name Store.

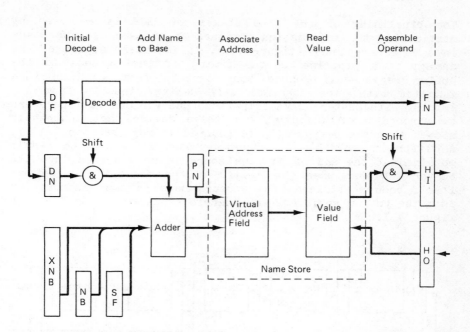

Figure 4.5 The Basic Components of the Primary Operand Unit

In the second stage the name and base are added together to form the address of a 64-bit word. This address is concatenated with the 4-bit Process Number (PN) and presented to the Associative Field of the Name Store. If the address is found, access is made to the 64-bit word in the Name Store Value Field. If the required address is not in the associative store a request is made to the Store Access Control Unit, and the value returned from store, together with its address, is written into an empty line in the 32-line Name Store (section 6.1.2). This number of lines was chosen both on the results of software simulation (section 2.3) and on technological considerations. Thus, for example, the modules needed to make up a 32-word associative store and a 32-word flip-flop store could each be fitted on to one platter.

The next stage of processing is the assembly of the operand. A 32-bit integer, for example, may be taken from either half of the 64-bit store word, but must always appear at the least significant end of the data highway when presented to a succeeding unit. Registers FN and HI form the input to the Central Highway of the Processor and register HO is connected to one of its outputs to receive operands resulting from store orders.

67

## 4.2.1 Design of the PROP Pipeline

The pipelining of the five stages in PROP is achieved by staticising the information obtained at the end of each stage in a buffer register (figure 4.6). An important aspect of the design of a pipeline is the timing of the strobes to the buffer registers, because some outputs from a stage (the function bits, for example) will derive directly from its inputs. With master/slave flip-flops the various registers can be strobed simultaneously, but these devices are inherently slower than the D-type flip-flops used in MU5 (section 3.1.1). A different technique is therefore used in which the result obtained at the end of any one stage is only copied into its buffer register when the result of the following stage has itself been staticised. The strobes used to copy information into the buffer registers are therefore staggered, as shown in figure 4.7.

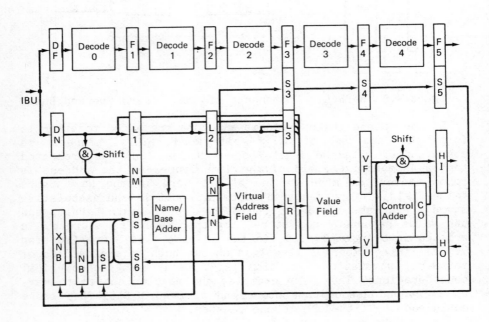

Figure 4.6 The Complete Primary Operand Unit

The shaded portions of figure 4.7 show the progress of one instruction through the PROP pipeline. It is first copied into DF and DN (function and name respectively) and the Decode 0 logic carries out the decoding of the instruction necessary to control the first stage. The decoding logic of figure 4.5 is spread out in the pipelined version into separate decoders for each stage. In many cases, however, the necessary decoding cannot be carried out in sufficient time to control the action of a given stage. In these cases it is carried out in the previous stage, and the various control signals appear as additional function digits, along with the original function, as inputs to the stage requiring them.

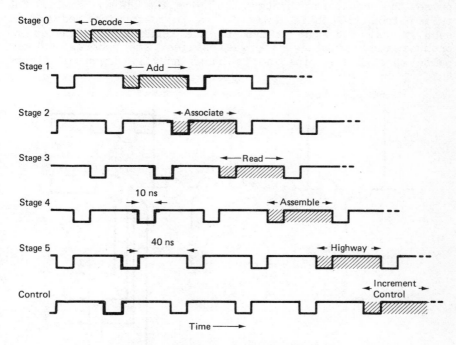

Figure 4.7 The Basic PROP Timing Diagram

The next pipeline strobe is timed to arrive no earlier than when the outputs of the first stage have settled and are ready to be strobed into the registers F1 (function), NM (name) and BS (base). The addition of name and base now takes place and after the appropriate time has elapsed, the result is copied into IN, the Interrogate Register. The output of IN is concatenated with PN, the Process Number, to form the input to the associative field of the Name Store. The result of the association is then copied into the PROP Line Register (PLR), the output of which accesses the line in the Value Field containing the required operand. The Value Field output is copied into the Value Field register (VF), and thence, after assembly, into the Highway Input register (HI).

Once an instruction has reached HI, PROP must wait until it has been accepted by another unit before taking any further action. Instructions therefore proceed through PROP in series

69

of 'beats', the rate at which these beats occur being
determined by the maximum operating rate of PROP and the
acceptance rates of the succeeding units. The generation of a
beat is initiated by the setting of a 'data gone' flip-flop
(figure 4.8), which when any other necessary conditions at the
end of the PROP pipeline have been satisfied, allows a 20 ns
pulse to propagate through the pipeline delay chain. The
pulses from the chain drive 10 ns pulse-forming modules at
each stage, and the delays in the chain are adjusted to
produce a 10 ns stagger between stages. The progress of one
pulse through the pipeline is shown heavily drawn in figure
4.7.

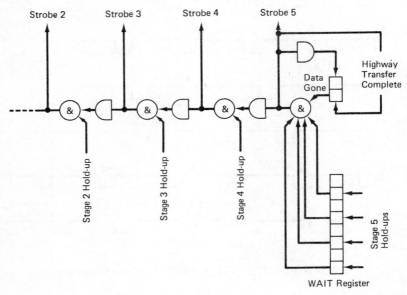

Figure 4.8 The Pipeline Delay Chain

Some problems arise as a result of the physical dimensions
of the Processor and the layout of the platters within it
[16]. Thus it is not feasible to locate all registers
pertaining to one stage in close proximity either to each
other or to the timing control logic. As a result, all the
registers of one stage cannot be strobed simultaneously, since
'far' strobes would have to be sent out in advance of 'near'
strobes by up to 20 ns. Alternatively, all 'far' registers
could be strobed late (the strobes and data must all travel
the same distance) but some control signals must travel back
from the far registers to the near registers, and the double
delay would slow the pipeline down. The problem has been
overcome in practice by deriving far strobes from the earliest
level of fan-out in each section of the delay chain, and by

70

designing for only three levels of logic in paths which involve data travelling from near to far registers. Thus the 50 ns within each stage is typically made up as follows

| | |
|---|---|
| Input Buffer Settling Time | 5 ns |
| Operation Within Stage | 30 ns |
| Inter-platter Cable Delays | 5 ns |
| Output Buffer Strobe | <u>10</u> ns |
| | |
| TOTAL | 50 ns |

So far we have assumed that each stage of the pipeline contains one 16-bit order. However, circumstances arise which prevent full utilisation of each stage. For example, the order code allows for multi-length orders (section 4.2.2) and some orders involve multiple accesses (sections 4.2.3 and 4.2.4). These can normally be dealt with by a purely logical control mechanism which does not affect the main pipeline timing, but may involve the creation of gaps (unused stages) in the pipeline. These gaps, or 'dummy orders', are distinguished by means of an additional function digit, which, when set, inhibits the actions of each stage, including the Control Register updating. Other conditions can also arise which require hold-ups within the pipeline and hence also produce gaps. They occur when some necessary information is not immediately available, and can arise from most stages of the pipeline. Apart from hold-ups which arise from the fifth stage, they cannot be detected in time for the next beat of the pipeline to be inhibited and therefore operate independently of the beat generating logic, by simply preventing subsequent beats from propagating back beyond the stage from which they arise (figure 4.8), and by causing dummy orders to be propagated forwards.

Hold-ups arising from the fifth stage are normally ones involving a complex action within PROP or an interaction with another unit, both of which require the pipeline to be stopped. The need for one of these hold-ups is indicated by the setting of one or more bits in a 'WAIT' Register as the instruction is copied into F5 (figure 4.8). On completion of the highway transfer the 'data-gone' flip-flop is set as usual, but the next beat is prevented from being released by the presence of the digit in the WAIT Register. Instead, a hardware routine is entered appropriate to the most significant digit in the WAIT Register. When the routine is completed the corresponding WAIT digit is re-set and either the beat is released or another hardware routine is entered appropriate to the next most significant digit in the WAIT Register.

71

## 4.2.2 Multi-length Instructions

Multi-length instructions are those using a 16-bit name or a 16, 32, or 64-bit literal operand. The actions required to implement these orders, and also the stack mechanism, are controlled by three digits in each of registers DF and F1 and the decoding logic between them. Thus following a DF strobe, the inputs to these three control digits in F1 take up states determined both by the function and the states of the control digits in DF. When the next beat pulse reaches F1, the F1 control digits take up their new states and are then copied back into the corresponding DF digits by the same beat pulse 10 ns later, so that the digits in DF and F1 act as a master/slave combination. For example, when a long name is used, the next beat copies a dummy order into F1 and the 16-bit name into DN, the DF strobe being inhibited. On the following beat the order enters F1 with the execute digit set to 1 and the 16-bit name in NM (figure 4.6).

16-bit literal operands are dealt with in the same way as 16-bit names, except that the content of DN is copied into L1 instead of NM, and thence into L2, L3 and VU as the order proceeds down the pipeline. 32-bit and 64-bit literal operands start off in the same way as 16-bit literals but require three and five phases respectively. Following the decoding of the literal, the next beat copies a dummy order into F1, and the first 16 bits of the literal into DN. The valid order itself proceeds to F1 on the subsequent beat and is then followed by dummy orders until the whole literal has been copied into the pipeline using registers DN, L1, L2 and L3.

For any size of literal the complete value is copied into VU from some or all of DN, L1, L2 and L3, as appropriate, when the order itself enters F4. For a 16-bit literal, sign extension, if specified, takes place to 32 bits between L3 and VU (a 6-bit literal is extended to 16 bits between DN and L1) and sign extension to 64 bits, again if specified, takes place between VU and HI. Figure 4.9 shows the pattern of the phases for a 32-bit literal superimposed on the pipeline timing diagram.

This technique for dealing with long literals was adopted because it avoided the need for the IBU-PROP interface to be extended beyond 16 data bits, and also the need to provide a 64-bit data buffer at each pipeline stage. The obvious penalty for this saving in hardware is the number of extra pipeline beats necessary whenever a long literal is used. However, for a parallel system to operate satisfactorily, a higher IBU data rate would also be necessary to ensure the availability of all parcels of a multi-length instruction.

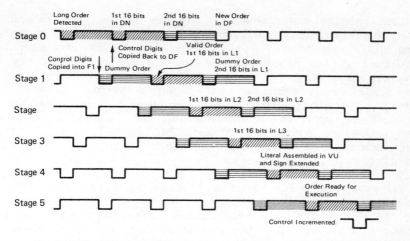

Figure 4.9 Pipeline Patterns for a 32-bit Literal

This requirement also applies in the serial system used in MU5. Various circumstances can arise where PROP requires an instruction from the IBU before it has been obtained from store and made available through the IBU Data Flow, particularly following unpredicted control transfers. In these cases a 'data valid' signal accompanying the function copied into DF is set to zero. PROP therefore treats this instruction as a dummy order and a gap occurs in the stream of orders in the pipeline.

In the case of multi-length instructions, it may not be possible to proceed even when the information copied into DF is valid, since sufficient additional instruction parcels may not be available to complete the instruction. Additional 'data available' signals are therefore copied into DF, along with the 'data valid' signal, to indicate whether there are two, three, four, or five instruction parcels immediately available. If the required number of parcels is not available for the order involved, a dummy order is propagated forwards and the strobe to the IBU is inhibited. In addition, however, the strobe to the DF function digits is inhibited so that successive pipeline beat pulses only copy in the 'data available' digits until sufficient parcels are available for the order to proceed normally.

4.2.3 The Stack Mechanism

The stack is used for storing and retrieving partial results and for procedure links and parameters. For example, during the evaluation of expressions such as

$$a = b*c + d*e$$

73

partial results are **stacked by the use** of the '*=' (stack and load) function. They are later unstacked by use of the operand form STACK (section 2.2.1). Stacked operands are therefore contained in the MU5 Processor storage system in exactly the same way as names, their addresses being generated relative to the Stack Front register (SF), which points to the most recently stacked operand within the Name Segment. Thus SF is advanced by both the '*=' function and functions concerned with procedure entry (STACK and STACK LINK), and all these functions require two operand accesses to be made. Hence they are divided into two phases.

For the STACK functions an access is first made for the specified operand followed by an access to the stack, while for the '*=' order the first access is to the stack, in order to store the content of the specified register, and the second is for the operand. For the stack writes the name/base adder is used to create the address SF+2 and at the same time SF is updated to this new value. The two phases of these orders are distinguished by extra digits carried through the pipeline with the function. These digits override the normal operand accessing mechanisms when access to the stack is required and also prevent the incrementing of the Control Register when the first phase passes the Control Point.

For the unstacking operation the access to the stack must use the current value of SF as the address, and SF must then be decremented. Two passes through the name/base adder are therefore required, one to present the address SF and one to create address SF-2. Thus this type of order is also split into two phases, one of which is essentially a dummy order serving simply to decrement SF.

The implementation of this stack mechanism within a pipeline gives rise to additional problems in relation to control transfer orders. An order implicitly changing SF does so while there are still several orders ahead of it, but not past the Control Point, and therefore not yet completed. Any one of these orders could be a control transfer order requiring that the partially processed orders behind it in the pipeline be abandoned. Should this situation occur, the SF Register may contain an incorrect value. The correct SF value could be maintained by preventing overlap in such situations, but this would seriously deteriorate the pipeline performance. The alternative solution adopted is to allow the SF register to change as and when required and to carry along the pipeline with the order the new value of SF created by it (registers S3, S4 and S5 in figure 4.6). When the Control Register is updated for the order, the value in S5 is copied into S6. Therefore when a control transfer occurs, the value in S6 is correct and is used to restore SF.

## 4.2.4 Register-Register Orders

Since all the central registers in MU5 serve dedicated
purposes, the need for register-register transfers occurs far
less frequently than in machines such as the PDP-11 and
System/360. Indeed, transfers between these dedicated
registers are not really compatible with a pipeline
organisation. However, it is sometimes convenient to use
orders such as

$$X + B$$
$$B \Rightarrow DO$$

where B (the Modifier Register) and DO (the Origin Field of
the Descriptor register) are specified as Internal Registers
(section 2.2.3). A general scheme for organising these
transfers was therefore implemented. It involves splitting the
order into two phases, one to obtain the operand from the
source register, and one to carry out the required operation
on the destination register. Since the Control Register can
only be incremented once the second phase is complete, it is
convenient to split the order before the Control Point, and to
use the hold-up and WAIT mechanisms to control the necessary
actions. In retrospect it is doubtful whether the engineering
complications required to implement these orders are justified
by the advantage gained in the software, and a different
solution to the overall problem would be sought in a
re-designed system.

The first action in the pipeline for a register-register
order is the setting of a hold-up digit in the Stage 3
function register, F3 (figure 4.6). When the next beat pulse
occurs a control digit is set in F4, the output of which is
fed back to F3 in order to act as a counter and to release the
hold-up. Thus when the first phase of the order reaches Stage
5, the second phase enters Stage 4 and a new order enters
Stage 3. The first phase of the order sets a WAIT condition
(section 4.2.1) and no further action takes place in PROP
until the appropriate operand is returned via the Central
Highway to register HO. This operand is then copied into
register VU to line up with the second phase of the order in
F4. A beat is then generated, without the Control Register
being incremented, to put the second phase of the order into
Stage 5 where it behaves as a simple order.

Slightly different actions are required in each of the two
phases for the two examples given above. In the first case,
the first phase of the order is sent to the B-unit accompanied

75

by a control digit which indicates that the '+' function should be ignored and the value in the B-Register simply routed on to the Central Highway. The second phase of the order proceeds normally to the A-unit with the operand being treated as a literal in SEOP. In the second case, the first phase of the order proceeds to the B-unit, where it is treated as a normal store order. The second phase is sent to the D-unit, again accompanied by a control digit which indicates that the '=>' function should be ignored and the operand simply loaded into the least significant half of the Descriptor Register.

## 4.2.5 Store Orders

An order of the type 'B => name' does not reach the B-unit until some time after the access has been made to the Name Store, so that the operand is not immediately available. Thus, in the absence of any additional technique, a hold-up equivalent to at least four pipeline stages would be needed to await the return of the operand from the B-unit. In the case of store orders involving registers within PROP (NB =>, etc.) or SEOP (DR =>, etc.) this delay is less important since these orders occur infrequently and 'ACC => name' orders are dealt with separately by the Secondary Pipeline (section 5.2.6). For the 'B => name' order, however, special action is taken in order to avoid the hold-up.

When a 'B => name' order enters Stage 4 of the PROP pipeline, the content of the PROP Line Register (PLR in figure 4.6) is preserved, for later use, in an additional register BW, and the order proceeds normally through the pipeline without impeding those following, except as described below. When the function is executed by the B-unit, the Central Highway copies the result into register HO, and sets a WAIT condition (section 4.2.1), which stops the pipeline before the next beat is generated. The information held in register BW is then used to select the appropriate line in the Value Field of the Name Store and the content of register HO is written into it. The additional information needed to select one half of the line for over-writing is held in the F2 Function Register, together with a 'B => outstanding' digit which indicates that the BW Register is in use. When the action of writing into the store has been completed, the 'B => outstanding' digit is re-set and the pipeline is re-started.

While the 'B => outstanding' digit is set, two pipeline hold-ups can occur, one at Stage 2 and one at Stage 4. The hold-up at Stage 2 occurs if a second 'B => name' instruction enters that stage. This hold-up prevents subsequent beats from propagating back beyond the input registers to Stage 3 (F3 etc.) and causes dummy orders to be copied into Stage 3. The hold-up at Stage 4 occurs if any instruction tries to access the same line in the Name Store as that indicated by BW. This hold-up prevents subsequent beats from propagating back beyond the input registers to Stage 5 (F5, etc.) and causes dummy orders to be copied into Stage 5. Both these hold-ups are automatically released when the 'B => outstanding' digit is re-set, or if the contents of the pipeline are discarded by the action of a control transfer before the 'B =>' order has left the end of PROP. If a control transfer occurs after a 'B =>' order has left the end of PROP, then the store updating action must still be carried out since the Control Register will have been incremented for this order.

## 4.2.6 Lock-outs

Two types of situation occur in which an order reaching the end of the PROP pipeline cannot be allowed to proceed until an action arising from a previously issued instruction has been completed. In such cases the earlier order will have set a lock-out digit as it left PROP, and the order which must be held up is copied into F5, but is not issued, until the lock-out digit has been re-set.

The first type of situation occurs when a B-function requires a secondary operand access. The order is sent from PROP to Dr and thence via OBS and Dop to the B-unit. Once an order has been accepted by Dr, PROP would normally be free to send orders using primary operands direct to the B-unit, but these would arrive ahead of the order proceeding through the SEOP. The B lock-out digit prevents this.

The second type of situation occurs when a comparison order is sent to the B-unit or A-unit (COMP or CINC, for example) or to the D-unit (SCMP). The final action of any of these orders is the setting of the Test Digits in the Machine Status Register in PROP, according to the result of the comparison (zero, negative or overflow). Subsequent orders which copy the Machine Status Register into store (STACK LINK, for example), must therefore be held up until the result is received. In addition, further comparison orders must also be held up. This is not a normal programming situation, but a faulty program could issue two comparison orders in succession before a conditional control transfer, and the control transfer following the second comparison order would proceed on the result of the first, leaving all subsequent pairs of comparison and conditional control transfer orders out of step. Thus any comparison order leaving PROP sets a lock-out digit and any order copying the Machine Status Register into store or any further comparison order is held up until the

77

lock-out is re-set by the return of the comparison result. Control transfer orders are not held up by this mechanism. Instead, these orders are held up after the operand has been returned to register HO (but before execution), so that the Central Highway transfer time can be overlapped with the execution of the previous comparison order.

## 4.2.7 Organisational Orders

The Organisational orders, which are all carried out by PROP, set a WAIT digit (section 4.2.1) as they enter Stage 5 of the pipeline, thereby holding up the next pipeline beat until the operand has been returned to register HO and the order executed. Some of these orders (conditional control transfers and conditional Boolean setting orders) must also wait for the return of any outstanding comparison order result to be returned to PROP before they can be executed, while orders altering the base registers, Name Segment Number or Machine Status Register cannot operate under the normal overlapped condition of the pipeline. An order altering the content of the Name Base, for instance, must be completed before a succeeding order can be allowed into register DF, since it may use the content of NB to form an address. In these cases the decoding logic in Stage 0 of PROP sets a 'no-overlap' digit which prevents further orders from being copied into DF until the order has been executed.

The manipulation of the base registers is carried out using the same adder as that used for address calculations (figure 4.6). If the order is of the type 'NB +', then the base forms one input to the adder, via the same route as that used for address calculations, and the operand forms the other input, in place of the name. The adder output is routed back to the inputs of all the base registers and when the addition is complete the appropriate one is updated. If the order is of the type 'NB =', then the actions are exactly as for the 'NB +' type except that no base register is selected as input to the adder, so that the operand is effectively added to zero before being copied into the base register. Clearly the operand could be copied directly into the appropriate register in this case, at the expense of fifteen AND/OR selection gates, together with fan-out gates to drive the selection inputs. The saving in time thus made would only be about 10% of the total order time, however, which was not felt to be sufficient to justify the extra hardware involved.

The control transfer orders are carried out in a similar way using the Control Adder. Thus for relative transfers the operand is added to the current value of the Control Register before the latter is updated, while for absolute transfers the

78

operand is added to zero. Absolute transfers also update the Segment Field of the Control Register by copying the operand directly to the appropriate bits.

All the conditional control transfers run with normal overlap since, although their actual result is not known until they are executed, the IBU can attempt to predict their result (section 4.1), and if it is correct the pipeline will contain valid functions behind the control transfer when it is executed. The unconditional jumps, on the other hand, only run with overlap if the IBU has predicted that they will jump, and the Sequence bit (section 4.1.1) is set to 1. If subsequent instructions were allowed into the PROP pipeline behind an unpredicted unconditional jump, then these would have to be discarded when the control transfer was executed and the IBU would also have made additional, unnecessary pre-fetches.

## 4.2.8 PROP and IBU Interrupts

Four program-generated interrupts and one hardware-generated interrupt can arise from the different stages within PROP. Action is taken to deal with both internal and external interrupts at Stage 5, so for each internal interrupt a digit is carried through the pipeline from the stage at which it is generated. Should the contents of the pipeline be discarded as a result of a control transfer, these unprocessed interrupts are also discarded. The program-generated interrupts are 'Illegal Function' ('B => Literal', for example), 'Name Adder Overflow' (which can arise either as a result of an address calculation or the execution of an Organisational order such as 'NB +'), 'Control Adder Overflow' (an overflow into the Segment Field of the Control Register during the execution of a relative control transfer), and 'Illegal V-store Access' (which occurs in user mode if an order specifies a V-store location as its operand). The hardware-generated interrupt occurs if more than one line in the Associative Field of the Name Store indicates equivalence (section 6.1.1). In each case PROP does not execute the instruction, but sets the appropriate digit in the Program Fault or System Error V-lines (section 6.5.1), and when the order reaches Stage 5, all orders in the pipeline are discarded and the Interrupt entry orders are requested from the IBU (section 4.1.2).

Three types of IBU interrupt can arise, one from a hardware malfunction (multiple equivalence in the Jump Trace) and two from the use of the pre-fetching mechanism. Thus, the address counter associated with the Advanced Control Register (section 4.1.2) may produce a carry-out from its most significant digit, indicating an overflow into the Segment Field (Control Segment Overflow), or, alternatively, an address generated by

79

the incrementing of the Advanced Control Register may cross a page boundary and cause a Non-equivalence in the Current Page Register (CPRNEQ) when the request is sent to SAC. For an IBU priority request or a PROP request, the latter condition would immediately produce an interrupt, but for an IBU ordinary request the occurrence of the CPRNEQ is signalled to the IBU separately.

After either Control Segment Overflow or CPRNEQ has occurred, the IBU continues to send instructions to PROP, but the ones corresponding to the illegal or unobtainable addresses have an interrupt digit set with them. In many cases a control transfer will have been obeyed before the first marked order reaches Stage 4 of PROP, and the interrupt will have been discarded, but should the interrupt be genuine, the action taken in PROP depends upon which interrupt is involved. Thus the Control Segment Overflow interrupt is treated in exactly the same way as a Control Adder Overflow in PROP, whereas the CPRNEQ interrupt causes a dummy control transfer to the current Control Register address, and hence forces an IBU priority request to the failing address. This then causes an immediate interrupt when CPRNEQ is detected by SAC.

Multi-length instructions cause an additional problem in the case of CPRNEQ. The forced priority request is to the address of the first 16 bits of the instruction, which may be the last 16-bit word of a page. In this situation the failing address is accessed by an ordinary request subsequent to the forced priority request and does not cause an interrupt when CPRNEQ is obtained. This condition was not catered for in the original design, and when it first occurred (after many months of Processor operation) the Processor simply went into a closed loop, continuously causing control transfers to the partially obtainable instruction. The problem was overcome by incorporating an additional flip-flop in PROP. This flip-flop is set whenever a dummy control transfer occurs for an IBU CPRNEQ and re-set when an interrupt is detected. While it is set, all IBU requests are treated as priority requests by SAC, so that they can all cause a CPRNEQ interrupt to be generated.

## 4.3 THE CENTRAL HIGHWAY

The Central Highway [17] provides the non-dedicated function and data paths within the MU5 Processor needed to connect the operand accessing units with the function execution units. These paths are shown heavily drawn in figure 4.10. The paths from PROP to Dr, from the B-unit to Dr, from Dop to the A-unit and between the units of the SEOP are dedicated routes and do not form part of the Central Highway system. Thus the Central Highway is principally concerned with loading functions and operands into the B-unit and returning store order values from the B-unit or A-unit to PROP or Dop. The data path consists basically of two sets of 64-bit wide gates (G1 and G2 in figure 4.10) which provide all the necessary interconnection routes. In the quiescent state the PROP input is held open and all others are closed. Any other input is opened only as a result of requests from the other units and a set of fixed priorities is invoked in the event of a clash. Thus PROP has priority over Dop at the input to G1 and the descending order of priority at G2 is G1, the B-unit and the A-unit.

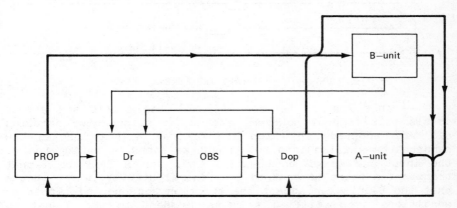

Figure 4.10 The Central Highway

## 4.3.1 PROP Requests

Whenever an order enters Stage 5 of the PROP pipeline, the 'data gone' flip-flop is re-set, and decoded information from Stage 4 is copied into a special register which determines the destination of the order. Orders destined for the B-unit or PROP travel via the Central Highway, while Dr is connected by a separate dedicated highway. A dummy order reaching Stage 5 has no destination and simply causes the generation of a beat 50 ns after the one which brought it into Stage 5.

The B-unit completes most functions within 45 ns, and can therefore accept a stream of such functions from PROP at a 50 ns rate. Because some functions take considerably longer, however, (multiply, for example) a handshake mechanism must be implemented between PROP and the B-unit. Figure 4.11 shows the minimum hardware needed to implement a handshake system between two units and a schematic timing diagram of its operation. Assuming a delay of 5 ns per circuit and a cable delay of 1.8 ns per foot, however, the maximum distance between units for a 50 ns operating rate is approximately 8 feet.

81

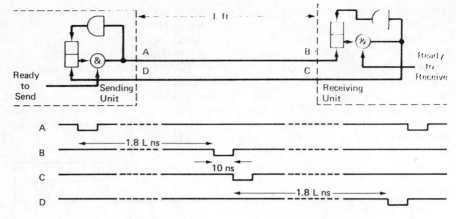

Figure 4.11 A Basic Handshake System

The cable lengths between PROP and the B-unit are almost double this figure, however, and so an alternative solution has been adopted, in which the Central Highway breaks the handshake mechanism into two handshake loops by making use of the input buffer of the B-unit. Thus for a PROP to B-unit transfer, a pulse is sent to the Central Highway, which checks that the B-unit can accept the function and operand. If these conditions are satisfied a pulse is sent to the B-unit to strobe the input buffer and to set the input buffer busy. At the same time a pulse is sent to PROP, which can then initiate a further transfer. As soon as the B-unit has received the function it determines whether it is a short or long order. If it is a short order it sends a buffer free signal to the Central Highway immediately, to complete the second loop of the handshake. If it is a long order then the buffer free signal is not sent until the order has been transferred into the arithmetic unit proper and been completed. Thus the buffer free signal indicates that the B-unit can accept the function currently being sent to it plus a further function after 45 ns. Since PROP can only send orders out 50 ns apart, any order it sends to the B-unit is guaranteed to be accepted.

In the case of a PROP to PROP transfer, the Central Highway simply checks that PROP is ready to receive the operand and if or when it is, the Central Highway sends a control pulse to PROP which causes the operand to be strobed into its input buffer (HO) and also returns a signal which indicates that the transfer is complete. Although PROP actually initiated the request, HO may nevertheless be busy as a result of the execution of a 'B => name' order. Since PROP continues with the processing of subsequent orders once a store order has been sent to the B-unit (section 4.2.5), the transfer of the operand back to PROP is initiated by the B-unit (section

4.3.3) and can occur at any time relative to the subsequent sequence of events in PROP.

## 4.3.2 Dop Requests

Dop makes requests to the Central Highway in order to send operands to the B-unit or PROP. Thus when a B-function requires a secondary operand, the instruction is first sent from PROP to Dr. After the necessary actions in Dr, OBS and Dop have taken place (Chapter 5), Dop sends a request pulse to the Central Highway. Provided that there is no PROP initiated transfer in progress, the Central Highway sets up the data path from SEOP into G1 and checks that the B-unit input buffer is free. When both conditions are satisfied a control pulse is sent to the B-unit to strobe its input buffer and a transfer complete signal is sent to Dop. At the same time a pulse is sent to PROP to re-set the B lock-out digit (section 4.2.6).

A Dop to PROP request occurs when an Organisational order requires a secondary operand, or when a Name Store non-equivalence in PROP requires a store word to be returned from the OBS Name Store (section 6.1.2). It proceeds as for a transfer to the B-unit, except that no lock-out is involved, and as in the case of PROP to PROP request, HO may be busy as a result of an outstanding 'B => name' order. The Dop to PROP route is also used when the contents of one of the registers in Dr is to be written to store or is required for a register-register transfer (section 4.2.4). This is because there is no direct route from Dr on to the Central Highway. Such a route would have considerably reduced the execution time of these orders, but was impracticable because of pin limitation problems.

## 4.3.3 B-unit and A-unit Requests

The B-unit and A-unit make requests to the Central Highway as a result of executing a store function or a register-register order (section 4.2.4). A control signal accompanying the function indicates whether the operand is to be returned to PROP or Dop. This control signal is preserved with the function and sent to the Central Highway along with the request for a transfer. Upon receipt of a request, the Central Highway checks that no higher priority transfer is in progress, opens the appropriate data path, and if or when the receiving unit is free, sends a control pulse to both the receiving and sending units to complete the transfer.

# 5 The Secondary Instruction Pipeline

The Secondary Instruction Pipeline (figure 5.1) is mainly concerned with accessing and processing the data structure elements specified as secondary operands by means of descriptors. It consists of three major sections, the D-unit [18], the Operand Buffer System [19] and the A-unit. The D-unit is itself made up of two units, the Descriptor Addressing Unit (Dr) and the Descriptor Operand Processing Unit (Dop). Although these two units are actually separated in the Processor, by the Operand Buffer System (OBS), their actions are complementary and they will be considered together in this chapter. The D-unit and the Operand Buffer System can be considered as a Secondary Operand Unit (SEOP), corresponding with the Primary Operand Unit in the Primary Instruction Pipeline.

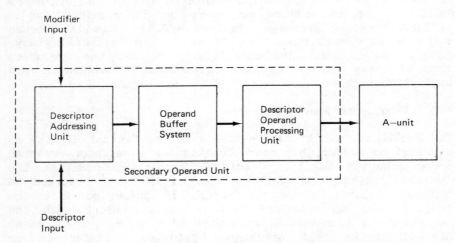

Figure 5.1 The Secondary Instruction Pipeline

Instructions enter the Secondary Instruction Pipeline from PROP. For an instruction specifying an array element as its operand, the descriptor supplied by PROP is loaded into the DR Register within Dr, and Dr proceeds to generate the required address using the content of the B-Register as a modifier.

This address is then sent to OBS, which, like the Name Store in PROP, is invisible to the programmer and its only function is to improve the instruction execution rate. OBS makes the necessary store request and sends the required 64-bit word to Dop, which contains masking and shifting circuitry to select the array element from the appropriate position in the word. Dop is controlled by a combination of a control field generated by Dr (at the same time as the address) and the original function code, which accompanies the instruction as it passes through the pipeline. Instructions leaving Dop are normally sent direct to the A-unit, and exceptionally returned to PROP or the B-unit via the Central Highway, or to Dr via an additional, dedicated route. In the case of the store-to-store functions, the operand processing takes place entirely within the D-unit. The operation of these functions and of the A-unit are dealt with in Chapter 7.

## 5.1 THE D-UNIT

The basic tasks of the D-unit are comparatively simple. They involve the formation of the address of an array element, by the addition of the modifier to the origin address contained within the descriptor, and the subsequent selection of that element from within the corresponding store word. These tasks are complicated, however, by a number of factors, such as the existence of different descriptor types and different operand sizes, the possibility of an operand straddling across two store words, and the need for bound checking. In addition, the two 64-bit descriptor registers, DR and XDR, can be manipulated in whole or in part by various functions. Also the origin and length fields of one or both of these registers must be incremented and decremented, respectively, during each cycle of the execution of the store-to-store orders (section 7.4). For both this task and the bound checking operation, it would clearly be desirable to use a subtractor, separate from the adder used either to increment the origin or to add the modifier and origin, since the appropriate additions and subtractions could then proceed in parallel. However, the alternative solution of employing one adder to carry out these tasks sequentially appeared in the early stages of design to require less hardware, and was somewhat regrettably chosen. This not only decreases the execution rate for array element accesses, but also leads to some restrictions on the programming use of the bound checking facility, since a bound check failure is only detected after the corresponding access has moved irretrievably along the pipeline. The hardware structure of the existing Dr unit is thus as shown in figure 5.2.

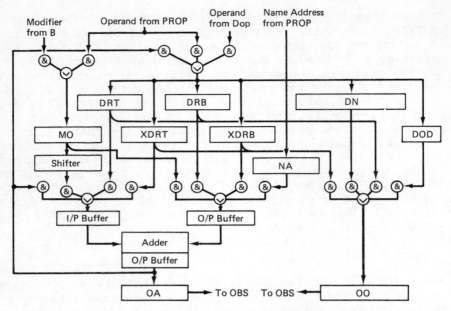

Figure 5.2 The Descriptor Addressing Unit

The two descriptor registers each consist of a top and bottom half (DRT and DRB, XDRT and XDRB). DR is the main descriptor register, used for array accesses and the destination address in store-to-store orders. DRB contains the origin and DRT the type and 'number of elements' field. XDR is similarly divided and is used to hold the source address required by some of the store-to-store orders. DR and XDR are normally loaded from PROP, but may in some circumstances be loaded from Dop.

The 32-bit modifier is held in register MO, which is loaded from the B-unit during an array access or from PROP during the execution of functions such as MOD, SMOD, etc., which manipulate DR or XDR. The true output of MO is connected to one side of the 32-bit adder via a shift network, and the complementary output directly to the other side. The modifier normally refers to the position of an element within an array, regardless of its size, and must therefore be shifted relative to the origin, which always refers to a byte address. The complementary output is used in the bound checking operation, where the subtraction of the modifier from the bound (equal to the number of elements in the array) is performed by adding the complement of the modifier to the bound and forcing a carry into the least significant digit position of the adder. Following the formation of the address, the output of the adder is passed on to OBS, via the OBS Address buffer (OA).

86

This address may also be used internally for the updating action of the store-to-store orders and for array accesses which involve elements straddling store-word boundaries (section 5.1.2).

Register DN is a 64-bit temporary buffer used for holding primary operands (names, literals or internal register values) associated with those ACC functions which do not require a secondary operand access. These functions pass through the Secondary Instruction Pipeline en route to the A-unit in order that the correct program sequence be preserved (section 2.3), but must not disturb the contents of the descriptor registers in Dr. The contents of the descriptor registers themselves also pass through the primary operand route to OBS (via the OBS Operand Buffer, OO) when required for orders such as 'DR =>'. A route through Dr is also required for addresses of names used with ACC functions and held in the OBS Name Store. This is provided via register NA, which is loaded from PROP and can be gated as an input to the Dr address adder. Register DOD is concerned with D-unit interrupts (section 5.1.5).

Orders leaving Dr are forwarded to OBS, which obtains the operand (section 5.2) and sends it to Dop. Control information generated by Dr during the address formation is buffered with the function in OBS, and is supplied to Dop with the store word. Using this information, Dop selects the required array element from within the store word, and in the case of a load order, routes it to the least significant end of its output highway, ready to be sent to the appropriate execution unit. In the case of a store order, Dop updates the appropriate part of the store word and returns the updated version to OBS.

Dop consists of two sections (figure 5.3), one with a 64-bit data path used for operands associated with computational orders, and one with an 8-bit data path used for operands associated with the store-to-store orders (section 7.4). The main input register (FR) has masking facilities which permit the selection of left or right hand masks to any bit position over the full 64-bit width, while the shift mechanism allows any circular shift from 0 to 63 bits in single bit increments. This is achieved by three levels of logic, the first allowing shifts of 0, 16, 32 or 48 bits, the second shifts of 0, 4, 8, or 12 bits and the third shifts of 0, 1, 2 or 3 bits. The output of the shifter is copied into the main output register (GR) if the order is destined for the A-unit or the Dr unit, or gated directly on to the Central Highway if the order is destined for PROP or the B-unit. The route from GR back into FR is used during the execution of store orders.

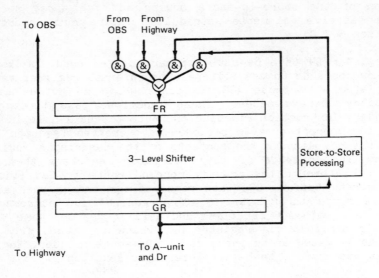

Figure 5.3 The Descriptor Operand Processing Unit

Figure 5.4 illustrates the actions taken for a load order requiring a 16-bit operand. The store word containing the operand is loaded into FR (a), and the shifter routes the required 16-bit operand to the least significant end of the input to GR  At the same time, the most significant 48 bits of the input to GR are set to zero by inhibiting the appropriate section of the data path in the third level of the shifter (b). GR is strobed when sufficient time has elapsed for the shifter outputs to settle, following the receipt of a store word in FR, and when the previous order in GR has been accepted by another unit.

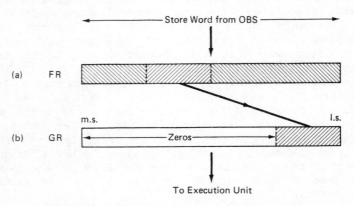

Figure 5.4 Dop Actions for a Load Order

88

The actions for a store order are more complex. The order first passes through Dop as if it were a load order, en route to the appropriate execution unit, and is only processed by Dop when the execution unit indicates that the required operand is available. The operand is received from the Central Highway (figure 5.3) and is copied into the least significant end of register FR (figure 5.5(a)). It is then shifted to its eventual alignment in the store word, copied into GR (b) and copied back from GR into FR (c). The store word of which it is to form part is then sent again from OBS and selectively copied into FR around the operand, using the masking facility (d). The updated version of the store word is then returned from FR back to OBS.

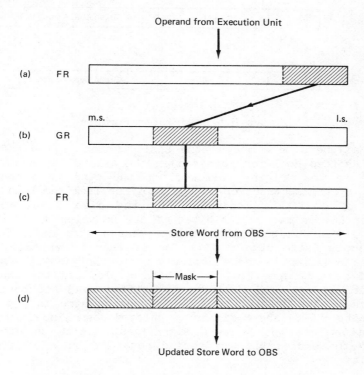

Figure 5.5 Dop Actions for a Store Order

## 5.1.1 Vector Accesses

The actions taken within Dr for secondary operands depend upon the instruction type and the descriptor type. The instruction can specify two pairs of alternative actions giving rise to four variations. Thus the access may or may not involve modification ([B] or [0] respectively), and the descriptor may be loaded with the instruction or may be the one currently

held in the DR Register (S[] or D[] respectively). The actions
corresponding to the different descriptor types (figure 5.6)
fall into three main categories, vector accesses corresponding
to Types 0 or 2, string accesses corresponding to Type 1
(section 5.1.2) and special actions corresponding to Type 3
(section 5.1.3).

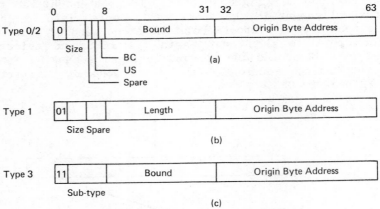

Figure 5.6 Descriptor Formats

For a Type 0 or 2 access the basic action is the addition
of the shifted Modifier (or zero in the case of an unmodified
access) to the Origin, followed, in the case of a modified
access, by the subtraction of the Modifier from the Bound. The
amount of shift is controlled by the Size bits held in
register DR, or may be inhibited if the Unscaled digit (US in
figure 5.6(a)) is set. If an 8-bit operand size is specified,
for example (size bits = 011), or if the unscaled digit is
set, the Modifier is added directly to the Origin; if a 64-bit
operand size is specified (size bits = 110) and the Unscaled
digit is not set, the Modifier is shifted up 3 bit positions
relative to the Origin; if a 1-bit operand size is specified
(size bits = 000) the Modifier is shifted down 3 positions. In
the latter case the 3 least significant digits do not pass
through the adder, but are copied into the output buffer as
'Dop bits'.

The Dop bits are carried through OBS together with the
function digits and control the operation of Dop. Figure 5.7
shows the Dop bits used to control the shifting and masking in
Dop. The first nine of these define the positions of the most
significant and least significant ends of the operand. Thus
the Most Significant Byte Address digits (MSBA) refer to the
arithmetically most significant (left hand) end of the
operand, and are simply the least significant three digits
from the adder. Since the descriptor origin is a byte address,
and since OBS is only concerned with providing 64-bit words to

90

Dop, only the most significant 29 digits from the adder are required as a store address. The Most Significant Bit Address digits indicate the position of the most significant bit of the operand within the most significant byte and only take on non-zero values for vector accesses to 4-bit or 1-bit elements. For these sizes the Modifier is shifted down by 1 or 3 bit positions respectively, and the bits shifted below the adder constitute the Most Significant Bit Address digits. Thus for a 4-bit access, bit 31 of the Modifier defines which half of the byte is to be selected, and for a 1-bit access bits 29, 30 and 31 of the Modifier define the single bit to be used.

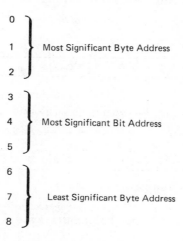

Figure 5.7 Table of Dop Bits

The Least Significant Byte Address digits (LSBA) refer to the arithmetically least significant (right hand) end of the operand. For operands of less than 16 bits only one byte is ever necessary, and the LSBA digits are identical to the MSBA digits. For 16-bit and 32-bit operands, which must lie on 16-bit or 32-bit word boundaries respectively, it can be seen from figure 5.8 that in the 16-bit case, the least significant of the LSBA digits must always be 1, while the other two must equal the corresponding MSBA digits, and that in the 32-bit case, the two least significant LSBA digits must always be 1, and the most significant LSBA digit must equal the corresponding MSBA digit. For 64-bit operands, which are aligned on 64-bit word boundaries, the LSBA digits are all set to 1.

Once the address and Dop bits have been formed by Dr, they are copied into the output buffer registers, and a request is sent to OBS, thus allowing Dr to proceed with the bound check. Normally, asynchronous communication between two units would

91

require that the output buffer be set busy at this point, and
not freed until OBS acknowledged acceptance of the request. In
order to overcome the 30 ns communication delay caused by the
physical separation of Dr and OBS, however, OBS guarantees
always to accept a first request within 80 ns of its being
sent. Thus Dr records the fact that it has sent one request to
OBS and declares the output buffer free immediately. The
output buffers can then be overwritten if necessary, and a
second request sent (provided it is not less than 80 ns after
the first) before OBS acknowledges receipt of the first
request. The first request must be acknowledged, however,
before the buffers can be overwritten for a third request.

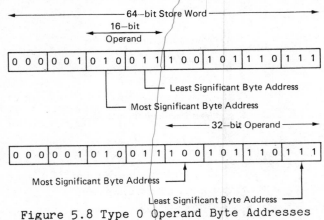

Figure 5.8 Type 0 Operand Byte Addresses

The bound check involves determining whether or not the
Modifier lies in the range

$$0 \leq \text{modifier} < \text{bound}$$

The check against the implicit lower bound of zero simply
involves checking the sign of the Modifier, while the check
against the explicit upper bound involves a full subtraction.
Thus the Bound is routed to one side of the Dr adder, the
inverse of the Modifier to the other side, and carry forced
into the least significant digit. When the subtraction is
complete, the adder output is tested for a zero or negative
result, and provided that neither of these conditions, nor a
negative modifier value is detected, Dr is ready for next
instruction. If any of these fault conditions is detected,
however, the Bound Check Fail digit is set in the DOD Register
(section 5.1.5). Unless the corresponding inhibit is set in
DOD, an interrupt is signalled to PROP, which takes
appropriate action (section 4.1.2). The whole action of
checking the Modifier can itself be inhibited if the Bound
Check Inhibit digit (BC in figure 5.6(a)) is set. In this

92

case, and in the case of an unmodified access, Dr is ready for the next instruction as soon as the address and Dop bits have been copied into the output buffer.

## 5.1.2 String Accesses

The Type 1 string descriptor (figure 5.6(b)) differs from the Type 0 vector descriptor in that only 8-bit (1-byte) elements may be specified, and a length (equal to the number of bytes) is specified instead of a bound. This type of descriptor is used principally in conjunction with store-to-store functions, but may also be used with computational functions to handle items of variable length within a data structure (section 2.2.4). In the case of store-to-store orders the strings are handled one byte at a time, and can therefore be of any length up to the maximum allowed by the 24-bit length field of the descriptor. In the case of computational orders, 64 bits (8 bytes) at most can be handled, and if the string length is greater than 8 bytes, only the first eight are actually supplied. A further distinction between Type 1 and Type 0 descriptors is that in the Type 1 case, operands are only obliged to start on byte address boundaries, so that a 32-bit (4-byte) operand for example, does not have to start on a 32-bit word boundary and may even straddle a store-word boundary. In this case two store words must be accessed and Dop selects and combines the appropriate parts of each.

The actions taken in Dr for a Type 1 are initially similar to those for a Type 0 access, involving the addition of the Origin and Modifier to form, in this case, the address of the most significant byte of the operand. The formation of the address of the least significant byte requires a second addition in which the Length (or 8 if the Length is greater than 8) is added to the address of the most significant byte. Until this addition has been performed, by routing the adder output back to one input and the Length to the other (figure 5.3), no request can be sent to OBS. This is because both OBS and Dop require a control digit, the Extra Store Word (ESW) digit, to be sent with the request if the operand crosses a store-word boundary. If a store-word boundary is not crossed, the processing of the order in Dr is finished as soon as this request has been sent to OBS. If a store-word boundary is crossed, a second OBS request is made.

The value obtained after the second addition actually addresses the first byte beyond the required operand (figure 5.9), and the check for store-word boundary crossing must take this into account. The LSBA digits (figure 5.7) must also be set up correctly.

93

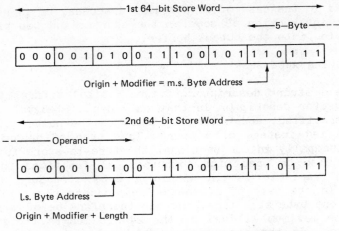

Figure 5.9 Type 1 Operand Byte Addresses

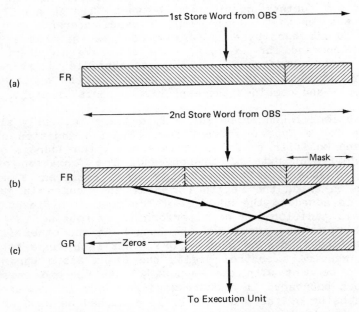

Figure 5.10 Dop Actions for an ESW Load Order

The actions taken in Dop for an ESW load order involving an operand such as that illustrated by figure 5.9 are shown in figure 5.10. The first store word is loaded into FR from OBS (a), as in the single word case (figure 5.4), but before being shifted into GR, the second store word is selectively copied

94

over it with the appropriate operand bytes being protected by the masking facility (b). FR is then shifted into GR, with zeros in the byte positions arithmetically more significant than the most significant byte of the operand (c). Since the shifter operates circularly, shifting the least significant bytes of the operand to the least significant end of GR aligns all the bytes correctly. As in the case of a single word access, the actions for an ESW store order are correspondingly more complex.

5.1.3 Special Descriptor Accesses

The Type 3 descriptor format (figure 5.6(c)) is basically of the vector type, but bits 2-7 are used to specify the following sub-types, each of which involves some special action

>           Real Address
>           Read/Store Direct
>           Read & Mark
>           Indirect
>           Escape

The actions in Dr for Real Address, Read/Store Direct and Read & Mark descriptor accesses are similar to those for Type 0 accesses, except that a fixed operand size of 64 bits is assumed. Real Address and Read/Store Direct accesses cause special action in OBS and SAC, however (sections 5.2.7 and 6.4), and Read & Mark accesses cause special actions in OBS and in the Local and Mass Stores (section 6.6.2).

The Indirect Descriptor causes the 64-bit operand addressed by its Origin to be accessed from store and then loaded into DR and treated as a new descriptor. This new descriptor can itself be Indirect, in which case the whole action is repeated. Since this action can occur any number of times, the system must be capable of being interrupted and re-started at any point in the event of a CPR non-equivalence (CPRNEQ). At such a re-start the original order is re-issued from PROP, but the existing descriptor in DR must be used; rather than the original one, so that an S[] order must be treated as a D[] order. This is achieved through a special bit contained in the link preserved at the time of the interrupt, and automatically re-set after the order has been re-issued to Dr.

All descriptor accesses are initiated in the first instance by the setting of a 'START' flip-flop and either an 'S[]' or a 'D[]' flip-flop, and during the course of the corresponding actions in Dr, these flip-flops are all re-set. For an access using an Indirect Descriptor, Dr sends a request for the

95

64-bit operand to OBS with the function digits modified to appear as 'D =', and then itself sets the 'START' and 'S[]' flip-flops again. No immediate action occurs, however, since an 'Operand Outstanding' flip-flop is also set. When the order reaches Dop, the operand is returned to Dr, and the 'Operand Outstanding' flip-flop is re-set. This allows the forced S[] request to be started. If the new descriptor is also Indirect, the cycle is repeated, but when a String or Vector Descriptor is encountered, the forced request is treated normally, with modification if appropriate, and sent to OBS accompanied by the original function digits.

When an attempt is made to access an operand by means of an Escape Descriptor, Dr initially carries out its normal Type 0 actions, but instead of sending a request to OBS, it sends a special control signal to PROP, sets an 'Escape' flip-flop internally, and terminates the order. PROP abandons the order and signals the IBU to send the two fixed instructions (section 4.1.2)

```
          STACK LINK    literal 0
          JUMP          D[0]
```

which in effect force a procedure call to the address given by the first element in the vector addressed by DR. The software is free to store 'parameters' in subsequent elements. Either of the forced instructions could cause a CPRNEQ interrupt, and the detail of the mechanism has to guard against the errors this could produce.

The Escape Descriptor is used principally in Algol programs to evaluate 'thunks' (section 2.2.4). The associated instructions evaluate the required operand, set up a Type 0 descriptor in DR which addresses it, and exit to the link, thus causing a return to the calling instruction. This time, however, it is executed as a D[] request rather than an S[] request, due to the presence in the link of the same bit as that used for an interrupted Indirect descriptor access. The same effect can also be achieved as a result of using the MOD order (section 5.1.4), rather than by an S[] request, in which case the Escape Descriptor mechanism is invoked during the first execution of the order instead of the actions required by MOD. When the order is re-executed, DR contains a Type 0 descriptor and the MOD order is executed normally.

5.1.4 Structure Access Orders

In order to allow flexibility in accessing data structures, a number of orders are provided for direct manipulation of the Origin, Bound and Type fields of the DR and XDR registers.

Typical of these are the MOD order, in which the operand is used to increment the origin and decrement the Bound in DR, and the XMOD order, which operates in the same way on XDR. In either case, a bound check is carried out as for a descriptor access and an interrupt is generated if the check fails.

More complex than the MOD type of order are the SUB1 and SUB2 orders. These are concerned with accessing structures defined by 'dope' vectors (section 2.2.5), and each involves the accessing and manipulation of the dope vector 'triples'. From a performance point of view, these orders are little short of disastrous, since little or no overlapping can occur in the pipeline during their execution. In the sequence common to both SUB1 and SUB2

```
B - XD[0]
B * XD[1]
DB = XD[2]
MOD B
XMOD 3
```

the individual orders are created by Dr, which performs several cycles of operation in order to generate the necessary function and operand requests to OBS. An immediate problem which arises is that any one of the three vector accesses could cause a CPRNEQ to occur, and once the order has been partially executed it cannot be re-started from the beginning. This and other problems associated with these orders have been solved in MU5, but with little elegance, and the details are best left to the reader's imagination.

5.1.5 D-unit Interrupts

Four different types of interrupt can arise within Dr and Dop as a result of descriptor accesses or the execution of structure access and store-to-store orders. They are

> Bound Check Fail
> Non-Zero Truncation
> Short Source String
> Illegal Access

Should any one of these errors occur, a corresponding digit is set in the DOD register (figure 5.2). In the Illegal Access case, the setting of the digit in DOD always causes a 'D Interrupt' signal to be sent to PROP, while in the other three cases this signal can be inhibited by the presence in DOD of a corresponding 'Interrupt Inhibit' digit.

97

The Bound Check Fail has already been discussed (sections 5.1.1 and 5.1.4). A Non-Zero Truncation (NZT) error arises if an array element being returned to store exceeds its specified length. Dop detects this situation and sets the NZT digit in DOD. A Short Source String (SSS) error cah arise during the execution of the SLGC store-to-store order (section 7.4), in which the bytes of a source string and a destination string are logically combined and returned to the destination string. If the source string runs out before the destination string has been filled, the SSS digit is set in DOD and the order is terminated.

Illegal Access interrupts can be generated in a number of ways. A descriptor access using a Type 0 descriptor can specify a 128-bit element, for example, but the hardware can only deal with elements up to 64 bits in length, and an interrupt would be signalled in this case. The store-to-store orders, which are concerned with manipulating strings of bytes, are obliged to use Type 1 string descriptors, and specifying any other type therefore generates an interrupt. Among the Type 3 descriptors, the Real Address and Read/Store Direct types are reserved for use by the Operating System and an interrupt occurs if an attempt is made to use either of these types in a user program.

## 5.2 THE OPERAND BUFFER SYSTEM

The Operand Buffer System (OBS) is invisible to user programs and exists simply to match the average accessing rate of array elements to the average rate of execution of instructions in the A-unit. Since array processing usually involves large arrays, OBS does not attempt to buffer large amounts of data in the hope that it will be used repeatedly. Instead it streams requests from its input stage out to SAC and queues the functions as they await the return of their operands from store. At the output stage of OBS these functions are re-connected with the stream of store words returning from SAC. In order to implement this scheme, however, sufficient operand buffers must be provided to accept data from all outstanding store requests. Because the buffer size of 128 bits is larger than the average operand size, and because of the sequential nature of many array calculations, these buffers may frequently contain the operands corresponding to new requests from Dr. Thus by performing an associative search on these buffers at the input stage of OBS, many store requests can be avoided. The eight buffers incorporated into OBS for this purpose constitute a Vector Store. In addition, for the reasons outlined in section 2.3, OBS contains a Name Store, and since literal operands must sometimes be sent through the Secondary Instruction Pipeline to the A-unit, a

98

Literal Store is also needed (figure 5.11).

A request sent to OBS from Dr normally consists of a function, accompanied by control information, and either a valid address without an operand (a vector or name address, for example), or a valid operand such as a literal, which has no address. In the latter case, the operand is simply written into the Literal Store, while in the former case the address is looked up in the Vector Address or Name Address Store, and the appropriate action taken according to whether or not a match is found.

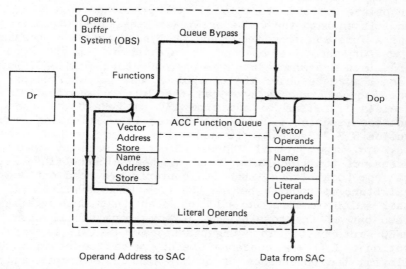

Figure 5.11 Overall Diagram of the Operand Buffer System

The function queue is only used for ACC instructions. Thus if an instruction sent from Dr is destined for the A-unit, it is written into the Queue, and when it reaches the output of the Queue, the Operand Store provides the appropriate operand store word to be sent to Dop with the function. If the function is destined for the B-unit, PROP or Dr, the Queue is bypassed by copying the function into the Queue Bypass Line, which allows it to overtake ACC functions in the Queue. This is done for two reasons; firstly the B-unit, PROP and Dr are situated at earlier positions in the Processor pipeline and are mainly concerned with supplying operand addresses to OBS in order to keep the A-unit (which is executing the 'useful' part of the program) busy, and although they use secondary operands relatively infrequently, there would be no point in queuing these functions behind ACC functions. Secondly, in the case of an ACC order in the Queue causing a CPRNEQ, this order will lodge at the head of the Queue and will be joined by

99

subsequent ACC orders released by PROP before action is taken on the CPRNEQ interrupt. The CPRNEQ procedure itself requires access to secondary operands for use with B functions, and must therefore be able to bypass the Queue when the latter is blocked.

The normal operation of the Operand Buffer System can be considered in terms of a number of functional control processes as shown in figure 5.12. The Input Process receives requests from Dr and decodes the function. It presents the operand address to the Virtual Address Store and makes a new entry when no match is found. The function, together with the appropriate Operand Store line number, encoded as a 'Tag', is then written into the Queue or Bypass Line. The Output Process reads a function from the Queue or Bypass Line and passes it on to Dop when its operand is available from the Operand Store. Data transfers into the Operand Store from SAC, Dop or Dr are also made under the control of the Output Process. The Store Request Process provides the interface with SAC, and organises transfers to and from SAC on behalf of other OBS processes (section 6.2.3). The Buffer Line Selection Process (section 6.2.2) selects the next line to be freed when a new entry into the Virtual Address Store is made by the Input Process. If the line to be freed has been altered since it was read from Local Store, then its contents are read out and the Local Store is updated before the line is overwritten. In the detail which follows it will be seen that much complexity arises out of the possibility of any store access causing a CPRNEQ interrupt. The Organisational Facilities of OBS (section 6.2.4) are concerned mainly with the actions taken following the occurrence of such a CPRNEQ interrupt and are controlled by means of V-lines.

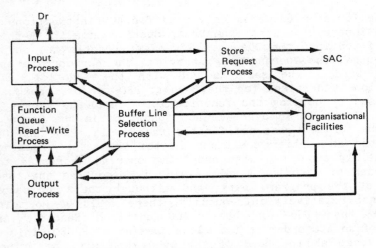

Figure 5.12 OBS Control Processes

100

## 5.2.1 The OBS Input Process

The Input Process controls the actions of the first two stages of OBS, which are mainly concerned with finding or creating an entry in the buffer stores for the operand associated with each order (section 6.2.1). The position of the entry is encoded as a Tag which is then carried through OBS, and if necessary SAC, with the order. In the output stage of OBS this Tag is used to obtain the operand from the buffer stores, and in the case of an order requiring an operand from SAC, the Tag is also returned with the corresponding store word, enabling the correct entry to be made into the Operand Store.

In the case of a literal operand, a new Tag is always generated, and as well as being sent to the Queue or Bypass Line, it is also used to make an immediate request to the Output Process for the literal to be written into one of the Literal Buffers. A better organisation of the system would have been to have the Literal Buffers as part of the Queue, in order to avoid the time penalty involved in writing into the buffer store, but cost and platter space considerations prevented this.

For orders destined for the Bypass Line, the Control Register in PROP is not incremented until and unless CPR equivalence is obtained. These orders are abandoned by OBS in the event of a CPRNEQ, and are therefore prevented, by a 'Function Hold', from proceeding beyond the input stages until the check for CPR equivalence has been successfully completed. Certain Queue functions are also held up and may be abandoned in this way. An ACC COMP order, for example, returns a result from the A-unit to the Test Digits in the Machine Status register in PROP, and since the latter is preserved by the interrupt entry instructions, but cannot be written to store while a COMP result is outstanding (section 4.2.6) such an order must not be allowed to lodge in the Queue as a result of a CPRNEQ.

## 5.2.2 The Queue Read/Write Process

To avoid long delays in OBS in cases where functions pass through a largely empty Queue, the Queue is implemented as a six-line random access store addressed by two counters, the Queue Read Counter and the Queue Write Counter (figure 5.13). Information is entered into the 'tail' of the Queue at the location addressed by the Queue Write Counter, and is read out again when that location has become the 'head' of the Queue, as a result of being addressed by the Queue Read Counter. Thus if the Queue is empty when a new request is received, both counters address the same location and the time for the function to pass through OBS is around 200 ns. If the Queue had been organised as a straightforward pipeline, this time would have been around 800 ns. The operation of the Queue Counters is organised by the Queue Read/Write Process, which accepts read requests from the Output Process and write requests from the Input Process (figure 5.12).

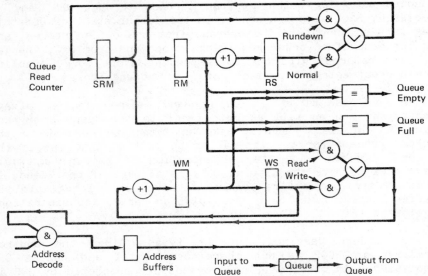

Figure 5.13 The Queue Function Addressing System

A write operation is requested by the Input Process when a function is ready to be transferred into the Queue. Provided that the Queue is not full, and that a read request (which has higher priority) is not outstanding, the write sequence is started as soon as the Queue Read/Write Process has finished its previous cycle of operation. The address of the tail of the Queue is held in the Write Counter Slave register (WS in figure 5.13), which is therefore selected for decoding. The new function, Tag, and Dop, bits are then written into the line addressed by WS, and at the end of the cycle WS is updated from the Write Counter Master WM. WM is incremented at the start of a write cycle to allow a check for the 'Queue Full' condition to be carried out in parallel with the write operation. The Queue becomes full if WM addresses the same location as the Second Read Counter Master (SRM) which normally indicates the position of the function which was last read from the queue, and which may be read again following a CPRNEQ (section 5.2.5). When Queue Full occurs, further write cycles are inhibited until a read cycle causes SRM to be incremented, and the Queue Full condition to disappear.

Read cycles of the queue are initiated by the Output

102

Process, which specifies whether or not the read count should advance for a particular cycle. This enables a read/re-cycle to take place when the operand required by a function read from the queue is found to be unavailable. If the operand is available, a counter advance is required, and the position of the next line to be read is specified by the Queue Read Counter Slave RS. In this case RS is normally copied into both read counter masters RM and SRM. If the operand is unavailable, no advance is required, and since the next line to be read is already specified by RM, no copying takes place.

During a read cycle, the contents of RM are selected to address the Queue. RM is also compared with the Write Counter Master WM, and if a match is found, the 'Queue Empty' condition occurs. Queue Empty indicates that the line currently being read has not yet been filled by the write sequence, and hence its contents are non-valid. When appropriate, RS is incremented at the end of the cycle to indicate the line to be read by the next cycle.

## 5.2.3 The OBS Output Process

The Output Process controls the interface which passes orders from OBS to Dop, and organises all accesses to the Operand Store. The issuing of an order from OBS to Dop involves extracting a function from the Queue or Bypass Line and passing it on to Dop with the appropriate store word read from the Operand Store. The Operand Store may be accessed from various sources (section 6.2), so that Operand Store lines may be filled, altered, used to update the Local Store, etc.

Provided that the Queue is not empty, the Output Process normally requests another read cycle of the Queue Read/Write Process as soon as action on the preceding function has been completed. When a Queue Read/Write Process response indicates that the Queue has been read, the Output Process action starts. The Queue Tag is selected and is used to address the Operand Store for a read cycle, and to access the corresponding digit in the 'Full Register' (section 6.2). The Full Register contains one digit for each line in the Operand Store indicating whether or not its contents are valid. Following a non-equivalence in the Virtual Address Store, for example, it indicates whether or not the store word has been returned by SAC. If the Full digit is 0 for the selected line, a second request is made to the Queue Read/Write Process, but the Queue Read Counter is not advanced, so that the same function is read from the Queue as before. The Output Process cycles again, and the sequence is repeated until the required store word is found to be available. The store word is then read out and sent to Dop together with the function and Dop bits. The next cycle of the Queue Read/Write Process will then advance the Queue Read Counter, so that the next function in sequence is extracted from the Queue.

In the case of a Bypass function, a request for action is made to the Output Process as soon as a function is transferred into the Bypass Line. The action taken by the Output Process in this case is similar to that for a function from the Queue so that if the Output Process finds that the store word required by the Bypass function is available, it reads it out and sends it to Dop, together with the function and Dop bits, whereas if the store word is not available, it re-cycles until the store word becomes available, and then sends the function, Dop bits and store word to Dop.

## 5.2.4 Queue Management after a CPRNEQ

When a store request made to SAC from any unit in the MU5 Processor causes a CPRNEQ, subsequent requests from all units are abandoned by SAC. Thus OBS requests subsequent to one causing CPRNEQ are not answered, and the first such function to reach the head of the Queue effectively blocks the Queue to all subsequent Queue functions. Meanwhile, however, SAC informs Dr and PROP of the CPRNEQ and these units take alternative action. Functions trapped in the Queue cannot be re-executed from PROP, since the Control Register is incremented for them as soon as they are accepted by Dr. Furthermore, it is essential that in this situation it should still be possible to execute Bypass functions, so Dr and the input stages of OBS should not contain Queue functions after the Queue has been blocked. For this reason action is taken on every request from Dr to OBS to regulate the number of entries in the Queue.

Thus whenever action is initiated in Dr for a Queue function, the contents of a 'Queue Gauge' are raised up by one position, or by two in the case of a String Descriptor access crossing a store-word boundary. The Queue Gauge is lowered by one whenever a CPRNEQ reply is received from SAC in response to either a Queue function access or a 'CHECK ONLY' request. A CHECK ONLY request is one made specially for this purpose by OBS to SAC when the operand for a Queue function is already in the OBS buffers. Once such a request has passed the CPR equivalence checking stage in SAC and a reply has been sent to OBS, it is abandoned. Thus, since any new order entering Dr can cause one or two Queue entries to be made, an output is taken from the Queue Gauge indicating whether or not the OBS Queue contains room for two or more new entries. If, at the end of the current order in Dr, there is room for two more new entries, the order terminates normally and a new order can be accepted. If there is not room for two more new entries, one of three situations may occur. If the next order does not require a Queue entry, the current order terminates normally and action for the next order is begun. If the next order requires a Queue entry, termination of the current order is held up until sufficient entries have been deleted from the Queue Gauge, or else a CPRNEQ reply is received. In the latter case the next order, which has not yet been accepted by Dr, and for which the Control Register has therefore not been incremented, is abandoned, and the interrupt entry sequence (section 4.1.2) is entered instead.

The address causing CPRNEQ is available as a V-line in SAC (section 6.4.3) and is examined by the CPRNEQ interrupt procedure which establishes the location of the required block using only primary operands or bypass functions. If this block is currently contained in the Local Store, then it is only necessary to set up a CPR. If the required block is currently contained in some other level of the storage hierachy, however, then a block transfer is required between storage levels before a CPR can be loaded (section 9.3).

If a CPR can be loaded, the interrupted process can be re-entered immediately. The OBS store requests which were abandoned when the CPRNEQ occurred are then remade under the control of a 'Re-start' sequence (one of a set of organisational commands controlled by the V-store mechanism (section 6.5)), after which the execution of the process can continue. If a block transfer is required as a result of the CPRNEQ, then a significant delay is involved, and a change to another process is necessary if efficient use is to be made of the Processor. In order to effect this change, the Queue must be cleared, and the functions of the interrupted process preserved, so that when the Processor is ready to resume the interrupted process, the Queue can be restored to its former state, ready for the Re-start sequence. Two further organisational commands, the 'Dump' and 'Undump' Sequence are used by the Operating System to preserve and restore the Queue for this purpose. The Dump may take place to any address specified by the software, and a number of dumped queues may thus be in store at any time.

5.2.5 Double Access Orders

Double access orders originating in the Secondary Instruction Pipeline (cf. double access orders originating in the Primary Instruction Pipeline (section 4.2.4)) are of two types, those involving one operand which, due to the addressing flexibility available through the Type 1 descriptor mechanism, is partly contained in one 64-bit store word and partly in an adjacent store word (section 5.1.2) and those involving two operands which constitute the source byte and destination byte respectively of a store-to-store order pair (section 7.4). In either case, Dop can only process these double accesses as an entity, and special action is required in the case of CPRNEQ.

If the access is for an ACC order, then the Input Process enters the two phases of the order into the Queue normally. If a CPRNEQ occurs for the first access, then this will cause both accesses to lodge in the Queue, and the normal techniques used for Queue management after a CPRNEQ can be applied. If a CPRNEQ occurs for the second access, however, then the first order will have been issued to Dop, but must be abandoned, and must be re-issued when the Queue is re-started. These actions require the use of the two Read Counter Masters, RM and SRM, (figure 5.13), one of which records the position in the Queue of the first phase of the order, while the other addresses the second. RM and SRM normally advance synchronously when functions are read from the Queue, but when the first phase of a double access order is read, its address is frozen in SRM, until the second phase has been read using RM, which continues to increment normally. If the two phases are issued to Dop without interruption, RM and SRM are resynchronised when the next function after the double access pair is read and RS is copied into RM and SRM. In the situation where the second phase causes a CPRNEQ, the Output Process receives a 'Run Down' signal from SAC, after the first phase has been sent to Dop, indicating that no further operands will be returned (section 6.4.3), and it therefore sends a control signal to Dop which causes the first phase of the order to be abandoned. The Output Process also makes a last read request to the Queue Read/Write Process, accompanied by a control digit which causes SRM to be copied into RM. The counters are thus resynchronised and address the first phase of the double access order again. The first phase is then ready to be re-issued to Dop when the process is re-started, or is available to the Dump Sequence for preservation and subsequent restoration and re-issue by the Undump and Re-start Sequences.

5.2.6 Store Orders

As in the case of orders which write to a primary operand (section 4.2.5), special action is taken to deal with store orders in the Secondary Instruction Pipeline. In this case, however, the commonly occurring store orders are 'ACC => name' and 'ACC => vector', rather than 'B => name'. Thus, just as a 'B => name' order does not reach the B-unit until some time after the required access has been made to the PROP Name Store, an 'ACC =>' order does not reach the A-unit until some

106

time after the required access has been made to the OBS Operand Store. A similar arrangement to that in the Primary Instruction Pipeline is used to avoid the consequential hold-up.

When an 'ACC =>' order is sent from OBS to Dop, the Dop bits and the Tag are preserved in an AW register and the Full digit of the corresponding line in the Operand Store is set to 0. When the operand becomes available from the ACC it is copied into the Dop input buffer and a request is made to the OBS Output Process. The Tag held in AW is used to re-access the Operand Store and the required 64-bit store word is sent to Dop, together with the Dop bits held in AW. Dop performs the appropriate merging of the store word from OBS and the operand from the ACC (section 5.1) and then signals to OBS that it requires to write the altered store word back to the Operand Store. This action is performed by the Output Process, again using the Tag in AW to address the Operand Store. The Full bit of the line, which was cleared when the store order was originally sent to Dop, is now set to a 1. As long as the Full bit is zero, any subsequent order trying to access the line is held up at the output stage of OBS, just as if the store word had not been returned from SAC following a non-equivalence in the Virtual Address Store.

5.2.7 Special Descriptor Actions

Special action is necessary in OBS for Real Address, Read/Store Direct and Read & Mark descriptor accesses, since it is a requirement of these accesses that no entry should be left in the OBS store. The Input Process proceeds normally for these accesses, and enters the address into the empty line in the Name part of the Virtual Address Store. The free name line is used because each of these Descriptors refers specifically to a 64-bit quantity, and the use of the line is to be transitory. The appropriate request to SAC is then made but the order is held up in the input stages. In addition, the action of the Buffer Line Selection Process, which normally creates a new empty line at this point, is suspended. Provided that CPR equivalence is obtained from SAC, the order is released by the Input Process, enters the Queue or Bypass line as appropriate, and is then passed on to Dop as soon as the required operand is received from SAC. When the normal OBS action for this order is complete, including, if necessary, the receipt of the response to a write order, the Buffer Line Selection Process is allowed to continue its line freeing sequence with the constraint that for the next name access it must re-allocate the line used for the special descriptor access.

# 6    Store Organisation

During the running of a process in the MU5 Processor, the information referred to by the virtual addresses it generates may exist in any one of the several real stores which make up the MU5 storage hierarchy (figure 6.1). Thus most operand requests are satisfied by the high-speed integrated circuit stores contained within the Processor, but some require access to a higher level of storage. Interactions between the Processor and the Local Store are organised entirely by hardware, but interactions between other levels in the hierarchy involve a combination of both hardware and software techniques. The software aspects of the system are discussed in Chapter 9, while in this chapter we consider the hardware techniques.

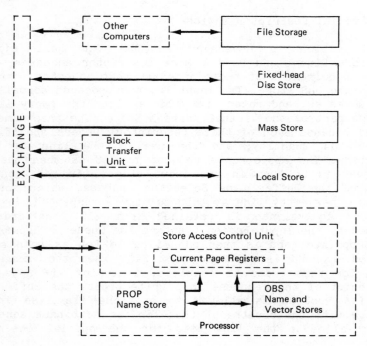

Figure 6.1 The MU5 Storage Hierarchy

Addresses are generated within three units of the Processor, instruction addresses in the IBU, and operand addresses in PROP and SEOP, both of which contain high-speed associatively addressed integrated circuit stores. When an operand access cannot be satisfied by this level of storage, the hardware automatically sends a 'Main Store' request to the Store Access Control Unit (SAC). SAC co-ordinates the interaction between the Processor and its Local Store and between both of these Units and the Exchange. It also contains the Current Page Registers (CPRs) which effect the translation of the virtual addresses sent as 'Main Store' requests by the Processor into the real addresses required for accessing the stores. Normally these addresses refer to the Local Store, but may refer to some other store in the complex (the Mass Store, for example), by suitable loading of the real address field of the CPRs. In the event of the CPRs giving non-equivalence, an interrupt is generated, and the Operating System organises any necessary transfer of pages (section 9.3) and the loading of a CPR. The interface between the hardware and software components of the store organisation system is provided through the V-store, which is also described in this chapter. In addition, the Operating System may use Real Address descriptors (section 5.1.3), for which the CPR address translation mechanism is bypassed, to address certain areas of real store directly.

## 6.1 THE PROP NAME STORE

We saw in Chapter 2 how the original single Name Store developed into two parts, a 32-line store in PROP (section 4.2) dealing mainly with names used by the B-unit, PROP and SEOP, and a 24-line store within the Operand Buffering System (section 5.2) dealing mainly with names used by the A-unit. The PROP Name Store [20] constitutes two stages of the PROP pipeline. Its address field (figure 6.2) is 20 bits wide, 4 bits for the Process Number (PN), 15 for the address within the Name Segment and 1 bit to distinguish 4 lines which are reserved for Level 0 interrupt procedures (section 2.3.1). The segment address is not included since it was assumed that the Name Segment would usually be segment zero. In the rare event of a process using a Name Segment different from zero, the Operating System must purge the Name Store on each entry to and exit from that process. In any case it was not expected in general that the names in use by a process would still be in the Name Store after another program had run. The PN bits are really provided to allow brief and rapid excursions through Operating System modules which run as separate processes. Each of the 28 normal lines also has a bit in each of three status registers. These are the Line Used register (LU), indicating whether the line contains valid information, the Line Altered

register (LA), indicating whether the contents of the value
field have been overwritten by the action of a store order,
and the Line Pointer register (LP), indicating the line of the
Name Store to be used when a new name is next entered into it.

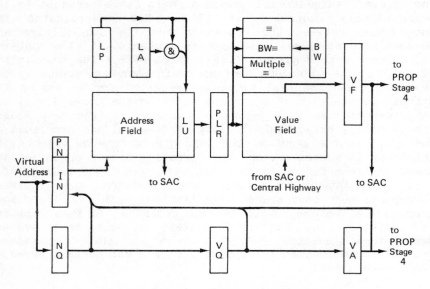

Figure 6.2 The PROP Name Store

### 6.1.1 Normal Operation

The normal action in the PROP pipeline is for a virtual
address generated in the first two stages to be copied into
the Interrogate Register (IN) and concatenated with the PN
bits, at each pipeline beat. If a match is found in the
associative store, and the corresponding Line Used digit is
set to 1, then an equivalence has occurred, and on the next
pipeline beat a digit is set in the PROP Line Register, PLR.
The digit in PLR then selects a register in the Value Field,
and the 64-bit word is read out and copied into the Value
Field Register (VF) by the next beat. At the same time, checks
are made to determine whether

(1) an equivalence occurred

(2) a 'B Write Equivalence' occurred

(3) multiple equivalence occurred

The check for equivalence simply requires an OR operation
on the digits in PLR. If no digit is set, however, this

110

indicates non-equivalence, and the Name Store is updated by transferring a new word into it and discarding an old one. It would clearly be inefficient to enter software to organise this one-word transfer, so the transfer is controlled directly by hardware. A 'B Write Equivalence' occurs if the line giving equivalence is the target line of an outstanding 'B => name' order, and this causes a pipeline hold-up (section 4.2.5) until the operand value has been returned from the B-unit and written into the Name Store. A multiple equivalence occurs if a hardware malfunction in the associative field causes more than one line to give equivalence. In this case a System Error interrupt is generated (section 4.2.8).

When a Name Store entry is replaced the hardware must take into account the effect of store orders. To maintain the speed advantage of the Name Store, store orders only update the value of an operand in a Name Store. (This arrangement is significantly different from the IBM Cache Stores, for example, where both the buffer and the main store are updated together). Thus the old word may have to be copied back to the Local Store before it is overwritten. The decision concerning which line to replace requires the use of a replacement algorithm, and the effects of various replacement algorithms were studied by simulation before the Name Store was built [21]. These varied from a simple cyclic replacement algorithm, requiring a minimum of additional hardware for its implementation, to a multiple-use digit algorithm requiring, for a 32-line store, 32 5-digit counters. Very little difference in performance was found among these different algorithms, and the simple cyclic one was therefore chosen.

The actions which take place when a non-equivalence is detected also depend upon whether the order is destined for the A-unit and whether the required operand is already in the OBS Name Store. The OBS Name Store is meant to keep names used by ACC functions and the PROP Name Store to keep those used by non-ACC functions. Thus for a non-ACC order the normal situation is for equivalence to occur in the PROP Name Store, while for an ACC order the normal situation is for a non-equivalence to occur in the PROP Name Store and equivalence to occur in the OBS Name Store. However, the same name might be accessed by both kinds of orders, and the hardware must guard against the possibility that a name is in the 'wrong' Name Store.

6.1.2 Non-equivalence Actions

A PROP Name Store non-equivalence is detected as the corresponding order enters Stage 4 of the PROP pipeline. It is signalled by a 'non-equivalence' digit set in register F4,

111

which creates a hold-up, and causes the normal control signals decoded for the instruction to be overridden. The address of the required operand is in register VA at this stage, and register VF contains zero. When the next beat occurs, and the order is copied into Stage 5, the control signals set up by the 'non-equivalence' digit cause a WAIT condition to be set (section 4.2.1) and a special order is sent via Dr to OBS. This order carries the non-equivalence address (including the Name Segment number) through to OBS and causes OBS to access its Name Store. If OBS finds equivalence, it returns the 64-bit store word to PROP via Dop and the Central Highway, while if it finds non-equivalence, it makes an access to SAC on behalf of PROP so that the 64-bit store word will be returned direct to PROP from the Local Store.

The setting of the WAIT condition in PROP causes the initiation of the next beat to be held up until the appropriate actions have been completed (figure 6.3). The first actions are the preparation of a line in the Name Store to receive the new address and store word and the copying of the new address, currently held in register VA, into the Interrogate Register (IN). The Name Store line to be replaced is indicated by the Line Pointer Register (LP), which contains one bit corresponding to each line in the Name Store and has, at any time, only one digit set to a 1. Thus LP is simply copied into register PLR (using the set/re-set inputs of the flip-flops), in order to select the line for replacement. Two possible conditions are checked, however, and if necessary dealt with, before the line is ready to be overwritten with the new address and value. The first is that the selected line may be the target line of an outstanding 'B => name' order (section 4.2.5). If it is, LP is moved on to select the next line. This is done by first copying the content of PLR back into LP, and then copying LP into PLR. The outputs from PLR are routed back to the Line Pointer with a 1 digit shift, thus implementing the simple cyclic replacement algorithm. The second condition is that the contents of the selected line may have been altered by the action of a store order. This is checked using the appropriate digit in the Line Altered register. If it has, the virtual address and value are read out, and a write request is made to SAC. The selected line is then ready for overwriting.

The next action which occurs depends on whether the store word is returned from SAC or OBS, or on whether a CPR non-equivalence occurs, in which case no store word is returned, but the interrupt sequence is entered instead. If the store word comes from SAC, then when it arrives the address and value are written into the Name Store, the content of PLR is copied back into the Line Pointer in preparation for

112

the next non-equivalence, and the corresponding bits in LU and LA are set to 1 and 0 respectively.

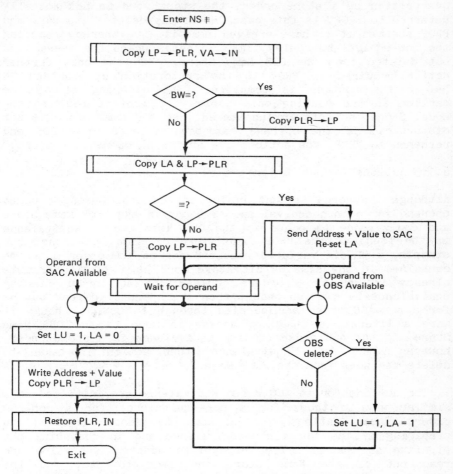

Figure 6.3 The Name Store Non-equivalence Routine

Although the actions needed to update the Name Store are complete at this point, the contents of the PROP Line Register and Interrogate Register no longer correspond to the orders in Stages 2 and 3 of the pipeline, and must be restored. PLR is restored first by copying the address in register VQ into IN, and after a delay to allow for association, PLR is re-strobed. (Preserving a previous copy of PLR for use at this time would not be satisfactory, since it might be the line newly overwritten.) The address in register NQ is then copied into IN, and the actions are complete. Had a longer PROP pipeline beat time been adopted at the outset of the design, these complications could well have been avoided.

113

In the case where OBS indicates that the required store word is in its Name Store, then if all 64 bits are to be overwritten by a store order, the store word is not actually returned to PROP. In this case OBS simply deletes its copy and PROP assumes it to have arrived immediately, thereby reducing the non-equivalence delay time. In cases where the operand is not deleted from the OBS Name Store, then the only further action required in PROP is the restoration of PLR and IN before the routine is complete. (The clearing of a line earlier in the routine only copies its content back to the Local Store and sets it 'unaltered', so the Name Store is not disturbed.) If the operand has been deleted from OBS and returned to PROP, the actions are as for an operand from SAC.

## 6.1.3 Actions for ACC Orders

Although the normal situation for an ACC order using a named operand is for non-equivalence to occur in the PROP Name Store and equivalence to occur in the OBS Name Store, equivalence may be found in the PROP Name Store on some occasions. For example, a 32-bit variable required for an ACC order might be contained in the same 64-bit store word as a 32-bit variable already in use by B orders. Unless the ACC order finding equivalence is a store order, then the operand is read out as for a non-ACC order and carried through to OBS as though it were a literal, so that no access is made to the OBS Name Store. If the ACC order finding equivalence is a store order, however, (ACC Write Equivalence) then action is taken to delete the word from the PROP Name Store.

The actions for an ACC Write Equivalence are initiated in a similar way to those for a non-equivalence for a non-ACC order. These actions are similar to those involved in preparing a line for a non-equivalence and in restoring the pipeline at the end. The appropriate address and value are read out of the Name Store and sent to SAC, and the appropriate digits in the LU and LA digits are then set to zero, in order to mark the line empty. When the order reaches OBS its operand will not, of course, be found in the OBS Name Store, and the normal OBS non-equivalence actions will be initiated (section 6.2.1). It will now be clear that the management of the name stores of MU5 is complex by comparison with the Cache approach. The complication was thought acceptable because it gives rise to a high 'hit-rate' and a high rate of instruction execution between 'misses'.

## 6.1.4 Organisational Facilities

Ideally the Name Stores should be transparent to the software. They mostly are, but some parts of the paging and program changing software need to take account of their existence. The organisational facilities in the PROP Name Store are provided for this reason. They are controlled by the use of V-lines, and apply to the 28 user lines. An organisational facility is activated when the appropriate V-line is specified as the operand of a store order. Thus, writing to one of the V-lines associated with the PROP Name Store causes all the Line Altered and Line Used digits to be re-set to zero, and another causes the Line Pointer to be re-set to point to Name Store line 0. Re-setting the Line Used and Line Altered digits effectively destroys information contained in the store since the Local Store is not updated for those operands which have been altered. The purge facility allows the store to be emptied without loss of information. The Line Pointer is re-set to line 0 when a purge is initiated and each line is then read in turn. As each line is read, it is checked for being altered, and if it is, an access is made to SAC to return its value to the Local Store. The line is then set unused and the pointer is incremented. This facility is normally used by the CPRNEQ interrupt procedure if the CPR being overwritten has references to it within the Name Store. The software can check for this situation by using the search facility.

A Name Store Search requires two V-lines to be set up, one containing a mask corresponding to the page/block size involved, and one the virtual block address. When the address is set up, association occurs over all non-masked digits, and one or more lines may give equivalence (the multiple equivalence interrupt is suppressed in this case). The output from the equivalence detecting logic is used to set one of the Test Register digits, so that a subsequent control transfer order will jump ·to the appropriate sequence of instructions according to whether or not references to the block address exist in the Name Store.

## 6.2 THE OBS STORE

The Operand Buffer System buffers three kinds of operand, vectors, names and literals. The vector and name parts require both Virtual Address and Value Fields, while the literal part requires only a Value Field to provide temporary storage for the literal operands of functions in transit through the OBS Queue (section 5.2). Thus the Virtual Address Store contains 32 associatively addressed registers (figure 6.4). Of these, 24 are dedicated to name entries, and are 33 bits in length (4 Process Number bits, 14 Segment bits and 15 bits addressing a 64-bit word), while the remaining eight are dedicated to vector entries, and are 32 bits in length (4 Process Number bits, 14 Segment bits and 14 bits addressing a 128-bit word).

115

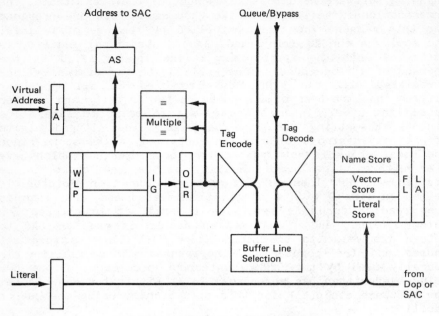

Figure 6.4 The OBS Store

In addition, each line in the Virtual Address Store has a corresponding bit in each of two Status Registers, the 'Write Line Pointer' (WLP) and the 'Ignore Register' (IG). The Write Line Pointer normally has two bits set, one pointing to the next free line to be used in the event of a vector non-equivalence and one pointing to the next line to be used in the event of a name non-equivalence. The Ignore Register corresponds to the Line in Use Register in the PROP Name Store, except that the meaning of the digits is inverted. A bit set in the Ignore Register causes any equivalence occurring in the corresponding line in the Virtual Address Store to be ignored.

The Operand Store contains 24 lines for holding 64-bit words, eight lines for holding 64-bit literals and nominally eight lines for holding 128-bit words, although these are actually implemented as 16 lines each holding a 64-bit word. Corresponding to each line in the vector and name fields is a digit in each of two further Status Registers, the 'Full' Register (FL) and the 'Line Altered' Register (LA). The Full Register indicates whether the contents of a name or vector line in the Operand Store are available. When the Full bit of a line accessed by the Output Process (section 5.2.3) is not set, then either it is waiting to be filled by the return of a store word requested from SAC, as a result of a

116

non-equivalence in the Virtual Address Store, or to be updated from Dop by an outstanding store order. The Line Altered Register is exactly equivalent to the Line Altered Register in the PROP Name Store. If the Altered bit of a line is set, then its contents have been altered by the action of a store order.

## 6.2.1 Normal Operation

In the PROP Name Store the address and value fields constitute adjacent stages of the pipeline and the action in the event of non-equivalence is to inhibit the normal operation of the pipeline until the Name Store has been updated. In OBS the address and value fields are separated by the Queue, and the basic aim of the system is to stream requests out to SAC while queuing up functions awaiting the return of the corresponding operands. The normal operation of the OBS Store is therefore different from that of the PROP Name Store. When an address is copied into IA for association in the Virtual Address Store, it is also written, at the same time, into a free line in each of the name and vector areas, as selected by bits in the Write Line Pointer. The outputs of the associative registers are combined with the corresponding bits in the Ignore Register and copied into the OBS Line Register (OLR), so that the latter will only contain a 1 if equivalence occurred between the interrogate address and a line already in use. The position of this bit in OLR is encoded into a Tag (section 5.2.1) and copied into the Queue or Bypass Register according to the type of function. In the output stage of OBS this Tag is used to access the Operand Store.

In the case of non-equivalence, no digit will be set in OLR, but the only action now required to create a new entry in Virtual Address Store is the re-setting of the appropriate digit in the Ignore register. In this case the Tag is supplied by the Buffer Line Selection Process (section 6.2.2), which must then create a new free line so that the normal action of association/writing can be carried out on the next address.

## 6.2.2 The Buffer Line Selection Process

The function of the Buffer Line Selection Process is to ensure the availability of a free line in both the name and vector parts of the Virtual Address and Operand Stores prior to each cycle of the Input Process, and to update the Local Store when necessary. In order to carry out this function, it uses the Tag system to access and manipulate the information contained in the Status Registers associated with the buffer stores. In addition, before freeing a line for re-use, it checks that the line is not currently referenced by a function in the Queue or Bypass Line. This 'Referenced' Status is obtained by comparing

117

the Tag for the line to be cleared with the contents of the
Tag Queue and Bypass Tag Buffer.

A Buffer Line Selection Process cycle is initiated whenever
an Input Process cycle is started, the latter indicating
whether a name, vector or literal cycle is required. The line
freeing sequence uses three counters, one each for names,
vectors and literals, to determine the line to be freed, so
that the replacement algorithm is cyclic in each case. In the
case of a literal cycle the new line will always be needed,
while in the case of a name or vector cycle the delay incurred
in the event of a non-equivalence is minimised by overlapping
the two activities. In the case of equivalence, no new line is
needed and the Buffer Line Selection Process cycle is
abandoned. If non-equivalence occurs, the Input Process
re-sets the Ignore bit of the name or vector line
corresponding to the bit in WLP, and the corresponding Tag is
written into the Queue or Bypass Line and sent to SAC with the
store request. The new line to be freed is then selected by
incrementing the appropriate counter. Provided that the 'Full'
and 'Referenced' signals indicate that the line is not waiting
to be filled from SAC or Dop, and that it is not currently in
use by a function in OBS, then it can be freed. Otherwise the
selected counter is re-incremented until an available line is
located. The position of this line is then set in WLP, and the
corresponding Ignore bit set. If the selected line is not
Altered, then the line may be freed ‧immediately by clearing
the Full bit, whereas if it is Altered, its contents must
first be sent back to store via SAC.

6.2.3 The Store Request Process

The Store Request Process organises data transfers between OBS
and SAC, making requests to SAC on behalf of the Input Process
(section 5.2.1), the Buffer Line Selection Process (section
6.2.2) and the Organisational Facilities (sections 5.2.7 and
6.2.4). The Input Process makes a request for a transfer from
Local Store whenever a name or vector operand is required, but
no action is taken by the Store Request Process until the
result of the association of the input address is known. If
non-equivalence is obtained, a store request is made to SAC
accompanied by the Tag generated by the Buffer Line Selection
Process. The Tag is carried through SAC and returned to OBS
with the required store word, and is then used by the Output
Process to select the appropriate line in the Operand Store
when writing in the store word. The data returning from SAC
may be a 64-bit word or 128-bit word, but as in the case of
the SAC IBU interface (section 4.1.1), the data highway is 64
bits wide, and a 128-bit word is returned as two successive
64-bit words. If equivalence is obtained, a request is still

made to SAC, but a control digit accompanying the request indicates to SAC that the request is a 'CHECK ONLY' request and no store access is required (section 5.2.1).

## 6.2.4 Buffer Store Organisational Facilities

The Buffer Store organisation facilities in OBS are similar to the organisational facilities in the PROP Name Store (section 6.1.4) and are similarly controlled by the use of V-lines. Thus writing to one of the OBS V-lines causes the Ignore, Full and Altered bits to be cleared, effectively destroying all the information contained in the stores, while writing to another V-line can initiate Clear or Purge actions. The Clear facility involves scanning through the Vector and Name lines of the store, and updating the Local Store whenever a line is found to have been altered. The Altered bit is then cleared, but the line remains otherwise unaffected. The Purge facility is similar to Clear, but in addition, the Ignore bit of each line is set so that the store is left in an empty state. The Search facility is used in the same way as the PROP Name Store Search to check that a CPR which is about to be overwritten is not required by an entry in the Buffer Store. The result is combined with the result from the PROP Name Store Search so that the Test Digit indicates whether or not references to the block address exist in either store.

## 6.2.5 Interactions between the PROP and OBS Stores

The interactions which occur between the PROP and OBS Stores as a result of name accesses have already been described. Additional interactions occur, however, if a descriptor access is made into the Name Segment (Name Segment Equivalence). The checking of name addresses in the PROP Name Store normally occurs for all functions as part of the PROP pipeline actions. A name address arising from a descriptor access is generated at a later stage in the pipeline than the PROP Name Store, however, although earlier than the OBS Name Store. Thus in the case of Name Segment Equivalence (NSE) occurring, the OBS Name Store can be checked normally, whereas special action must be taken to check the PROP Name Store. This is one of the most difficult problems arising in MU5 from the use of the naming concept and a pipeline structure in its design. The ad hoc solution adopted is far from ideal and arises partly from pin limitation problems around platter boundaries.

The occurrence of a Name Segment Equivalence is detected by Dr, which does not send its normal accept signal to PROP, but instead signals that an address check with the PROP Name Store may be required. The order is passed on to OBS in the normal way, together with an NSE control digit (figure 6.5). This

119

digit causes a hold-up in OBS and also causes OBS to treat the access as a name rather than a vector. The association of the address takes place in OBS, and if non-equivalence is found, an access must be made to the Local Store. Before this can occur, however, the PROP Name Store must be checked. OBS therefore makes a special request to SAC, since no direct route exists to PROP, with a control digit set to indicate that the request should be sent to the PROP Name Store. If the PROP Name Store contains the address, the word is returned to SAC, its Use digit is set to zero and a proceed signal is sent to OBS. If the PROP Name Store does not contain the address, the proceed signal is sent immediately.

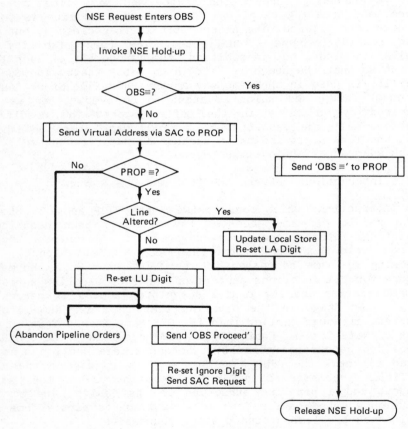

Figure 6.5 Name Segment Equivalence Actions

When OBS receives the proceed signal it clears the Ignore bit of the free line in the name field of the Virtual Address store, makes the normal request to SAC for the required store word, and clears the NSE hold-up. At the same time, if the

120

operand was found in the PROP Name Store, PROP abandons the orders in its pipeline and re-executes them all by forcing a control transfer to the order following that which found Name Segment Equivalence. This is essential since the descriptor access could be writing to the operand concerned, and this operand could also be required by the order in Stage 4 of the PROP pipeline at the time when the Name Segment Equivalence occurred. In this case an out-of-date value would have been obtained from the PROP Name Store. If OBS equivalence occurs, then no check in PROP is required. This case is signalled to PROP and the NSE hold-up is cleared immediately.

## 6.3 THE LOCAL STORE INTERFACE

Operand accesses which cannot be satisfied by the stores in PROP and OBS, and all instruction accesses, cause requests to SAC. In most cases these requests are directed to the Local Store, the individual stacks of which are linked to SAC (and to the Exchange) through the Local Store Interface (figure 6.6). The operation of this logic is largely controlled by SAC, but is best explained before the operation of SAC itself. The stacks themselves are individually controlled by timing circuitry in the Interface, so that under normal running conditions the stacks are interleaved and requests to separate stacks are overlapped to give a higher overall access rate.

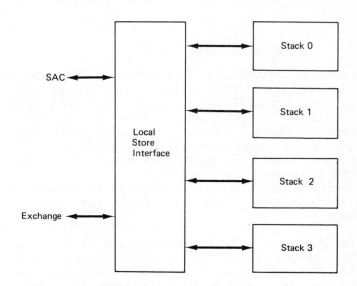

Figure 6.6 Overall Diagram of the Local Store

A request is initiated when SAC sends an address to the Address Buffer AB (figure 6.7) and in the case of a write

121

request from the Processor, data to Buffer DB. Data corresponding to write requests from the Exchange is also copied into DB, but only when the address corresponding to the request has passed through SAC, in order to be fitted into the stream of Processor requests, and sent back to AB (section 6.4.2). Data read out of a stack is copied into register DS or DE to be sent to SAC or the Exchange according to the source of the request.

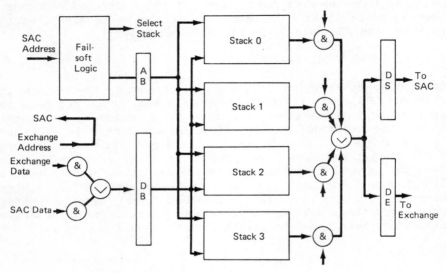

Figure 6.7 The Local Store Interface

SAC contains four busy flip-flops to indicate the busy status of the stacks. Each time a request is sent to the Interface, the appropriate flip-flop is set to busy and while the flip-flop is set, any subsequent request to the corresponding stack · is held up. Subsequent requests for different stacks can proceed, however, since SAC contains four parallel output buffers. During the stack read/write cycle, a pulse is generated and returned to SAC to re-set the corresponding busy flip-flop. This pulse is timed to arrive in SAC so that the next request can reach the stack just after the completion of its cycle.

In the fully interleaved condition a stream of requests for sequential instruction or vector addresses can be processed at a rate of four 128-bit words per store cycle time (260 ns). In practice the data rate of the Processor is limited to one 128-bit word per 50 ns (equivalent to 160 Mbps), so that, under ideal operating conditions, the store speed is not a limiting factor. The addressing of words within the stacks is organised, in this case, as in figure 6.8(a). If a stack failure occurs, however, then a Fail-soft capability allows the store to be re-configured, so that the best use can be made of the remaining stacks, and self-test functions can be performed on a malfunctioning stack, either manually or under Processor control. The Fail-soft logic, which re-orders the address bits according to the contents of the Fail-soft V-line, can also change the stack number to which a given address corresponds, and part of this logic is therefore situated within SAC. By setting an appropriate Fail-soft Mode, the addressing can be re-organised to be sequential through the remaining stacks, so that if stack 1 fails for example, setting Fail-soft Mode 5 allows addresses 0-12K to be used starting at stack 2 (figure 6.8(b)). If two stacks are out of commission together, then the remaining two can again be interleaved, as in figure 6.8(c). Ten different Fail-soft modes are available altogether, so that if any one or two stacks are out of commission, the remaining stacks can be addressed sequentially from address 0.

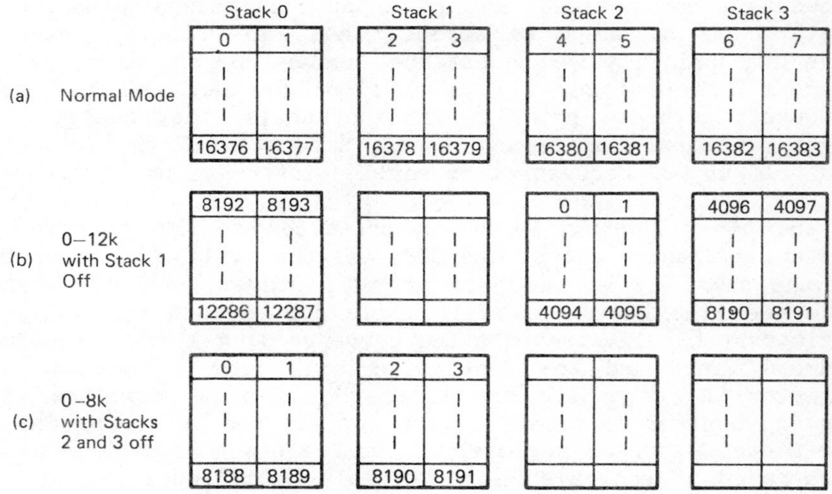

| | | Stack 0 | | Stack 1 | | Stack 2 | | Stack 3 | |
|---|---|---|---|---|---|---|---|---|---|
| (a) | Normal Mode | 0 | 1 | 2 | 3 | 4 | 5 | 6 | 7 |
| | | 16376 | 16377 | 16378 | 16379 | 16380 | 16381 | 16382 | 16383 |
| (b) | 0–12k with Stack 1 Off | 8192 | 8193 | | | 0 | 1 | 4096 | 4097 |
| | | 12286 | 12287 | | | 4094 | 4095 | 8190 | 8191 |
| (c) | 0–8k with Stacks 2 and 3 off | 0 | 1 | 2 | 3 | | | | |
| | | 8188 | 8189 | 8190 | 8191 | | | | |

Figure 6.8 Local Store Address Organisation

## 6.4 THE STORE ACCESS CONTROL UNIT

The Store Access Control Unit (SAC) forms the interface between the MU5 Processor and all but the fastest level of storage in the MU5 Storage Hierarchy (figure 6.1). It accepts virtual address requests from the Instruction Buffer Unit and the Primary and Secondary Operand Units, translates them into real addresses using the 32 CPRs [22] and passes the requests on to the appropriate real store, either directly in the case

123

E

of the Local Store or via the Exchange in the case of the Mass or Disc Stores. For a read request, data returned from the store is routed back to the requesting unit via SAC. In addition, SAC controls most of the V-store within the MU5 Processor and also detects the occurrence of CPR non-equivalences, access permission violations and parity failures.

The various actions required to implement these facilities are carried out by an asynchronous pipeline mechanism which attempts to minimise the service time for a single request while at the same time providing the maximum possible repetition rate [23]. The main registers and interconnecting highways within this pipeline are shown in figure 6.9. When SAC receives a request from PROP, OBS or IBU, it waits, if necessary, until it is in a position to accept the request, copies the address and relevant tag and control information into the Stage A address register SA, and sends an accept signal to the requesting unit. In the event of more than one request being present at the input, it makes a priority decision as to which to accept. Thus IBU Priority requests have high priority for acceptance, above PROP or OBS requests, whereas IBU Ordinary requests, although they are the most frequent, have low priority since otherwise they could, if a tight predicted loop were entered, saturate SAC with requests and hold up OBS requests from earlier instructions.

The block address in SA is presented to the associative Virtual Address Field of the CPRs (figure 6.11) which operates in the same way as the PROP and OBS Stores, and the signal from the line giving equivalence is copied into the SAC Line Register (SLR). SLR selects the corresponding line in the Real Address Field and the content of this line is copied into register RA. Meanwhile the line address bits, together with tag and control information, are copied from SA through SB to the Stage C address register SC, and a check is made for the occurrence of equivalence or multiple equivalence, as in the case of the Name Stores (section 6.1.1). If equivalence occurs, the concatenation logic takes the appropriate page and line digits (according to the page size) from RA and SC respectively and forms the real address. In the case of a Real Address descriptor access (section 5.1.3), the output from RA is ignored, and the whole of the address taken from SC, thus bypassing the CPR mechanism. In all cases the real address is routed to the Local Store or the Exchange via DA (in the case of an IBU request) or via DB or DC (in the case of an OBS or PROP request). If non-equivalence or multiple equivalence occur, an interrupt is generated, the failing address is preserved in NA, and the access is abandoned (section 6.4.2).

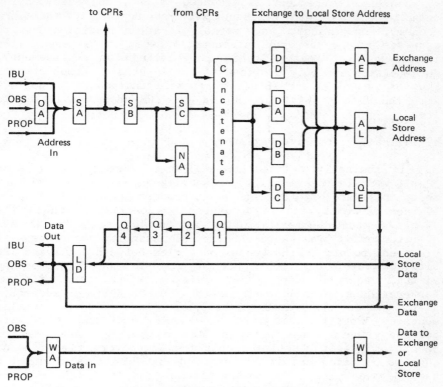

Figure 6.9 The SAC Pipeline

For requests to the Local Store, the address is copied into AL and the tag and control information into register Q1. The four Q registers form a queue for the tag and control information as it waits to be connected with the corresponding data being returned from the Local Store. Since SAC controls the Local Store (section 6.3) and only sends requests out to free stacks, the replies are always guaranteed to come back in the same order as the outgoing requests. Thus information copied into Q1 is automatically moved into the furthest available empty register in the queue and data returning from the Local Store is copied into the Local Store data register LD, together with the information in Q4, thereby emptying that register. Requests to Exchange are sent through AE, with their tag information in QE. Once set, QE remains busy until a response is received from Exchange, since Exchange requests occur infrequently compared with Local Store requests and are not overlapped. Data returning from the Exchange is accepted when there is a suitable gap in the flow of data from the Local Store, and all replies to read requests are sent back to the appropriate unit together with a 'data available' pulse.

125

When a write request is accepted by SAC, the accompanying data is copied into register WA. For reasons of hardware economy, and because, under normal operating conditions, write requests only occur very infrequently (when an 'altered' line in the Name or Vector Stores is selected for replacement), data buffers are only provided at the input and output stages. Thus registers WA and WB act as a small independent pipeline, with the data in WA being copied into WB when the latter is free.

## 6.4.1 The Current Page Registers

MU5 is nominally defined as a 32-bit computer, with each 32-bit word in the virtual store having an address of the form shown in figure 6.10(a). The 4-bit Process Number allows up to sixteen currently active processes to co-exist, each with a 14-bit Segment Number allowing up to 16K segments of 64K 32-bit words. The actual size of quantity addressed at different points in the Processor varies between 1 bit and 128 bits, however, and the number of bits in the corresponding virtual address varies accordingly. Thus the minimum instruction size is 16 bits and the Control Register addresses 16-bit words, while the Instruction Buffer Unit normally accesses 128-bit words from store and sends addresses with correspondingly fewer bits to SAC. Similarly, names may be 32-bit or 64-bit quantities, but the Name Store always holds 64 bits per line and is addressed using 15 digits within the Name Segment. The line number of the line in the Name Store giving equivalence with the virtual address presented to it forms, in a sense, a real address. This address is never communicated to software, or to other parts of the hardware, however, nor can such an address originate from outside the Name Store. In the case of a non-equivalence, the virtual address is sent to SAC, where the CPRs produce a corresponding Main Store real address to be sent, normally, to the Local Store, to access the required operand. In the event of a non-equivalence in the CPRs, software action is required either to move a block of data into the Local Store and to set up a CPR to address it (using V-store operations) or simply to set up a CPR to point to a block of data already contained in the Local Store. In the former case the block of data must be moved into the Local Store via the Exchange, from the Mass or Fixed-head Disc Store using real addresses appropriate to each store. Thus real addresses referring to the Local, Mass and Fixed-head disc Stores must be communicated both between software and hardware and between Units connected to the Exchange. The real address format used in the CPRs is therefore defined by the Exchange addressing format (figure 6.10(b)), which can refer to any one of sixteen Units.

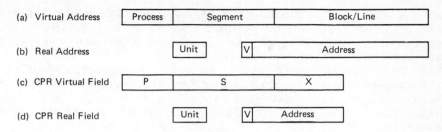

(a) Virtual Address | Process | Segment | Block/Line |

(b) Real Address | Unit | V | Address |

(c) CPR Virtual Field | P | S | X |

(d) CPR Real Field | Unit | V | Address |

Figure 6.10 Real and Virtual Address Formats

Within each Unit the address is three bytes long, with the most significant bit indicating whether the remaining 32 refer to real store or V-store. Thus 8 million 32-bit words of real store can be directly addressed within any one Unit. The positioning of the real address digits in relation to the virtual address digits is arranged so that there is a one-to-one correspondence between the line number in a virtual block and the line number in the corresponding real page, and also so that for real address accesses the four most significant segment address bits form the Unit number. The corresponding address formats used in the CPRs are shown in figure 6.10(c) and (d) and figure 6.11 shows the CPR overall diagram.

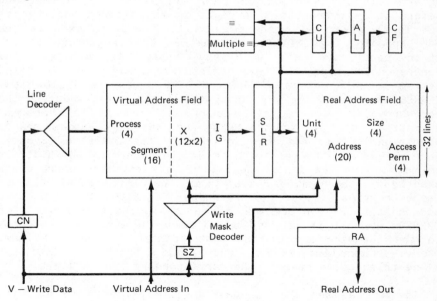

Figure 6.11 The Current Page Registers

The associative, virtual address field is made up of two major parts, the Process Number and Segment Number (PS) field and the X field. The PS field is constructed in the same way as the associative stores in PROP and OBS, while the X field requires two flip-flops per bit in order to implement the dynamically variable page size facility. This requires pages of different sizes to co-exist in the CPRs, and it is therefore necessary to store in the CPR associative field information about the position of the block/line boundary for each CPR in use. Bits in the X field which are less significant than this position are masked so as to give equivalence regardless of the interrogate information.

The real address field contains 4 bits for the Exchange Unit number, 20 bits for the page address within a Unit, 4 size bits and 4 access permission bits. A 20-bit page address corresponds to the minimum page size of 16 words, and for larger pages up to twelve of the least significant bits of the field may be unused. In addition each CPR has a bit in each of four Status Registers. These are the Altered Register (AL), the CPR Used Register (CU), the CPR Found Register (CF), and the Ignore Register (IG), all of which form part of the V-store.

The Altered Register corresponds to the Line Altered Registers in the PROP and OBS Name Stores, and is used in an analogous manner by the Operating System to determine whether or not to copy a block of information out of Local Store before it is overwritten. A digit in the Altered Register is set for a given CPR whenever a write access is made to the corresponding page. Digits in the CPR Used register, on the other hand, are set when any access is made to the corresponding page, and this register is used by the Operating System to help determine which CPR to overwrite following a CPRNEQ. Digits in the CPR Found Register are set whenever the corresponding CPR gives equivalence during a 'Search' operation (similar to the PROP and OBS Name Store search operations). This register is used by the Operating System, when releasing a Process or Segment, to determine which digits to set in the CPR Ignore Register. This register corresponds exactly to the Ignore Register in the OBS Virtual Address Store (section 6.2.1). The CPR Number Register (CN) is used to address the CPR for overwriting following the occurrence of a CPRNEQ, so that it is used by software in a manner analogous to the hardware use of the Line Pointer in the PROP Name Store. Overwriting a CPR automatically brings it into use since this action re-sets the corresponding Ignore digit.

It can be seen that there are many points of similarity between the Current Page Registers and the associative stores

128

in PROP and OBS. This similarity could have been extended further, by the use of hardware CPR loading, but this facility was consciously rejected at the design stage to allow full flexibility for software investigation of different organisations. The major responsibility for the management of the CPRs is therefore placed on software in MU5, with hardware providing sufficient facilities for this to be possible, through the V-store mechanism, and to ensure a clean transition from User Process to System Process.

## 6.4.2 SAC Interrupts

SAC interrupts fall into two classes, those concerned with the inaccessibility of data (CPRNEQ, CPR Multiple Equivalence, Access Violation, etc.), and those concerned with erroneous data (parity faults). SAC is also indirectly involved with the occurrence of any interrupt, since there may be several instructions in the Secondary Pipeline at the point when PROP detects an interrupt, and any one of them could cause a SAC interrupt to be generated. If PROP were to act on a non-SAC interrupt immediately, and obey the two fixed instructions causing entry to the appropriate interrupt procedure, a CPRNEQ for an outstanding request in the Secondary Pipeline could be erroneously treated as a System Error (section 6.5.1). PROP guards against this possibility by sending the dummy 'interrupt order' through the Processor (section 4.1.2) before obeying the fixed instructions.

The occurrence of a CPRNEQ causes an interrupt signal to be sent to PROP for all virtual address requests except IBU ordinary requests, for which CPRNEQ is dealt with separately by the IBU (section 4.2.8). A request generating a CPRNEQ also causes SAC to enter a 'Run-down' mode of operation and inhibits strobe pulses to register NA (figure 6.9). During normal operation of SAC, NA is strobed at the same time as SC, so that following a CPRNEQ it contains the failing address, and may be examined as a V-line by the CPRNEQ interrupt procedure. After entering its Run-down mode, SAC discards all normal requests until the request from PROP corresponding to the first of the two fixed instructions causing entry to the CPRNEQ interrupt procedure, which restores SAC to normal operation. During Run-down, all requests ahead of the failing address are processed normally, and the Run-down condition is then signalled to OBS, so that the Queue can also be set into a Run-down state (section 5.2.5).

CPR Multiple Equivalence is basically similar to multiple equivalence in any of the other associative stores in the Processor. It occurs when two or more associative lines give equivalence at once, but whereas this condition can only arise

129

in the IBU, PROP and OBS stores as a result of a hardware failure, it can also arise in the CPRs as a result of a software failure. An Access Violation occurs whenever the access type bits associated with a request do not correspond with the Access Permission bits read out from the CPRs with the real address. SAC records the occurrence of any Access Violation in an Access Violation V-line, the outputs from which cause an appropriate interrupt.

Parity checks are carried out by SAC on all data returning from the Local Store and the Exchange to ensure that it has correct parity (odd parity in each byte) and in the event of a parity failure being detected, returns zeros to the requesting unit and sets the appropriate digit in a SAC Parity V-line in order to cause an interrupt. Additional checks are made on the address and control information associated with requests coming from Exchange, and in the event of a parity failure in either of these fields, the appropriate digit is set in the SAC System Error V-line and the Exchange Request Parity V-line.

## 6.5 THE MU5 V-STORE

Although the MU5 V-store does not form part of the main storage hierarchy, it plays an essential part in the management of the hierachy and in the general running of the Processor. The V-store is nominally divided into 128 blocks each containing 256 lines, although in practice only eight blocks are used, and within each block only a few lines actually exist. The lines are nominally 64 bits long but apart from those in System V-store, contain at most 32 useful bits.

The System V-store is used by the hard-wired Interrupt Entry instructions (section 4.1.2) to access the necessary links. These are contained in segment 8192, the first of the common segments in the virtual store, and the mapping of the System V-store addresses into this area is achieved by simple address digit manipulation in PROP. PROP V-line requests (section 6.5.1) are dealt with internally by PROP itself, but all others are dealt with by SAC, since it already has data path connections with most of the units containing V-lines, and actually contains much of the V-store itself.

The SAC V-store consists of two parts, one concerned with providing the facilities needed by the Operating System to manage the CPRs (section 6.4.1) and one concerned with the interrupts generated within SAC itself (section 6.4.2). Within the CPRs, the Real and Virtual Address fields of the CPR addressed by the CPR Number Register can be accessed as V-lines, as can the four Status Registers (the Ignore,

130

Altered, CPR Used and CPR Found Registers) and the NA Register in SAC, which contains the address giving non-equivalence.

## 6.5.1 The PROP V-store

The Primary Operand Unit contains V-lines concerned not only with the control of the organisational facilities within its own Name Store (section 6.1.4) but also with the general running of the Processor, particularly the interrupt system. The System Error V-line, for example, contains flip-flops which record individual system errors which arise in different parts of the Processor. Among these are the occurrence of multiple equivalence in any of the associative stores, and the occurrence of a CPRNEQ during some interrupt procedures. The Program Fault V-line, on the other hand, records the occurrence of errors within a process, examples being arithmetic faults and bound check failures.

PROP also contains an Instruction Counter, a 16-bit parallel master/slave counter which is normally decremented by 1 whenever the Control Register is incremented, or whenever a store-to-store order cycle is completed in the D-unit. When it reaches zero an interrupt is generated. This counter is used by the software for scheduling purposes, and in order to ensure reproducibility of user statistics, despite variable system activity, counting can be inhibited for System Processes by the setting of a digit in the Machine Status Register.

## 6.5.2 The Operating Console V-store

The Operating Console of the MU5 Processor includes various control and mode switches, which can be accessed as read-only V-lines and provides for communication with, and direct control of the Processor. In addition, it contains a program-readable digital clock, which also provides regular interrupts and a programmable loudspeaker. This facility is useful for test and diagnostic purposes, but has also led, inevitably, to the writing of music-playing programs. These programs, which play four-part harmony, also provide a visual display by assuming a piano keyboard layout for a set of display lamps.

The mode switches indicate the availability of Local and Mass Store stacks (for use with the Fail-soft facilities (section 6.3.1)) and also whether each of the clock interrupts is allowed or inhibited, etc. The control switches allow the Processor to run at full ('Auto') speed, in which case PROP beats occur normally, or to run at a selected clock rate, in which case each PROP beat is held up until the next clock

131

pulse occurs. The source of instructions can also be altered, so that instead of being taken from the IBU, PROP can obey functions set on console handkeys, or read in directly from a Teletype.

The three most frequently used Operating Console controls are the 'Re-set', 'Interrupt' and 'Go' switches. The 'Go' switch injects a single pulse into PROP to cause one pipeline beat, which, in 'Auto' mode, is sufficient to set the Processor running. The 'Interrupt' switch sets the Engineers Interrupt digit in the System Error V-line, while the 'Re-set' switch re-sets all essential timing and control flip-flops in the Processor to their 'initial' state. Thus from being stopped, the Processor is normally re-started by operation of the 'Re-set' 'Interrupt' and 'Go' switches in sequence. For commissioning purposes these three switches can be set to inject their pulses in the correct sequence at a selected clock rate. Since the Processor is asynchronous, very many of the faults which occurred during commissioning simply caused it to stop, thus preventing continuous observation by oscilloscope. By using the continuous 'Re-set', 'Interrupt', 'Go' system, a continuous trace could once more be obtained. Certain faults only occurred several seconds or even minutes after a Processor re-start, however, and in order to obtain an observable oscilloscope trace of signals near to the fault point, it was necessary to re-start the Processor with the central registers, CPRs, stores, etc., set up to a state close to the fault point. Thus, during the running of a fault-producing process, the contents of the central registers, CPRs and stores can be 'photographed' at a selected CPRNEQ prior to the fault, and preserved on disc. At a subsequent re-start the information on the disc can be used to restore the 'photographed' state of the Processor before the fault-producing process is itself re-started.

## 6.6 THE MU5 EXCHANGE

We saw in Chapter 2 how the idea of the MU5 Exchange [24] arose out of the need to provide a simple, fast and flexible means of allowing a number of computer and storage devices to communicate with each other. The present MU5 Exchange has a theoretical maximum capacity of 16 Units, but technological considerations have limited the number of Units to a practical maximum of ten. These Units each provide a set of parallel inputs to a multiple width OR gate and each is connected, via its own buffer register, to the output of this OR gate (figure 6.12). The Exchange operates by time sharing the OR gate between the Units. Thus the transfer of a block of words from the Fixed-head Disc Unit to the MU5 Local Store, for example, involves a succession of 64-bit word transfers from the Disc, as 'Sending' Unit, to the Local Store as 'Receiving' Unit, with the OR gate connecting these Units for the duration of each word transfer rather than for the whole duration of the block transfer. Other transfers can therefore be accommodated during this period, so that the 1905E computer, for example, can make read requests to the Mass Store. Two transfers are required for a read request, one in which, in this case, the 1905E as Sending Unit sends the address and appropriate control information through the Exchange to the Mass Store as Receiving Unit, and subsequently one from the Mass Store as Sending Unit to the 1905E as Receiving Unit in order to return the data read out from the specified location in the Mass Store.

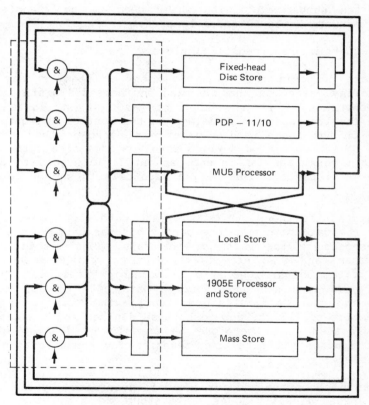

Figure 6.12 The MU5 Exchange System

The requests from different Sending Units arrive at the Exchange completely asynchronously, and much of the control logic within the Exchange is therefore concerned with scheduling transfers through the actual OR gate on a priority basis. A substantial proportion of these transfers are paging transfers between the Local and Mass Stores. Since these are

133

both passive Units, the transfers are activated by the Block Transfer Unit (section 6.6.4), itself connected as a Unit to the Exchange and physically housed within the same logic bay. The Exchange is also concerned with checking the parity of information passing through it, and, being connected to each Unit, it acts as a focal point for parity errors arising within any Unit in the complex.

6.6.1 The Exchange OR Gate

The design of the Exchange OR gate is affected by two important criteria

(1) the number of digits which need to be transferred between Units in order to effect a transfer

(2) the time required to complete a transfer.

These criteria are to some extent related in any given technology, since on the one hand an increased width involves the control of a larger number of gates at any instant, and hence involves additional delays in the control fan-out logic, while on the other hand a data path narrower than the full width of the connected devices involves additional propagation delays through the fan-in and fan-out logic needed to connect the several parts of the device data path to the OR gate data path.

In practice the width of the data path was chosen to be 8 bytes (64 data bits plus one parity bit per byte). This figure corresponds to the width of the data paths within the MU5 Processor, and also exceeds the minimum width necessary for some of the Units to be able to communicate at all. Thus the Fixed-head Disc has an effective data rate of 0.5 µs/byte, while the storage modules constituting the Mass Store have a cycle time of 2.5 µs, and both these devices and the data path between them must therefore be capable of dealing with at least 5 bytes (40 bits) per transfer for communication to be possible.

The width of the address field is determined by the size of the largest directly addressable store which might reasonably be expected to be connected to the Exchange, with the additional constraint that it is convenient to make this field an integral number of bytes. Allowing one digit to select V-store or normal addresses within a Unit, a 3-byte address (24 address digits plus 3 parity digits) allows up to 8M words to be addressed. This compares with 256K words available in the Mass Store, the largest directly addressable store currently connected to the Exchange.

134

The control field contains some information which is copied directly through the OR gate from the Sending Unit to the Receiving Unit (the tag bits, for example), some information which is copied through the OR gate and is also used by the Exchange Control System (section 6.2.2) and some information (the Unit number) which is transmogrified by the Control System before being sent to the Receiving Unit. In all, 14 control digits pass between Units via the Exchange, making the total width of the OR gate 113 bits, and some additional control signals pass between the Exchange Control System and each of the Units.

The timing of transfers through the Exchange is dependent on the nature of the communication between a Sending Unit and the Exchange and between the Exchange and a Receiving Unit. A Sending Unit initiates a transfer by sending a Strobe Outwards signal (SO) to the Exchange (figure 6.13), timed to arrive as soon as the data, address and control information in the Sending Unit output buffer has become valid at the Exchange (allowing for cable length, etc.). This output buffer is necessary since, at the time SO is sent, either the Receiving Unit may not be free, or a higher priority transfer may be in progress, and the Sending Unit therefore has no means of knowing when the transfer will actually occur.

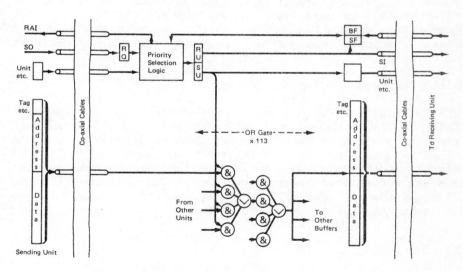

Figure 6.13 Exchange Control and Data Paths

The timing control logic of the Exchange itself is governed by a free running oscillator, so that the Exchange operates synchronously, at a rate of one transfer per 100 ns. Each transfer requires two 100 ns periods or 'slots' for its completion, one for the actual transfer through the Exchange OR gate, and a previous one in which the Exchange control logic determines which of the incoming requests to service. Within the Exchange these two activities are overlapped for successive transfers. When a request has been selected for servicing in one time slot, the information from the Sending Unit is gated into the OR gate in the next time slot by the appropriate decoded output from the Select Unit Register (SU in figure 6.13). The output signals from the OR gate then propagate to the input buffers of all the Units but only the buffer corresponding to the Receiving Unit of the current transfer is strobed, at the end of the slot. A Strobe Inwards pulse (SI) is then sent to the appropriate Receiving Unit, thereby completing the transfer as far as the Exchange is concerned. The Receiving Unit, on receipt of SI, deals with the data in its buffer at its own convenience and then returns a signal to the Exchange indicating that its buffer is free to be overwritten by a further Exchange transfer.

The input buffers for all the Units are contained on the same platters as the OR gate itself, in order to minimise the transfer times. Although the data could in principle be allowed to propagate over the long cables connecting the Exchange to the Units as wide pulses, with a narrow control pulse accompanying them, variations in cable delays and the deterioration in edge times of signals propagated over these long distances would in practice lead to the need for a much longer Exchange slot time in order to ensure reliable operation.

## 6.6.2 The Exchange Control System

The Exchange Control System, in conjunction with the Exchange Priority System (section 6.6.3), provides the gating and strobing signals necessary to organise transfers through the OR gate. Transfers can be initiated by any Unit sending its SO signal to the Exchange, accompanied by the necessary data, address and control information. Two of the control digits RO (Read Outwards) and WO (Write Outwards) are encoded to indicate the type of transfer, as follows

| RO | WO | TYPE OF TRANSFER |
|----|----|------------------|
| 0  | 0  | Data Available |
| 1  | 0  | Read Request |
| 0  | 1  | Write Request |
| 1  | 1  | Read & Mark Request |

Read requests and write requests normally originate from Processor Units and are sent to Store Units. The processor

136

sends the Unit number and real address within the Unit in either case, and the data in case of a write request. In the case of a read request, the Receiving Unit accesses the required data and subsequently initiates a data available transfer back to the original Sending Unit. Read & mark requests (section 5.1.3), involve a reading and writing action, and are therefore accompanied by both address and data, as for a write request. The data is used to mark the addressed location, after the data already contained in it has been read out and sent back to the original Sending Unit by means of a data available transfer.

Before taking any action on an incoming request, the Exchange must know that the Receiving Unit is free to accept an incoming request. The Exchange therefore keeps a record of the state of each Receiving Unit by means of two flip-flops per Unit, the Buffer Free and Store Free flip-flops (BF and SF in figure 6.13). The Buffer Free flip-flop is re-set to the busy state whenever a transfer is made to a Unit, and no further transfers can be made to that Unit until the Unit itself has sent a signal to set the Buffer Free flip-flop, after it has assimilated the information in the buffer. The Store Free flip-flop is essentially identical to the Buffer Free flip-flop in many Units, but serves a distinct purpose in Processor Units which can both initiate read requests (and hence receive data available replies) and themselves be accessed by read or write requests from other Units. Thus if a Unit's Buffer Free and Store Free flip-flops are both in the free state, then it can accept any type of transfer, whereas if the Buffer Free flip-flop is in the free state but the Store Free flip-flop is in the busy state, then it can only accept a data available transfer. If the MU5 Processor is interrupted by another Unit writing to its Peripheral Window V-line for example, it can prevent further similar interrupts occurring during the servicing of this interrupt by maintaining the Store Free flip-flop in the busy state, while at the same time remaining free to accept data available replies corresponding to its own read and write requests.

The first action at the start of each slot time is the strobing of the incoming SO signals into register RQ. When sufficient time has elapsed for the RQ register flip-flop outputs to settle, those requests for which the states of RO and WO, and the BF and SF of the Receiving Unit, are such that the transfer is possible become candidates for selection by the Exchange Priority System (section 6.6.3). The latter encodes the Unit number of the selected Sending Unit, and selects the appropriate Receiving Unit number for copying into registers SU and RU at the start of the next time slot. The value in SU, which when decoded, selects the appropriate

137

inputs to the OR gate, is sent to the Receiving Unit as the Unit number in the control information field. For a write request or data available transfer this information is irrelevant to the Receiving Unit, but for a read or read & mark request the incoming Unit number value is preserved in the Receiving Unit and is then returned to the Exchange as the Unit number with the subsequent data available transfer. The value in RU, which selects the appropriate buffer and BF and SF flip-flops for updating and the Unit to which SI is to be sent, is discarded at the end of the transfer.

If all Units connected to the Exchange could only accept one read request before returning a data available reply, then the Unit number sent with the read request could equally well be preserved within the Exchange. By sending it to each Unit, however, those Units within an internal pipeline or parallel accessing structure can accept sequences of read requests from different Units and guarantee to return each data available reply to the appropriate requesting Unit. A further possibility is that one Unit may send out several requests before receiving data available replies, and must be able to distinguish between these replies when they arrive. This is achieved by means of the tag bits, which are used in a similar fashion to the tags used by OBS to distinguish between replies it receives from SAC. The Block Transfer Unit (section 6.6.4) for example, has four separate channels capable of controlling data transfers between Units, and data available replies corresponding to requests from one channel are distinguished from those for another channel by means of the tag bits sent with each read request. A Receiving Unit passes the tag bits through its system, along with the Unit number, and returns both tag and Unit number to the Exchange as part of the corresponding data available reply.

6.6.3 The Exchange Priority System

The Exchange Priority System determines which request is to be serviced next by the OR gate when more than one request is present in the RQ register. Each Unit attached to the Exchange is assigned a priority inversely proportional to its Unit number, so that Unit 0 has highest priority. The priority of a request which has become a candidate for selection by the Priority System is determined by the priority of the Sending Unit or Receiving Unit associated with it, according to the type of request. For all except data available requests, the Sending Unit priority always applies, while for data available Requests, the Sending Unit priority applies only if the Receiving Unit is not a crisis time device. If the Receiving Unit is a crisis time device, then the Receiving Unit priority applies.

138

Units are classified into four priority categories, Peripheral Processing Units (PPUs), Central Processing Units (CPUs), Stores (Mass and Local), and the Block Transfer Unit. PPUs have highest priority since they are generally concerned with organising transfers which involve crisis time devices. The Fixed-head Disc, for example, with a 4 μs crisis time, is classified as a PPU, and is connected as Unit 0. CPUs normally maintain an intense traffic to and from their own local stores, via dedicated highways, and only make occasional requests to stores via the Exchange. Apart from PPU transfers, most of the store transfers are paging transfers between the Mass and Local Stores organised by the Block Transfer Unit. Since this Unit can control up to four block transfers simultaneously, it can easily saturate the Mass Store, and although CPUs have a crisis time extending to infinity, it would be unreasonable to hold up their requests for the duration of a block transfer. Thus CPUs have the second highest priority and the Block Transfer Unit has the lowest. The changeover from Sending Unit to Receiving Unit priority for data available requests from the stores, which have third highest priority, ensures that crisis-time Units are serviced promptly both in the outwards and inwards direction.

6.6.4 The Block Transfer Unit

The Block Transfer Unit (BTU) is closely associated with the Exchange in that its sole function is the transfer of blocks of information through the Exchange from one store to another, and it is physically housed within the Exchange logic bay. Transfers are carried out on a word by word basis, with the BTU making alternate read and write requests to the Source Unit and Destination Unit respectively. The BTU actually contains four channels, each capable of organising a transfer, and data available replies for the different channels are distinguished by means of the Exchange tag bits (section 6.6.2). Each channel is made up of a number of registers and a counter as shown in figure 6.14.

The registers form part of the V-store and in order to initiate a transfer, the initiating processor writes into registers S and D the page address and Unit number of the source page, and the page address and Unit number of the destination page. Register L is set up to contain the number N-1, where N is the number of word to be transferred. This facility corresponds directly to the variable page size facility in the Current Page Registers (section 6.4.1) and so problems of concatenating the overlapping digits of L and S or D do not occur since an N-word transfer must always start on an N-word page boundary within each store.

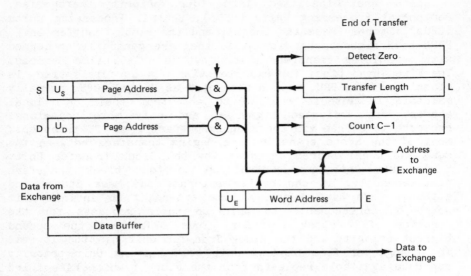

Figure 6.14 A Block Transfer Unit Channel

Each word transfer involves three Exchange requests, a read request to the Source Unit, a data available request to the BTU which buffers the data word, and finally a write request to the Destination Unit. Alternative schemes involving only two Exchange requests were considered as part of the BTU design exercise, but these suffered from obvious disadvantages, such as the fact that while the data could be sent directly from the Source Unit to the Destination Unit, provision has to be made for the transfer of the Destination Unit address from the BTU.

Once the write request has been accepted by the Exchange, the value in register L is decremented in preparation for the next read request. Thus transfers proceed from the highest to the lowest address within a block, thereby simplifying the detection of the end of the transfer, since the transfer is complete when register L contains zero, regardless of its initial content. The end of transfer is communicated to a processor by means of a message sent by the BTU to the 'communication window' specified in register E. Register E is loaded by the initiating processor at the start of the transfer and allows the initiating processor to deal with the end of transfer signal itself or to delegate the task to a separate processor. Furthermore, it allows the end of transfer to appear as an MU5 interrupt, by specifying the communication window as being the MU5 Peripheral Window. Alternatively the communication window can be a location in the Local or Mass Store which is polled by the interested processor.

140

# 7 The Execution Units

Computational functions are executed in three .units of the MU5 Processor, the A-unit, the B-unit and the D-unit. The A-unit is the main computational unit, capable of carrying out fixed-point (signed and unsigned) and floating-point operations, while the B-unit carries out fixed-point signed arithmetic, and is used mainly for calculating modifier values to be used during data structure accesses. Orders concerned with byte processing, the store-to-store orders, are carried out by the D-unit, with bytes being accessed by the descriptor mechanism in Dr and manipulated by the byte-processing logic in Dop. Addition is an important operation in all these units, and it is therefore convenient to present the general technique used for carrying out addition in MU5 before considering the design of the individual units.

## 7.1 ADDITION

Many techniques for performing fast addition have been proposed, but in practice most of them cannot be implemented successfully when circuit limitations such as fan-out, fan-in, etc., are taken into consideration. The method used in MU5 can be considered as deriving from two techniques, the Block-carry Adder and the Conditional Sum Adder [25], as well as relying on the particular properties of the flip-flop in the ECL logic family [26]. The basic problem with fast adders is that a carry generated at the least significant end of the adder may, in the worst case, be propagated through to the most significant end.

Thus in any parallel adder a carry may be generated or propagated at the kth bit position according to the state of its inputs $X(k)$ and $Y(k)$. A carry is generated according to a signal $G(k)$ given by

$$G(k) = X(k).Y(k)$$

and a carry is propagated from the less significant position $(k + 1)$ through to the next most significant position $(k - 1)$ according to a signal $P(k)$ given by

$$P(k) = X(k) \text{ v } Y(k)$$

The carry from bit position k is therefore given by

$$C(k) = G(k) \text{ v } P(k).C(k + 1)$$

By expanding, the carry at any bit position may be written as

$$C(k) = G(k) \text{ v } P(k).G(k + 1)$$
$$\text{v } P(k).P(k + 1).G(k + 2)$$

$$\text{v } \ldots$$
$$\text{v } \ldots$$

$$\text{v } P(N - 2).P(N - 1).Cin$$

where operands are N bits long.

For large values of N, however, such an expression cannot be implemented in a single AND-OR combination due to both fan-out and fan-in limitations of the circuits. P(k) appears k times in the expression and the OR gate must have a fan-in of k + 1. In the Block-carry Adder the N bits of the adder are divided into B block of r bits, and in each block two extra signals are produced. For block q these signals are

G(r,qr) - a carry appears from bit qr which may have been generated there or propagated through from any of the previous r - 1 bits.

P(r,qr) - a carry into bit (q + 1)r - 1 is propagated past these r bits.

Hence

$$G(r,qr) = G(qr) \text{ v } P(qr).G(qr + 1)$$
$$\text{v } P(qr) \ldots P((q + 1)r - 2).G((q + 1)r - 1)$$

$$P(r,qr) = P(qr).P(qr + 1) \ldots P((q + 1)r - 1)$$

and so

$$C(qr) = G(r,qr) \text{ v } P(r,qr).G((q + 1)r)$$

$$\text{v } \ldots$$
$$\text{v } \ldots$$

$$\text{v } P(r,qr)\ldots P(r,(B - 1)r).Cin$$

Figure 7.1 illustrates such a system. The signals C' are

142

combined with the G(k) and P(k) signals to form carries into
individual bits.

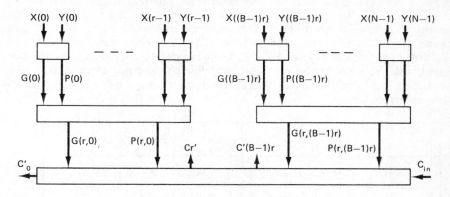

Figure 7.1 Block-carry Addition

When large numbers of bits are involved, the logic
expressions are still too complex for direct implementation,
and the system is developed further by grouping the B blocks
into S super-blocks. Thus B = N/r and S = B/t, where t is the
number of blocks in a super-block. This process may be
repeated as often as necessary, with each division adding two
logic stages to the carry path. Using the MU5 ECL logic
family, the fan-out and fan-in capabilities fix r and t at 4,
giving, for an 8-bit adder

$G(4,0) = G(0) \lor P(0)G(1) \lor P(0)P(1)G(2) \lor P(0)P(1)P(2)G(3)$

$G(4,4) = G(4) \lor P(4)G(5) \lor P(4)P(5)G(6) \lor P(4)P(5)P(6)G(7)$

$P(4,0) = P(0)P(1)P(2)P(3)$

$P(4,4) = P(4)P(5)P(6)P(7)$

$C(1,4) = G(4,4) \lor P(4,4)Cin$

$C(1,0) = G(4,0) \lor P(4,0)G(4,4) \lor P(4,0)P(4,4)Cin$

$C(2) = G(2) \lor P(2)G(3) \lor P(2)P(3)G(4,4) \lor P(2)P(3)P(4,4)Cin$

The second technique which is of interest is Conditional
Sum Addition. In this method two sums are formed, one assuming
the carry will be zero and one assuming it will be 1. The
correct one is then selected by the carry signal. As with the
Block-carry Adder, bits can be grouped together, as in the
example shown in figure 7.2. Considering the first level of
logic for bit 5, if the carry in is 0, then S5 = 1 and C5 = 0,

143

while if the carry in is 1, then S5 = 0 and C5 = 1. In the second level of logic, pairs of bits are considered. Taking bits 6 and 7, S7 will be the same as in the first level. If the carry in is 0, then C7 = 0 (from the first level) and hence S6 = 0 and C6 = 1. If the carry in is 1, then C7 = 1 and hence S6 = C6 = 1. The value of C7 need not be copied. Considering bits 2 and 3, C3 is always 1, regardless of the input carry, and hence the second row of values from bit 2 are selected in both cases. This procedure may be continued as necessary.

| 1 | | 1 | | 0 | | 1 | | 1 | | 0 | | 1 | | 1 | X |
|---|---|---|---|---|---|---|---|---|---|---|---|---|---|---|---|---|
| 0 | | 1 | | 0 | | 1 | | 0 | | 1 | | 1 | | 0 | Y |
| C0 | S0 | C1 | S1 | C2 | S2 | C3 | S3 | C4 | S4 | C5 | S5 | C6 | S6 | C7 | S7 | |
| 0 | 1 | 1 | 0 | 0 | 0 | 1 | 0 | 0 | 1 | 0 | 1 | 1 | 0 | 0 | 1 | C = 0 |
| 1 | 0 | 1 | 1 | 0 | 1 | 1 | 1 | 1 | 0 | 1 | 0 | 1 | 1 | 1 | 0 | C = 1 |
| 1 | 0 | | 0 | 0 | 1 | | 0 | 0 | 1 | | 1 | 1 | 0 | | 1 | C = 0 |
| 1 | 0 | | 1 | 0 | 1 | | 1 | 1 | 0 | | 0 | 1 | 1 | | 0 | C = 1 |
| 1 | 0 | | 0 | | 1 | | 0 | 1 | 0 | | 0 | | 0 | | 1 | C = 0 |
| 1 | 0 | | 0 | | 1 | | 1 | 1 | 0 | | 0 | | 1 | | 0 | C = 1 |
| 1 | 0 | | 0 | | 1 | | 1 | | 0 | | 0 | | 0 | | 1 | C = 0 |
| 1 | 0 | | 0 | | 1 | | 1 | | 0 | | 0 | | 1 | | 0 | C = 1 |

Figure 7.2 Conditional Sum Addition

This method of addition has the advantage that the maximum fan-in is 2, but the disadvantage that the maximum fan-out is N/2. If a conditional sum addition is performed on each group of 4 bits, however, fan-out is no longer a limitation. It is now only necessary to form carries at 4-bit intervals, and signals such as C1, C2 and C3 are not required. The carries C0, C4, etc., can be formed by a suitable block-carry network, and used by the conditional sum system to select the correct values of sum.

A further advantage can be gained from the properties of the ECL flip-flop. One of the characteristics of adders is that both phases of the carry signal are normally required. This requirement is eliminated by connecting the flip-flop as shown in figure 7.3, which is a logic diagram of the 2-bit sum module used in MU5. The signals S(k)|C = 0 and S(k)|C = 1 are formed from the true and inverse phases of the inputs X(k) and Y(k) and gated with an input strobe. These signals, applied to the set and re-set inputs of the flip-flop, cause the latter to take up the value of the sum corresponding to a carry in (Cin) of 0. If Cin is actually found to be a 1, the state of the flip-flop must be changed. Thus E(k) is connected to the

144

Data input of the flip-flop and Cin to the Gate input (cf. figure 3.5). The Clock input is the OR of $S(k)|C = 0$ and $S(k)|C = 1$, one of which will always occur. The Clock input therefore always starts and ends one gate delay after the set/re-set pulses, and since the D-type inputs override the set/re-set inputs (contrast TTL flip-flops), the correct result is always obtained. This type of adder has been termed a Sequential State Adder.

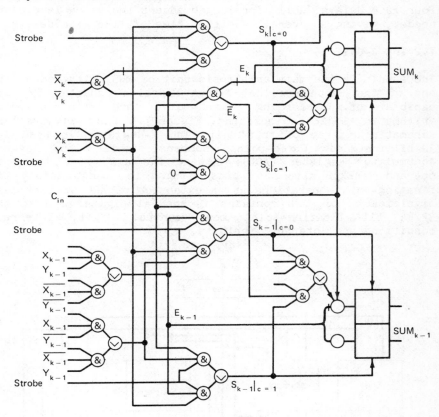

Figure 7.3 The MU5 Sum Macro Module

A modification of this system is used for the second, more significant digit ($S(k - 1)$), since Cin is simply the carry in to the first digit. $S(k - 1)|C = 0$ and $S(k - 1)|C = 1$ are formed from the inputs corresponding to bit positions k and k - 1 in order to allow for the case where a carry is generated at bit position k. The result is now only incorrect, and must be changed to $E(k - 1)$, if Cin propagates through the first bit, ($E(k) = 1$). Thus Cin is still connected to the Gate input of the second flip-flop, but the strobe to the Clock input is gated with $E(k)$.

145

The packaging of the adder in 2-bit macro modules requires carries to be generated at intervals of two bits, even though the basic block size is four bits. The carry logic is partially contained in a carry macro module which produces the generate and propagate signals over groups of four bits in two levels of logic and partially made up from standard modules. For a 16-bit adder one extra level of logic is needed in the carry path, giving an overall addition time corresponding to four gate delays, while for larger adders two extra levels are needed, giving an overall addition time of five gate delays.

## 7.2 THE A-UNIT

The A-unit is the main arithmetic unit of MU5, situated at the end of the Secondary Instruction Pipeline (chapter 5), and capable of performing fixed-point and floating-point arithmetic, logic and shifting. Figure 7.4 shows an idealised schematic diagram of this unit. The X-Register is used for 32-bit signed fixed-point numbers, while the 64-bit Accumulator Register (ACC) is used for all other types of operand. AEX, also 64 bits long, is used mainly in floating-point operations as an extension of ACC at its least significant end. AOD contains 13 special digits such as the 32/64 bit floating-point mode control digit, interrupt conditions and interrupt inhibits.

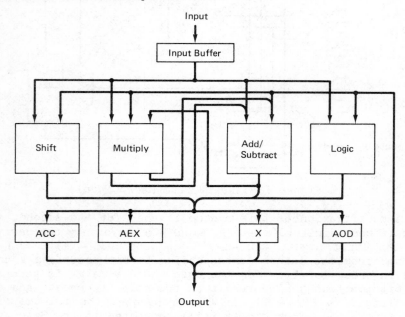

Figure 7.4 Idealised A-unit Schematic

Functions are executed by four main arithmetic/logic sections, each of which can receive operands from, and send operands to, any of the four registers. Loading of the registers (as a result of an '=' function) is achieved via the logic section, in order to reduce the number of internal highways. The add/subtract section performs all 64-bit additions and subtractions, forms 3 * D (where D is the multiplicand) for multiplication and carries out the final addition required for multiplication (section 7.2.3). It also contains the pre-arithmetic and normalising shift network required for floating-point operations, and the highway between this section and the registers is therefore notionally 128 bits wide. The shift section contains a unidirectional (left) shifter. Right shifts are achieved through the use of 'twist' gating connections at the input and output stages of the shifter which allow the order of bits in the operand to be reversed. The multiply section carries out multiplication of two signed 2's complement numbers up to 53 bits long (the mantissa size) and produces a signed 2's complement number up to 106 bits long. Thus it is capable of dealing with both 32-bit fixed-point numbers and with the mantissae of floating-point numbers. In the latter case the corresponding exponent arithmetic is carried out in the add/subtract section. The A-unit is actually required to carry out a variety of different orders, all of which are implemented by adaptations of these four sections. In particular, division (section 7.2.4) is performed by an iterative process involving multiplication, addition and shifts.

In practice, constraints introduced by the physical configuration of the hardware led to the logical configuration shown in figure 7.5. The principal differences between this scheme and the idealised scheme are that transfers between the registers and the shift section all take place via the add/subtract section, and the least significant half of a double-length result is fed to the appropriate part of AEX via a separate dedicated highway. This allows the main path from the execution sections to the registers to be only 64 bits wide. In addition, the extra input buffer incorporated into the A-unit is shown in figure 7.5. Input Buffer 2 holds the operand and function corresponding to the order currently being executed in the A-unit, which cannot normally be overwritten until the order has been completed. Individual orders require varying amounts of time for their completion, however, some more and some less than the typical average time required by the Secondary Operand Unit to supply successive functions and operands. Timing interlocks between the units prevent orders being sent to the A-unit before it can accept them, and without further buffering no advantage could be gained from the faster orders. For example, if Input Buffer 2

147

held a slow order and the next order was fast, then in the absence of Input Buffer 1, the A-unit would be held up, once it had completed both these orders, until the Secondary Operand Unit had had time to supply a third order. By incorporating Input Buffer 1, the overlap between the A-unit and the Secondary Operand Unit is ·improved and the third order can have been made available earlier. Clearly the general effect of Input Buffer 1 is to smooth out variations in the acceptance rate of orders into the A-unit and, depending on the actual sequences of orders, more buffers could improve the situation further. A law of diminishing returns operates, however, and one extra buffer was considered sufficient for the present design.

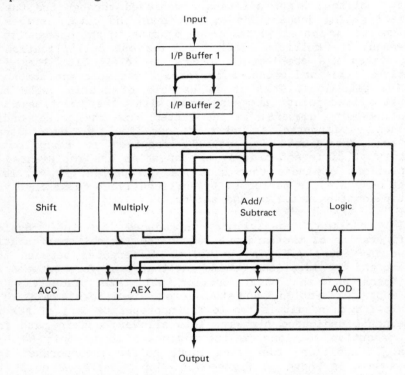

Figure 7.5 Practical A-unit Schematic

## 7.2.1 Number Representation

The number formats used in MU5 are shown in figure 7.6. Apart from the floating-point format they are fairly conventional. Even the floating-point format has no exceptional virtues relative to any other systems in use, except possibly the use of a hexadecimal radix, and was chosen by ICL during the 'convergence' exercise (chapter 1) because it met certain

148

customer requirements. In the absence of such virtues, it might have been better to adopt a number system compatible with that used by IBM, a course subsequently adopted by ICL for the 2900 Series.

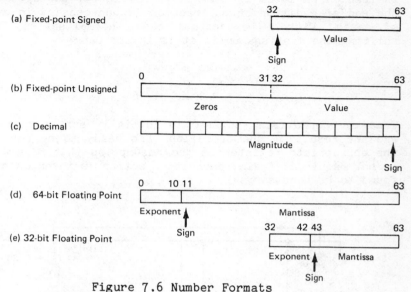

Figure 7.6 Number Formats

The virtue of the hexadecimal radix lies in the speed advantage which can be obtained during the execution of floating-point addition and subtraction (section 7.2.2). It is a fact that in many calculations most of the operands are of similar magnitude and with increasing radix value the number of occasions on which pre-alignment shifting is required for addition and subtraction decreases. This advantage must, however, be off-set against the reduction in accuracy caused by retaining fewer mantissa digits during normalisation and rounding.

7.2.2 Addition and Subtraction

The add/subtract section of the A-unit carries out addition and subtraction of both fixed-point and floating-point numbers and therefore contains not only an adder/subtractor, but also a shifter and exponent arithmetic unit. For floating-point addition or subtraction the exponents must be equalised and the mantissae correspondingly aligned before the addition or subtraction can be carried out. Thus the exponents are compared, and the mantissa of the smaller number is shifted right (towards the least significant end), until the exponents are equal. However, as a consequence of using a hexadecimal radix, the probability of such a shift being necessary is only

149

around 50% [27], and advantage is taken of this fact in MU5 by starting the addition or subtraction immediately, on the assumption that no shift will be necessary. Corrective action is then taken later if necessary. Similarly, normalisation at the end of addition or subtraction is unnecessary in over 80% of cases. With a hexadecimal base, normalisation involves shifting the mantissa until it is in the range

$$-1/8 \geq m \geq -1$$

or

$$1 > m \geq 1/16$$

Thus the normalising shifter is initially set to zero shift, and the result of the operation made ready to be copied into the appropriate register on the assumption that normalisation is not required. Again, corrective action is taken later if it found to be necessary.

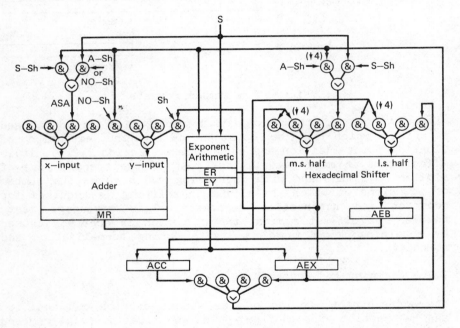

Figure 7.7 The Add/Subtract Section

Figure 7.7 shows the overall diagram of the add/subtract section of the A-unit. For floating-point addition the mantissae corresponding to the incoming operand and the ACC Register are routed to the x and y inputs of the adder respectively through the 'no shift' gates (NO-Sh) and the addition is started. At the same time, the 11-bit exponents are compared in the exponent arithmetic unit and the

150

difference set in the Exponent Result register ER. EY is set with the larger exponent value which is also the exponent of the floating-point result. The exponent arithmetic unit is actually 12 bits long, since an overflow condition may cause the 11th bit to indicate a shift of the wrong mantissa. The 12th bit is also used for checking floating-point overflow or underflow.

If ER is non-zero, then the first addition must be abandoned and a second addition initiated. If the difference is positive, then the S-Sh gates are opened and the incoming operand (S) is shifted by the number of hexadecimal digits indicated by ER. If the difference is negative then the A-Sh gates are opened, and the ACC Register content is shifted by one more hexadecimal digit than the number indicated by the inverse of ER. (Negating a 2's complement number involves inverting and adding 1; in this case the extra 1 is incorporated into the shift at the entry to the ASB gates by wiring the A inputs four bits shifted relative to the S inputs.)

The shifter itself is 105 bits wide so that bits shifted below the significance of the adder can be retained for double-length results. These bits are held in the Accumulator Extension Buffer (AEB) at the end of the addition, while the result of the addition proper is held in the Mantissa Result register (MR). The shifter is re-set to zero shift after the addition, in preparation for normalisation. Normalisation requires a left shift (towards the most significant end) and since, for reasons of economy in modules and platter interconnections, the same (unidirectional) shifter is used, the order of the digits is reversed. Thus MR is connected to the input to the least significant half of the shifter, and AEB to the most significant input, both either directly or via a 4-digit shift which allows for the super-normal case. The output from the shifter forms the input to the ACC Register and AEX, with the digits in an appropriately inverted order, and if no normalisation is required, the result can be copied in immediately. Where normalisation is required, an extra delay is incurred while the data paths through the shifter settle to the new conditions. Rounding occurs if the content of AEB is non-zero, the least significant digit of the ACC Register being forced to 1 in this case.

The fastest time for floating-point addition, when no pre-arithmetic or normalisation is involved, is 170 ns. Normalisation involves an additional delay of approximately 70 ns, and pre-arithmetic shifting an additional delay of approximately 125 ns, so that the longest floating-point addition requires 365 ns. The expected average time, however, is around 250 ns, when account is taken of the relative frequency of occurrence of the various cases [27]. These times are, in fact, considerably longer than those which could be achieved with the existing logical design. The extra time is mainly incurred because of layout difficulties and pin limitations which require extra cable delays and highway gates within the system.

Fixed-point subtraction is performed by inverting the subtrahend and adding an extra 1 (via the carry-in entry) to the least significant digit. In floating-point subtraction a difficulty arises in cases where the subtrahend mantissa is shifted before subtraction, since the position at which the extra 1 must be added is variable..This difficulty could be overcome by extending the subtrahend to double length at its least significant end and always adding the 1 to the least significant digit of the double-length value. This would require a complete double-length adder however, and an alternative approach has therefore been used. In the cases where the subtrahend is shifted (the incoming operand (S) in Subtract, or the ACC Register content in Reverse Subtract), this number is first complemented by a separate pass through the adder and then added to the minuend to form the result. The time taken for subtraction is obviously increased in this case, the actual amount being approximately 100 ns. This only leads to an average expected floating-point subtraction time 25 ns longer than the average floating-point addition time, however, when account is taken of the relative frequencies of occurrence of the different possibilities [27].

Fixed-point addition and subtraction both take approximately the same time as the fastest floating-point addition. This is because the same data paths through the adder and shifter are used, although only 32 bits are actually of significance. In the case of fixed-point signed arithmetic orders, an overflow can occur. This situation is detected by examining digits from the adder of higher significance, and its occurrence is recorded as a digit in the AOD Register. Unless the corresponding Interrupt Inhibit digit is set in AOD, an interrupt is signalled to PROP, which takes appropriate actions (section 4.1.2). In the unsigned case, overflow is not meaningful, and since unsigned arithmetic is performed on numbers in the 64-bit ACC Register, a 33-bit result may be returned.

7.2.3 Multiplication

In most computers multiplication is implemented as repetitive addition, and a number of techniques are available for enhancing its speed [28]. In MU5 the number of additions is reduced by decoding three multiplier digits at a time, and the time for a single addition is reduced by use of the carry-save addition technique.

| Multiplier Digit Pair | | Decoding | |
|---|---|---|---|
| 0 | 0 | (+) | 0 |
| 0 | 1 | + | D |
| 1 | 0 | + | 2D |
| 1 | 1 | + | 3D |

(a)

| Multiplier Digit Pair | | m.s. Digit of Previous Pair | Decoding | |
|---|---|---|---|---|
| 0 | 0 | 0 | (+) | 0 |
| 0 | 1 | 0 | + | D |
| 1 | 0 | 0 | − | 2D |
| 1 | 1 | 0 | − | D |
| 0 | 0 | 1 | + | D |
| 0 | 1 | 1 | + | 2D |
| 1 | 0 | 1 | − | D |
| 0 | 0 | 1 | (−) | 0 |

(b)

| Multiplier Digit Triple | | | m.s. Digit of Previous Triple | Decoding | |
|---|---|---|---|---|---|
| 0 | 0 | 0 | 0 | (+) | 0 |
| 0 | 0 | 1 | 0 | + | D |
| 0 | 1 | 0 | 0 | + | 2D |
| 0 | 1 | 1 | 0 | + | 3D |
| 1 | 0 | 0 | 0 | − | 4D |
| 1 | 0 | 1 | 0 | − | 3D |
| 1 | 1 | 0 | 0 | − | 2D |
| 1 | 1 | 1 | 0 | − | D |
| 0 | 0 | 0 | 1 | + | D |
| 0 | 0 | 1 | 1 | + | 2D |
| 0 | 1 | 0 | 1 | + | 3D |
| 0 | 1 | 1 | 1 | + | 4D |
| 1 | 0 | 0 | 1 | − | 3D |
| 1 | 0 | 1 | 1 | − | 2D |
| 1 | 1 | 0 | 1 | − | D |
| 1 | 1 | 1 | 1 | (−) | 0 |

(c)

Figure 7.8 Multiplier Digit Decoding

Figure 7.8(a) shows the decoding of multiplier digits taken two at a time. In order to carry out the multiplication, twice the multiplicand (2D) and three times the multiplicand (3D) are required. Furthermore, in order to produce the correct result in a 2's complement system, provision must be made for a subtraction to be performed in the last cycle when the multiplier is negative. By allowing subtraction in any cycle,

153

however, a further advantage can be gained, as shown in figure 7.8(b). In this case only 2D has to be formed, and the case of a negative multiplier is taken care of automatically. This particular scheme also has the advantage that the most significant digit of the pair indicates whether addition or subtraction is required. The method can be extended to more multiplier digits, but as the number increases, more pre-additions are required. Thus 3-bit decoding requires one addition to produce 3D, 4-bit decoding requires additions to produce 3D, 5D and 7D, and as more time is saved by reducing the number of product additions, more time is lost in forming multiples of the multiplicand. In MU5 three digits are decoded in each cycle, as shown in figure 7.8(c).

The carry-save addition technique relies on the fact that for repetitive additions it is unnecessary to propagate the carry. Instead, the result is in the form of a 'pseudo-sum' and 'pseudo-carry' which can be added to the next product to form a new pseudo-sum and pseudo-carry, as shown in figure 7.9. This arrangement requires the use of master/slave flip-flops for the pseudo-sum and pseudo-carry registers. Thus using the ECL D-type flip-flops (section 3.1.1) a second pair of registers is required. The minimum strobe width used with these flip-flops is 10 ns, although the propagation delay is only 5 ns, and since the carry-save addition can also be carried out in 5 ns, a second carry-save adder (CSA*) can be inserted between the two registers (figure 7.10) such that a single carry-save addition can be performed every 10 ns. Figure 7.11 shows the ECL logic required to implement the carry-save adder; xk and yk are the inputs to digit position k, one of which is a previous pseudo-sum result, and ck is the pseudo-carry in to position k.

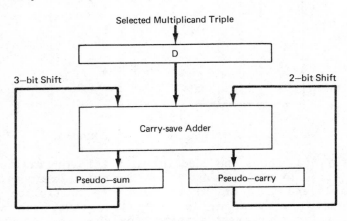

Figure 7.9 Simple Carry-save Adder Arrangement

154

At the start of a multiply order, the appropriate register content is fed to multiplicand register D0 and to the add/subtract section to form 3D. The latter is copied into register TD, and the incoming operand associated with the order (S) is copied into the multiplier register RR. The decoding and selection logic forms a double pipeline feeding the carry-save adders; since the two carry-save adders operate in anti-phase, the inputs to the D and D* registers must be correspondingly staggered. Thus signals decoded from the three least significant digits of register RR select D, 2D, 3D or 4D to be fed to register D1, and the content of RR is then fed to RR* where similar signals decoded from the next three digits select the appropriate multiple of D to be fed to register D1*. The content of RR* is then fed back to RR, with a 6-digit shift which causes the appropriate digits of the multiplier to be used in the next cycle. D, 2D and 4D are obtained simply by connecting digits k, (k + 1) and (k + 2) of D0 to the inputs corresponding to digit k of D1. In the second selection stage the true and inverse of D1/D1* are selected and copied into D2/D2* using the appropriate information copied from RR/RR* into RS/RS*.

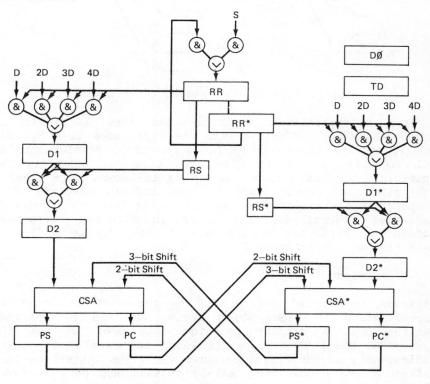

Figure 7.10 The Multiplier Section

155

F

Carry-save additions proceed until all the digits in the multiplier register have been used. During this time carry propagate additions of the digits shifted down below the significance of the adders are carried out in a special 3-bit adder, so that at the end only a single-length propagate addition is required to form the result. This is carried out in the main adder in the add/subtract section, to which the final pseudo-sum and pseudo-carry are sent.

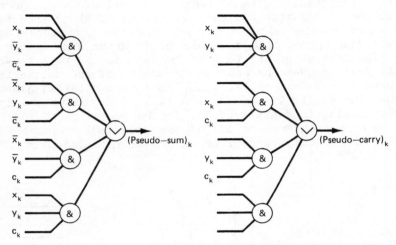

Figure 7.11 ECL Carry-save Adder Logic

This multiplication technique has been shown to be particularly cost-effective with the logic used in MU5 [28], and it appears to remain so for more recent developments in LSI circuits, though it might be better to use only two multiplier bits at a time. As far as is known, this type of multiplier was first used in the English Electric KDF9 computer, built around 1960, while the IBM System/360 Model 91 [29] used a variation of the scheme, in which more carry-save adders were used, and hence more multiplier digits handled in each (rather longer) cycle.

7.2.4 Division

Division is carried out in MU5 by means of a successive approximation technique which avoids the use of repeated subtractions. A similar technique was used in the IBM System/360 Model 91 computer [29] and it has also been used subsequently in the Cray-1 computer [30]. The latter provides better accuracy than MU5, mainly because MU5 retains fewer digits during the course of the operation. The successive approximations are obtained by an algorithm which is derived

156

by letting $X = 1/D$, where D is the divisor, and considering the function

$$f(X) = D - 1/X = 0$$

If Xn is the nth successive approximation to X and h is a small deviation from Xn, then

$$f(Xn + h) \sim f(Xn) + hf'(Xn)$$

where $f' = df/dX$. Now since $f(X) = 0$

$$f(Xn) + hf'(Xn) \sim 0$$

i.e.
$$h = - f(Xn)/f'(Xn) = (D - 1/Xn)/(1/Xn{\uparrow}2)$$

Let
$$X(n + 1) = Xn + h$$
then
$$X(n + 1) = Xn - DXn{\uparrow}2 + Xn$$

$$= Xn (2 - DXn)$$

Suppose that initially $X0 = R0 \sim 1/D$ from a table, then

$$X1 = R0 (2 - D * R0)$$

If we now write
$$R1 = 2 - D * R0$$
then
$$X1 = R0 * R1$$
and
$$X2 = X1 (2 - D * X1)$$

$$= R0 * R1(2 - D * R0 * R1)$$

If we again write
$$R2 = 2 - D * R0 * R1$$
and proceed, then
$$X2 = 1/D = R0 * R1 * R2$$

Now $D * R0$ can be written as D1, $D * R0 * R1$ can be written as D2, etc., and hence

$$D(i + 1) = D * R0 * R1 * \ldots Ri \to 1$$

Furthermore
$$Ri = 2 - Di$$

and if Di is fractional, then Ri is simply the 2's complement

157

of Di. (For the mantissae of floating-point operands this condition is true by definition, and fixed-point operands can be treated with a scale factor). Thus, once R0 has been determined, forming the reciprocal of the divisor involves only the multiplication and complementing of partial results, and if at each stage the dividend N is multiplied by Ri, the quotient Q = N/D is obtained as the end result. In practice the 2's complement operation is replaced by a 1's complement operation, which is faster but slightly less accurate.

The number of successive approximations which must be made depends on the required accuracy. Suppose

$$R0 = 1/D + e$$

where e is an error, then

$$D1 = D * R0 = 1 + De$$

$$R1 = 2 - D1 = 1 - De$$

$$D2 = D1 * R1 = (1 + De)(1 - De)$$

$$= 1 - (DE)\uparrow 2$$

$$R2 = 2 - D2 = 1 + (DE)\uparrow 2$$

$$D3 = D2 * R2$$

$$= 1 - (DE)\uparrow 4 \qquad \text{and so on.}$$

Since $D \leq 1$, then if $e < 2\uparrow-7$

$$(DE)\uparrow 2 < 2\uparrow-14$$

$$(DE)\uparrow 4 < 2\uparrow-28$$

$$(DE)\uparrow 8 < 2\uparrow-56$$

which corresponds to more bits than there are in the ACC Register. Hence D4 gives the correct answer provided that R0 is sufficiently accurate. The number of different values of R0 needed to obtain the required accuracy depends on the range of values of D. It can be seen from figure 7.12 that if D is small then 1/D varies rapidly with changes in D and many values of R0 are needed. This suggests that |D| should be normalised, and in fact bit normalisation of |D| reduces the required number of values of R0 to four. The range of D is then divided into four, and a pair of numbers generated from the second and third most significant bits. These numbers are

158

$$A = 4 * DMH/(DMH\uparrow2 + DH * D(H - 1))$$

and

$$B = 2/(DMH\uparrow2 + DH(H - 1))$$

where DMH is the middle of the interval and DH and D(H-1) are the ends of the interval. RO is then given by

$$RO = A - B * D$$

For example, if

$$D = 0.100$$

then

$$D(H - 1) = 0.100$$

$$DH = 0.101$$

$$DMH = 0.1001$$

and thus

$$A = 3.5776$$

$$B = 3.1801$$

Clearly A and B cannot be held in the floating-point ACC Register since their values are greater than 1, and values of RO/4 are used in practice. Furthermore, since 1/D = 2 is a possible value, Di must also be calculated as Di/4.

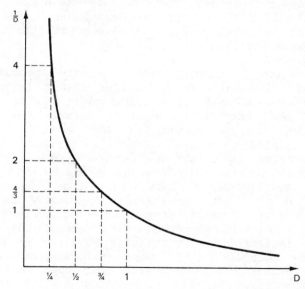

Figure 7.12 Graph of D Versus 1/D

The only additional hardware required for the implementation of this algorithm in the MU5 A-unit is

159

appropriate timing control logic, a means of determining R0, and an extra register for storing partial results. This register is connected to the output of the shift section (figure 7.5) and forms an input to the add/subtract section and to the multiply section. With careful layout of all the logic involved, a division time of 3 µs could be achieved, although in practice the time required is 4 µs. The Cray-1 computer uses a bigger look-up table (and hence requires fewer iterations) and also has a faster multiplier than MU5. This leads to a quoted time for division of 360 ns.

## 7.3 THE B-UNIT

The B-unit is a fairly straightforward arithmetic and logic unit which carries out fixed-point arithmetic, logic and shift operations involving an incoming operand and the contents of the 32-bit B-register. Its main use is in handling modifiers used in data structure accesses. Thus when a modified descriptor request is sent from PROP to Dr, a modifier request is sent, in parallel, to the B-unit. No function is executed as a result of this request, but as soon as any previous orders have been completed, the B-unit signals to Dr that the value on the dedicated modifier highway is valid. Dr always waits for this signal before commencing modification, since any previous value may have been invalidated by the execution of one or more B functions. The time taken to complete most of these functions is 45 ns, the main exceptions being Multiply and Shift, which take a variable time according to the values of the operands involved.

Multiplication is carried out by simple accumulation of subproducts, using pairs of multiplier digits in successive cycles, and once all significant multiplier digits have been considered, the order is terminated. Clearly the time for multiplication can be reduced if the operand with fewer significant digits is chosen as the multiplier. A test is therefore carried out at the start of each Multiply order in the B-unit to determine which operand to use as multiplier and which as multiplicand. Thus the time required for multiplication is 100 ns for starting up plus 45 ns for each cycle. The result of multiplying two 32-bit numbers together is normally a 64-bit number. However, one of the principal reasons for implementing the Multiply function in the B-unit was for the manipulation of dope vectors (the lack of a fixed-point multiply order on Atlas had been felt to be a significant omission in this respect), and a 32-bit integer result would normally be expected. Therefore, the less significant half of the result from multiplication is copied into the B-register, and a result with higher order digits causes an interrupt.

160

## 7.4 THE STORE-TO-STORE ORDERS

The store-to-store orders (section 2.2.6) are executed entirely within the D-unit and involve the use of the descriptor registers in Dr and the byte-processing logic in Dop [31]. These orders fall into two main classes, byte-string and string-string. The byte-string orders involve only one string, defined by a descriptor held in DR, while the string-string orders involve both a source string defined by XDR and a destination string defined by DR. Since the A-unit is inactive during the execution of these orders, the need for the extra descriptor register (XDR) could have been avoided by using ACC instead. This possibility was rejected in MU5 however, since the widely separated positions of XDR and ACC in the pipeline would have created significant timing problems in the hardware.

### 7.4.1 Operation of the Store-to-Store Orders

The store-to-store orders are controlled by logic in the Dr unit, which, by incrementing the origin field(s) of the descriptor(s) at each access, generates the appropriate series of addresses, and by decrementing the length field(s), until zero is reached, determines the point at which to terminate the order. The descriptors themselves are loaded into DR and XDR by preceding orders, while the filler/mask, which is the operand associated with the actual store-to-store order, is automatically transferred to Dop by a preliminary access during the execution of the store-to-store order itself. A 'Dop bit' accompanying this access indicates its special nature and causes the operand to be loaded into the filler/mask register within the store-to-store processing logic in Dop (figure 5.3).

During the execution of these orders, the main data path is used to extract bytes from the source and destination store words, and to return them to the destination store words as appropriate. Thus, for the SMVB and SMVF orders, for example, Dop performs 'load' operations to extract bytes from the source string, and for the SMVB, SMVF, BMVB and BMVE orders, performs 'store' operations to return bytes to the destination. For the logic orders, SLGC and BLGC, bytes are also extracted from the destination string before being logically manipulated and returned to the destination string. For the SCMP, BCMP and BSCN orders, only 'load' operations are required since the destination string is not updated.

The sequence of operations in a store-to-store order is best illustrated by reference to the patterns of bytes in the strings as the order proceeds. Figure 7.13(a) shows the

161

pattern of bytes in the destination string at the start of a
BMVE order. The origin of the descriptor initially points to
the first byte of the string, and the length is set to the
total number of bytes L. At the end of the first cycle, the
position is as shown in (b). The (masked) filler has been
moved into the first byte, but the origin and length are
unchanged; the only route to the OBS address highway is
through the Dr adder, and since the first address to be sent
must be that contained in the descriptor origin, the updated
value is not available for loading into the descriptor. For
the second and subsequent cycles, the address sent to OBS is
the origin plus 1. The origin is then updated with this new
value, and finally the length field is decremented by 1. The
string patterns are as shown in (c) and (d).

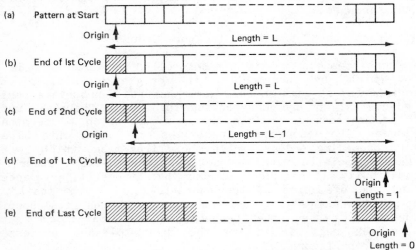

Figure 7.13 String Patterns in a Byte-string Order

The end of the move sequence is reached when the length
becomes equal to 1. This indicates that the last byte has been
filled, as shown in (d). Since the descriptor must point after
the end of the string when the order terminates, however, an
extra cycle is needed (without a store access) to increment
the origin by 1 and decrement the length by 1. The final
string pattern is shown in (e) and figure 7.14 shows the event
sequences in the various cycles.

The event sequence for a 'normal' cycle of a string-string
order is shown in figure 7.15. The source byte address is
generated first and sent to OBS, and then the source origin is
updated. The destination byte is then accessed in the same way
and the destination origin is updated. Finally, the two length
fields are decremented by 1. The order is normally terminated

162

when the destination length reaches zero, or when equality is found in SCMP. If the source length reaches zero before the destination length, the action taken depends on the order involved. SLGC is terminated immediately, and an interrupt is generated, whereas SMVF and SCMP are converted to the corresponding byte orders. This is illustrated in the complete event sequences for SMVF (figure 7.16).

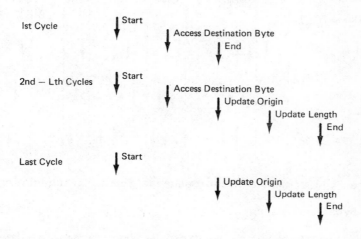

Figure 7.14 Event Sequence in Byte-string Order Cycles

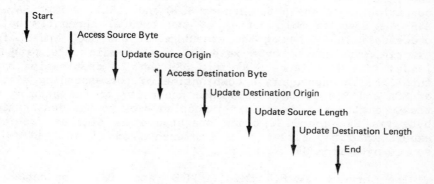

Figure 7.15 Event Sequence in a String-string Normal Cycle

In the first cycle, the origin fields are sent out directly as addresses and the two descriptors are left unchanged at the end of the cycle. 'Normal' cycles are then executed until the source string runs out. For subsequent cycles only the destination address is generated, and the function code

163

associated with these accesses is changed to BMVE, so that the rest of the destination string is filled with the filler byte held in Dop. The first of the BMVE cycles is also a 'last' cycle for the source descriptor, in which the origin and length fields are updated so that the descriptor finally points after the end of the string and has zero length.

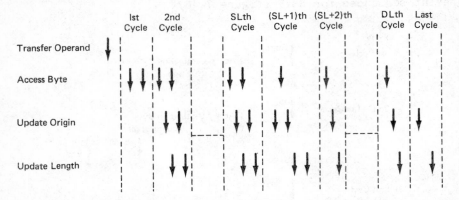

Figure 7.16 Complete Event Sequence for a String-string Order

7.4.2 Byte Processing

The additional hardware required in Dop to process the bytes selected by the main data path is shown in figure 7.17. Register DS contains the store-to-store operand (the filler, the mask, and the four LC digits which control the logical operation involved in the orders BLGC and SLGC), while SSA and SSB are used to hold copies of the byte(s) currently being processed. Thus, during the execution of the SLGC order, for example, the source byte selected by the main data path is loaded from GR (figure 5.3) into SSB and the destination byte into SSA. The appropriate combination of corresponding digits of SSA and SSB is then selected, according to the setting of the LC digits and the result is copied back to the destination byte via FR. The BLGC order operates in a similar fashion, except that the filler byte is taken from DS instead of a source byte from GR.

The orders SMVF, SMVB, BMVE and BMVB operate in correspondingly similar ways, except that they only involve the copying of source or filler bytes to destination bytes, and so the destination byte itself never needs to be copied into SSA. Both registers are used in SCMP, BCMP and BSCN, but during the execution of these orders the destination string is not updated, and no copying back to FR takes place. These orders terminate either when the destination string is exhausted or when the comparison logic indicates

164

non-equivalence (or, in the case of BSCN, equivalence) between the source and destination bytes. At termination, signals are sent to the Test Bits in the Machine Status register in PROP to indicate the cause of termination, and in the case of non-equivalence, whether the source byte was greater or smaller than the destination byte.

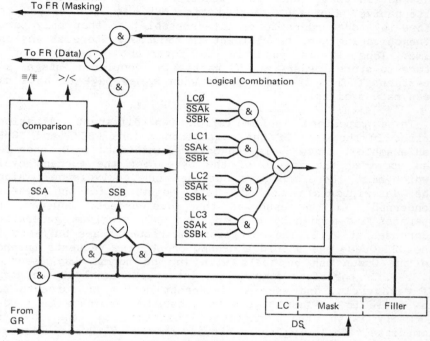

Figure 7.17 Byte Processing Logic

The mask digits in DS control the input gates to both SSA and SSB such that a zero is copied into these registers at any bit position for which the mask is set to 1. This arrangement affects SSA and SSB for all the orders, but is only relevant for SCMP, BCMP and BSCN. In the remaining store-to-store orders, the value in SSA or SSB for masked digit positions is irrelevant, since the mask digits in DS are also incorporated into the masking facility associated with FR. Thus digits in the destination store word in FR for which the mask is set remain unaltered when copying from the store-to-store byte processing logic takes place.

### 7.4.3 Special Store Management Problems

Since the addresses generated by the store-to-store orders are virtual addresses, the execution of a store-to-store order will generally involve the crossing of one or more page

165

boundaries, and hence require access to a page of data not currently available. A system which attempted to overcome this problem by ensuring the availability of all the necessary pages of data before the start of the order would involve different hardware constraints on the length of strings which could be handled in different implementations of the instruction set, and was therefore not considered. The alternative approach adopted in MU5 is to allow the store-to-store orders to be interruptable, so that only parts of each string need be resident in the Local Store at any one time. Thus it is possible to interrupt execution of a store-to-store order at a partially completed stage and re-start it from the same point when a new page of data has been made available.

In a pipelined implementation two different situations arise. In the case of the comparison orders (BCMP and SCMP, for example), a new cycle can only be initiated in Dr once Dop has compared the values of the bytes for the current cycle (which must therefore have obtained CPR equivalence), since the descriptor(s) must be left pointing to the byte(s) concerned. In the case of the move orders, however, Dr operates independently of Dop, and can continue generating addresses at will. The corresponding requests are buffered in the OBS Queue and should a CPRNEQ occur, the requests trapped in the Queue can be dealt with in the normal way (section 5.2.4). Dr therefore samples the interrupt signal at the start of each cycle, and when an interrupt occurs it converts the new cycle to a 'last' cycle in order to terminate the order normally with the origin(s) pointing to the byte(s) immediately following those already in the OBS Queue. Requests in the OBS Queue are automatically re-issued after a CPRNEQ has been serviced, and when an interrupted store-to-store order is re-issued, the first cycle generates the address(es) of the next byte(s) in sequence. Clearly for this system to operate properly, all the registers involved must be preserved and restored if the interrupt causes a process change. Unfortunately this fact was overlooked in MU5 in the case of register DS, and in practice each cycle of all the store-to-store orders must wait for CPR equivalence on the addresses it generates before the next cycle can begin.

# 8   The Software Tools

From the start of the MU5 project it was clear that the productivity of the software group would be a critical factor, and a lot of emphasis was placed on the provision of software tools. The project aim of designing the hardware to fit the software requirements meant that the software design had to run ahead of the hardware design. Also, since the evaluation of the completed system was to be based on its high-level language job processing ability, 'good' software would be required soon after the hardware commissioning was complete. It was felt very strongly that the only way to achieve good software was by expending effort in producing prototypes of each component, and that only by running them on other machines, or possibly on partially commissioned hardware, would the timescale be met. In fact during the 10 years from 1968 to 1977 the MU5 software group (of about 20 people) produced 10 operating systems and 15 compilers in addition to the software tools programs. Furthermore, it was recognised that to be useful as a basis for the design of their successors, these prototypes had to have a readily understandable external representation. It could not be assumed that there would be continuity in the staff to carry forward the experience.

## 8.1 INTRODUCTION

The software tools used on the MU5 project were intended to assist all phases of software production, namely

> Design and Specification
> Implementation
> Development
> Maintenance
> Documentation.

Although documentation, in the sense of final system documentation, appears at the end of the list, the MU5 software tools are mainly concerned with documentation. In the design phase the need is for documentation which records decisions and focuses the design effort. Owing to the iterative nature of design this documentation is subject to frequent change and its production needs to be automated. It is all too easy to lapse into the state where the documentation is obsolete, and the design only really exists in the minds of the designers. It is fairly obvious that the documentation must also be clear, concise, and easy to read. In the academic world of Computing Science a solution to all these problems has been sought through the disciplined use of better high-level languages (Pascal, for example)', and other approaches have been followed in commercial systems. The MU5 approach has been to develop a methodology to apply at a level above the programming languages, which provides a way of describing the programs before they are written. Wherever possible a graphical representation is used, although a word processing facility also exists to assist the production of written descriptions. In fact, it has been used to assemble and print the copy for this book.

## 8.2 DATA DRAW

In the early stages of the design of system software, given that its functional characteristics are understood, the first ideas that solidify relate to the content, layout and disposition of the data structures to be used by the software. The design of the main algorithms takes place around these data structures. This is particularly true of those parts of the Operating System that are main store resident, but even in virtual store, tables which are too large, or have a structure unsympathetic to the access pattern, can degrade performance. In both cases there will be interaction between the information content of the data structures and the choice of algorithms. Thus, a system called Data Draw was provided to produce a graphical representation of the data structures.

The structures represented are one dimensional. They contain entries subdivided into logical fields as in figure 8.1, but sometimes more implementation detail is added, because even at this early stage, implementation detail has to be considered in some parts of the system where it is felt that space and time will be critical.

The data draw input language is not particularly remarkable and it offers much more flexibility than the software designers have required. An example is given in figure 8.2 which is the encoding for the right hand part of figure 8.1.

The current design language (section 8.6.5) allows sufficient information to be given in the declarations for a pictorial representation of the data structures to be produced automatically, and is more convenient to use.

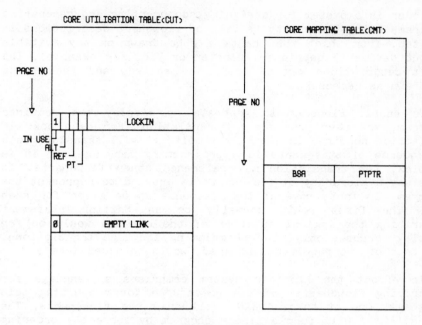

Figure 8.1 Store Control Tables

```
TITLE   CMT
SCALE   1
HEIGHT  32
SECTION1[12]LEFT -"PAGE NO">,ABOVE "CORE MAPPING TABLE(CMT)"
1["BSA",16]
2["PTPTR",16]
END
```

Figure 8.2 Encoding of Figure 8.1

As the ideas for the main algorithms in the system are formulated, they also need to be recorded. The emphasis here is on recording the ideas as they develop. At this stage they are in outline rather than detail form, and they relate to the logic of the situation rather than the detail of the implementation. This description of the system is for people, not computers. Later, the individual functions of the software, the context in which they apply and their interrelationships, clarify, and the programming detail emerges. In order to record this gradually evolving ('top down') design an automatic flowcharting system called Flocoder was produced.

169

## 8.3 FLOCODER

Flocoder is a system for designing, documenting and generating programs using flowcharts. A file of flowchart descriptions is created, from which the charts may be drawn on any suitable output device (lineprinter, plotter or VDU, for example). The chart descriptions may of course be edited, and the charts re-drawn as necessary.

To enable Flocoder to generate or display the required program, the user provides a 'translation' for each box. If the action required in a box is simple, it will translate into a sequence of statements in a programming language; if it is complex, the translation may reference other flowcharts. In this way a hierarchy of flowcharts is created to represent the program. In fact, several translations can be given for each box. The first would normally be an English statement describing the logical function of the box and would be for display purposes only. The programming language translations, for each of the required languages, would be added later.

In effect the Flocoder system comprises a language for describing flowcharts and two procedures for processing this language. One of these 'DRAW' will draw the flowcharts. The other 'FLIP' will form a linear program by correctly ordering the boxes and adding labels and 'goto's as necessary, although this latter representation is only seen by compilers.

The syntax of the Flocoder input language is simple and straightforward. Each statement in a chart description begins with the symbol '@' as the first character of a line, followed by a keyword, and continues until the start of the next statement. The keywords can be abbreviated to single letters since they are recognised by the first letter only; after that, all characters up to the next space or decimal digit are ignored. A complete chart description consists of

> A TITLE statement
> One or more COLUMN statements
> Zero or more ROW statements
> Zero or more FLOW statements
> Zero or more PARAMETER statements
> One or more BOX statements
> An END statement.

In the descriptions of these statement types which follow, the examples relate to the flowchart shown in figure 8.3.

170

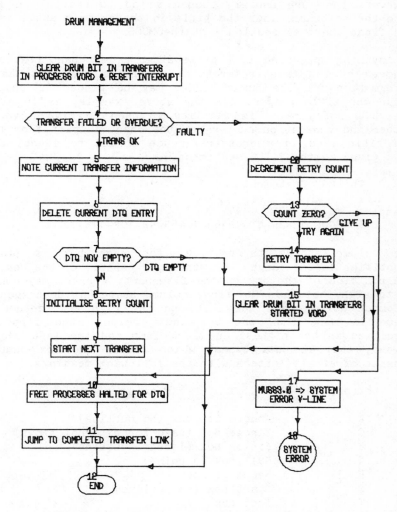

DRUM MANAGEMENT

2
CLEAR DRUM BIT IN TRANSFERS
IN PROGRESS WORD & RESET INTERRUPT

4
TRANSFER FAILED OR OVERDUE? — FAULTY

TRANS OK

5
NOTE CURRENT TRANSFER INFORMATION

6
DELETE CURRENT DTQ ENTRY

7
DTQ NOW EMPTY? — DTQ EMPTY

N

8
INITIALISE RETRY COUNT

9
START NEXT TRANSFER

10
FREE PROCESSES HALTED FOR DTQ

11
JUMP TO COMPLETED TRANSFER LINK

12
END

20
DECREMENT RETRY COUNT

13
COUNT ZERO? — GIVE UP

TRY AGAIN

14
RETRY TRANSFER

15
CLEAR DRUM BIT IN TRANSFERS
STARTED WORD

17
MUSS3.0 => SYSTEM
ERROR V-LINE

18
SYSTEM
ERROR

Figure 8.3 Flowchart Produced by Flocoder

8.3.1  The TITLE Statement

Example

@TITLE MUSS3(1,1)

The TITLE statement indicates the start of a new chart, and
gives a title, which serves two functions. First, it appears
on the flowchart whenever it is drawn, and thus serves to

171

identify the drawing. Second, it is used in cross-references within the code. A chart title may consist of any sequence of characters, terminated by a newline symbol. By convention, however, they are usually chosen so as to provide an index into the software. Thus the title in the example above is for the first chart of section 3 of the MUSS.

Anything appearing in a title after a left hand bracket is ignored by the cross-referencing mechanism, so that further information for the human reader may be placed in brackets after the title proper. (In the above example, as in all of the MUSS software, this facility is used to give a version number and generation number for the chart.) Apart from this, the title used in a cross-reference should be identical to that given in the TITLE statement.

8.3.2  The COL Statement

Example
        @COL 1S-2R-4T-5R-6R-7T-8R-9R-10R-11R-12F

The column statements provide, for each box: a numeric identifier in the range 1-63, the type (shape) of the box, and the position of the box on the flowchart. A chart may contain up to eight columns. The first column statement describes the leftmost column, and the last one the rightmost column. If there is more than one box in a column, the first one specified is the highest in the column and the last one the lowest, etc. The box types, which follow the box numbers, consist of single letters with the following meanings

|       Letter       |       Meaning       |
|--------------------|---------------------|
| A | Annotation box (no outline) |
| C | Circle box (used for external flows) |
| F | Finish box (lozenge outline) |
| N | Null box (a point) |
| R | Rectangle box |
| S | Start box (no outline) |
| T | Test box |

8.3.3 The ROW Statement

Example
                @ROW 5-20

Each row statement gives a list of boxes to be horizontally aligned. The ordering of the box numbers in the row statements has no significance. Normally the boxes within a column are placed a minimum distance apart, and may be imagined as being

172

connected to the box above (if any), or to the top of the diagram (in the case of the first box of a column) by invisible elastic. This means that boxes tend to be as high in their columns as possible. The effect of the ROW statement is to force horizontal alignment by 'stretching the elastic'.

### 8.3.4 The FLOW Statement

Example

@FLOW 1-2-4TRANS OK-5-6-7N-8-9-10-11-12

These statements specify the logical interconnections of the boxes. Text which is to appear at the point where a flowline leaves a box may also be specified in the flow statements. Any string of characters excluding newline and terminated by a hyphen is allowed. Except for test boxes, which may have two, there should be not more than one flowline leaving each box. Of course, the finish box will have no flow out.

### 8.3.5 The BOX Statement

Examples:

```
@BOX4.0
TRANSFER FAILED OR OVERDUE?
@BOX4.1
IF TRAN.COMP OF V.DRUM.CONTROL /= 1
! TRAN.FAIL OF V.DRUM.CONTROL = 1
```

These statements specify the text contained within each box, which may consist of any number of lines up to the start of the next statement. Several 'translation levels' may be defined for each box, corresponding to translations in several different languages. The example above gives translations in English at level 0 and the system design language (MUDL) at level 1. When the charts are drawn any translation level can be selected for display in the boxes. Figure 8.3 was produced by specifying level 0 (English) and figure 8.6 by specifying level 1 (MUDL). Similarly, the procedure FLIP can be instructed to generate code from any translation level.

In addition, it is possible to specify alternative translations for a box at a particular level. This facilitates the production of several versions of a program (in the same language) which differ in only a few boxes. It is a useful feature when the program is to be compiled for several machines. Alternatives are defined by appending an 'alternative number'. Thus

@BOX 3.2.4

specifies alternative 4 of level 2, box 3. The procedure FLIP may be instructed to select a particular alternative wherever it is defined, and the default (zero) elsewhere.

Flowchart cross-references may be inserted in the code by giving the name of the chart to be included, preceded by the character £ at the start of a line, thus

£MUSS3.1
£MUSS3.2
£MUSS3.3
£MUSS3.4

appear in the translation for BOX1 of MUSS3. As a result, the code for these subcharts will be inserted at the head of MUSS3 whenever code is generated for it.

A chart reference may also, where appropriate, include parameters consisting of character strings, enclosed in brackets, and separated by commas; thus

£TITLE(ABC,DEF)

Inside the chart definition warning characters can be used to reference the parameters. Each time code is generated for such a chart the actual parameter will be substituted.

8.3.6   The END Statement

Example
                                @END

This statement terminates the description of a flowchart.

8.4 SYNTAB

In sections 8.2 and 8.3 facilities have been described which are for general use. This section is concerned with a more specialised tool. It is a syntax processing package, which automatically generates the parser for a programming language, from a 'BNF-like' description of its syntax. It represents an approach to compiler writing which has developed out of the Compiler Compiler for Atlas [32] and the SPG system for the ICL 1900 [33]. Both of these earlier systems consisted essentially of two parts. First they included a BNF type of language, by means of which the syntax of the statements in a programming language were described, and second a system programming language, in which the procedures to generate code were written. The main difference between the two systems was that the Compiler Compiler was purely a compiler writing

174

system, while SPG was a more general system programming
language incorporating facilities for table-driven syntax
analysis, which made it convenient for compiler writing. In
both cases the compiler writing facilities could be used to
extend the basic language of the system. Although this feature
has some attraction, it also has disadvantages.

When a programming team are given a self-extensible
language, some of the less desirable traits of human nature
begin to show through. For example, the most prolific
producers of new statements do not always make the wisest
choice about what is needed. Nor are they over conscientious
about documentation. Thus the size of the system can mushroom,
and its operation and use moves into the folklore of the
project. In a fairly short time the group as a whole can
become separated from the reality of the hardware by a large
'fuzzy' layer of software, and the efficiency suffers.

Properly controlled, the facility to add new statements to
the system programming language can be very valuable, and its
control is only a management problem. Nevertheless, the
management of the MU5 project felt that it had enough
problems, and the decision was taken that the MU5 system
programming language would not be self-extensible. This
removed the need for the syntax defining facilities to be
closely integrated into the language. It was therefore decided
to have a system in which the parsing phase of the compilers
was generated by a pre-processor, and the rest of the compiler
was written in the standard system programming language. The
system is called Syntab. It accepts input in the form of
'BNF-like' formulae and produces a table-driven parser as
output. This parser is in the system programming language and
it will be seen, in the description given below, that psuedo
syntactic elements can be placed anywhere in the syntax, in
order to interrupt the parsing process and pass control to
user-provided code. This code may then take over the parsing
function, or generate code for those statements already
parsed.

The main statements of the Syntab system are the SYNE
definitions, which define the syntactic elements of the
language, for which a parser is required. They use a similar
notation to BNF, except for the ordering, which is arranged to
suit the left-to-right parsing algorithm. When a syntactic
element has several alternative forms, and if one is a stem of
another, it must come second. If one is a special case of
another, however, it must come first. Also, the first element
in an alternative must not recurse. For example, a character
string would be defined as

        SYNE<CH.STR>:=<CHARACTER><CH.STR>!<CHARACTER>

not as

        SYNE<CH.STR>:=<CHARACTER>!<CHARACTER><CH.STR>

nor as

        SYNE<CH.STR>:=<CH.STR><CHARACTER>!<CHARACTER>

   Parenthesis can be used in a SYNE definition, usually after
a common stem, to delimit a group of alternatives which have
no formal name. For example the above could be written

        SYNE<CH.STR>:=<CHARACTER>[<CH.STR>!<NIL>]

where NIL is built in to the system and has its usual meaning.

   Names denoting coded syntactic elements (COSYNES) can also
appear in SYNE definitions. They must subsequently be used as
labels on sequences of code written by the user to take over
control of the parsing process. There are several uses for
COSYNES, but the main one is to connect the interpretive
parser into the user-written code generation procedures. This
is often done in two stages. Some COSYNES scattered liberally
through the syntax will generate an analysis record, and
others placed at the ends of statements will transform this
analysis record into code. A number of COSYNES is built into
the system to assist this process. Also, there is a further
software package to assist in code generation known as the
Compiler Target Language.

8.5 THE COMPILER TARGET LANGUAGE

At an early stage in the design of the MU5 software it was
decided, as an aid to compiler writing, to introduce a
Compiler Target Language (CTL), into which the high-level
languages would be translated [34]. For each high-level
language a translator would be provided to convert from the
language to CTL, while a single compiler would convert from
CTL to machine code. The objective was to simplify the
individual translators by forcing the CTL to as high a level
as possible. For example, the CTL allows for declarations with
the characteristics of those found in high-level languages, so
that the name and property list management problems are passed
to the CTL compiler. This scheme also enables the mode of
compilation, for example, 'output semi-compiled form' or 'load
for immediate execution', to be determined within the CTL
rather than within each translator.

Subsequently, and as a result of the convergence exercise with ICL, a further role for the CTL emerged. The MU5 translators could be used on a wider range of machines, provided a CTL compiler could be written for each machine. This machine independence could extend to machines with structural differences, provided the data and address formats were compatible. This idea is summarised in figure 8.4. It is similar to the UNCOL idea [35] except that, whereas UNCOL attempted to span the significant differences between existing machines, the CTL has been designed to suit machines originating from MU5, or at least having a register structure on to which the MU5 dedicated registers could be mapped. There is, however, a more significant difference; the communication between the translators and the CTL compiler is two-way. Some of the CTL procedures return information to the translators. For example, there is a procedure for interrogating property lists. It is this two-way communication that makes it possible for the whole property and name list organisation to be handled by the CTL compiler.

The CTL does not have to be encoded in character form by the translators, then decoded by the CTL compiler. Instead, there is a CTL procedure corresponding to each type of statement, so that the CTL compiler is really a body of procedures rather than a written language. The main input parameter of each procedure is a vector, whose elements define the nature of the statement. In the case of an arithmetic assignment these elements comprise a sequence of operator operand pairs.

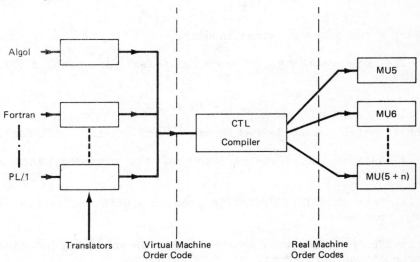

Figure 8.4 The Compiler Target Language

177

Only a small increase in compile time results from using the CTL procedures to generate code, because they form part of a natural progression from source to object code. However, a loss of run time efficiency could arise from the translators losing the ability to control completely the code which is generated. This problem does not arise with MU5 because of the high-level nature of the order code. For example, the addressable registers serve dedicated functions which correspond to identifiable features of the high-level languages. Also, the machine dynamically optimises the use of the fast operand store (section 2.2.2). For the other machines in the complex satisfactory optimisation can only be achieved at the price of complicating the CTL compiler.

In the overall software structure the CTL can be thought of as the instruction set of the MU5 virtual machine (section 9.1). Hence compatibility in the notional MU5 range of machines is at the CTL rather than the order code level. There is an associated written form of CTL, MU5 Autocode, which was used as the standard system programming language. The detailed facilities of the CTL are best described through this written form (section 8.6.2), and the example below assumes this description.

8.5.1  An Example of the Parametric Form of CTL

As an example of the way that CTL is used, suppose that an Algol translator wishes to translate

$$x := y + 10$$

where x and y are declared integer.

The corresponding Autocode statement (section 8.6.2.1) would be

$$I32, y + 10 => x$$

The translator must do two things to process this statement.

(1) Assemble a parametric form of the statement into a vector.

(2) Call the CTL.COMPUTATION procedure with the vector as parameter.

This CTL procedure then generates the corresponding MU5 binary instructions, semi-compiled or other forms.

Suppose that the translator is assembling the parametric

178

form into a vector CODE, then the elements of code are used as
follows

```
CODE [0] : Computation is in I32 mode and next operand
           is a name.
     [1] : Name y.
     [2] : Operator +, next operand is a constant.
     [3] : Constant 10.
     [4] : Operator =>, next operand is a name.
     [5] : Name x.
     [6] : Terminating mark.
```

This vector, in effect, contains an operator operand
sequence. Each word containing an operator also describes the
type of the operand following. The operator is held in the top
16 bits and the operand type in the bottom 16. Thus, in the
preceding example, since '=>' is operator 9, and a name is an
operand type '16', CODE[4] = 00090010 in hexadecimal.

A name is replaced at the lexical analysis stage by an
internal identifier, an integer, which is handed back to the
translator by the CTL.ADD.NAME procedure. Such integers are
placed in CODE[1] and CODE[5]. This form of operand assumes
the use of the standard form of name and property lists
mentioned previously. CODE[0], which is specially coded to
indicate the mode of the sequence, can be regarded as
describing a load operation. The complete hexadecimal
representation of the previous example is

```
CODE [0] : %80150010
     [1] : Integer corresponding to y (internal identifier)
     [2] : %00012001
     [3] : %0000000A
     [4] : %00090010
     [5] : Internal identifier corresponding to x
     [6] : %00320000
```

## 8.6 SYSTEM PROGRAMMING LANGUAGES

The software tools described above ease the task of providing
software and improve its design and documentation. However,
none can be said to be as essential as the programming
languages and their compilers. Four programming languages have
been used during the MU5 project, including the Autocode
mentioned in section 8.5, and to complete this account of the
programming tools, a brief summary of the role and
characteristics of each is given. They range from an assembly
language to a very high-level language.

## 8.6.1 XPL

This is the eXecutive Programming Language or basic assembly language. The question 'why use an assembly language on a machine designed specifically for high-level languages?' might well be asked. The short answer is perhaps 'lack of courage and confidence', but there is some pragmatic justification for this in an environment involving complicated prototype hardware. On the first day a system of this kind is ready for a test program, some functions will not have been commissioned, and all will be suspect. There are added problems, if these initial test programs are written in a high-level language. The compiling problem is easily solved in the case of MU5, because the compiler can be run on another machine in the complex, but the kind of control required over the code generated is the main problem. Also, and this is perhaps the strongest justification, the behaviour of these early test programs is never as intended. Many hours of combined hardware and software effort go into diagnosing 'funny' symptoms, and behaviour which defies logical analysis. During this time it seems inconceivable that the fault could be in any area under examination. Only full confidence that it cannot be due to external causes, such as a compiler, can maintain the concentration required to locate the fault.

These problems would, of course, be less severe with a simple machine, but a pipeline architecture with many operand buffers can be very pattern sensitive. This feature also means that some faults remain undetected until the system is running jobs. For this reason it was decided to extend the use of XPL, to the full Operating System and XPL compiler up to the point, in fact, where the system can recreate itself on MU5.

This is not as bad as it might seem. The existence of the Flocoder system makes the use of assembly language more palatable than is usually the case, and the MU5 instruction set lends itself to a very readable format. For example

```
B = 0
L1:X COMP LIST[B]
IF =, -> FOUND
B CINC 10
IF /=, ->L1
NOT.FOUND
```

is the assembly language encoding of a loop to find an element equal to the value in the X register in the one-dimensional array LIST.

## 8.6.2  MU5 Autocode

Two principal decisions have determined the overall
characteristics of the Autocode (and CTL). The first of these
was that they should be structurally the same language. It is
thus possible for the CTL compiler to generate the Autocode
equivalent of a program in any source language. A number of
minor advantages stem from this, ranging from the debugging of
compilers, to the hand optimisation of important programs. In
the light of past experience it was also considered
advantageous for the compilers to be written in the same
language that they generate. The second decision was that the
Autocode (and CTL) should be a high-level representation of
the MU5 machine code. For example, the declarations relate to
physical data items in the machine, rather than logical data
types. Also, the variables are typeless, as are operands in
the machine, permitting arbitrary manipulation using any kind
of arithmetic. Consequently, in MU5 Autocode, information
about data structures is embedded in the code, rather than
just in the declarations as it is in PL/1 or Algol 68.

```
          PROC SORT(A,N)
          PROC SPEC SUB.OF.MAX(S,I32,I32)I32
          V32,P,SUB
          V64,DUMP
                    PROC SUB.OF.MAX(A,P,N)
                    V32,SUB,I
                    P => SUB
                    CYCLE I = P+1,1,N
                    IF[R64,A[I]>A[SUB]]THEN
                    I => SUB
                    CONTINUE
                    REPEAT
                    RESULT = SUB
                    END
          CYCLE P = 1,1,N-1
          SUB.OF.MAX(A,P,N) => SUB
          R64,A[SUB] => DUMP
          R64,A[P] => A[SUB]
          R64,DUMP => A[P]
          REPEAT
          RETURN
          END
```

Figure 8.5 An Example of an MU5 Autocode Procedure

Practical considerations reinforced this decision. Firstly,
because the hardware and software of MU5 were to be
commissioned together, it was considered preferable for the
language to reflect the hardware. Secondly, the dependence of

181

the rest of the software on the CTL and the Autocode necessitated a short time scale for their development.

The overall form of the language can be seen from figure 8.5. This is a procedure for sorting an array into descending order using linear selection. In the following sections the form of declarations, the operations available, and the overall control structure are described.

8.6.2.1  The Autocode Computation Statements

Each arithmetic computation requires an implicit or explicit specification of the type and size of arithmetic required. The Autocode provides many arithmetic modes, but 32-bit integer is considered to be the fundamental mode. It was expected that only those modes justified by the style of use of any particular member of the MU5 range would be provided in hardware, the rest being provided by software. The arithmetic modes are signed and unsigned integer, real, and decimal, of size 32, 64 or 128 bits, and a Boolean mode. In the MU5 actually built 32-bit signed and unsigned integer, 32 and 64-bit real, and Boolean modes are provided in hardware, together with some functions to aid the software implementation of the other modes. The mode is normally specified at the start of each statement, unless it is 32-bit integer mode (in which case it may be omitted), and this is followed mainly by operator operand pairs. Each of these pairs generally corresponds to a machine instruction, hence the code compiled is closely controlled.

The operator precedence, in contrast to most high-level languages, is strictly left to right. There are several reasons for this. First, the operations in system programs are of a logical rather than an arithmetic nature, and they use operators for which precedence rules are not well established. Second, it is easier to ensure that efficient code is being compiled when the evaluation is left to right than when implicit stacking of partial results is taking place. Third, since different languages have different precedence rules, an equal precedence convention is the most convenient for use in the CTL. Precedence can be forced by the use of bracketed sub-expressions, which explicitly demand the stacking of a partial result on the opening bracket, and the application of a reverse operation on the closing bracket. This is shown in the following example

Algol    E := (A + B)/(C + D)

CTL      R64,A + B/(C + D) => E

182

In MU5 this statement would translate into

```
ACC = A
ACC + B
ACC *= C
ACC + D
ACC /: STACK
ACC => E
```

## 8.6.2.2  Operands and Declaratives

The names which are used to represent operands must be declared before use. Thus single pass compilation is possible. The user has control over the store layout and implicit declarations are not permitted. The scope of the declaratives is organised on a block structure basis. The basic items which may be declared are scalars, vectors and strings. The declaratives specify the operand size in the case of vector elements and 32 or 64 bits in the case of scalars. Vector element operands consist of the vector name and a subscript expression of arbitrary complexity. An example of the use of vector elements is

R64,X[I * N] + Y[J - 2] => Z

This statement translates into

```
B = I
B * N
ACC = X[B]
B = J
B - 2
ACC + Y[B]
ACC => Z
```

The Autocode also provides for more complicated data structures such as operands accessed through several levels of descriptors and multi-dimensional arrays. These cases are always explicitly described rather than being implicit. Hence, for example, if X is a vector of vector descriptors, X[I][J] causes element J of the Ith vector to be accessed.

The allocation of store for these data structures may be dynamic or static. In the latter case, store allocation is controlled by declared areas. An example of a static vector declaration is

VEC/$AREA[64,100]A

This declares a vector with 100 64-bit elements numbered 0-99

183

in the store area AREA. A descriptor of the vector is placed in the local namespace of the current procedure and may be referred to as A.

### 8.6.2.3 Autocode Control Statements

The order of execution of statements in a program is determined by various control statements. In MU5 Autocode these are intended to encompass the corresponding features of standard high-level languages. A Boolean facility similar to that of Algol 60 is also provided, since this is catered for at the hardware level in MU5. The general form of the conditional statement, and the conditional expression, is also similar to that of Algol 60. A relatively restricted looping facility is provided. Because there are significant structural differences in the 'do loops' of the various high-level languages, it is expected that compilers will, in general, generate the equivalent conditional statements. The simple facility provided deals only with the frequently occurring cases for which special hardware, such as test and count instructions, can be used.

A principal design consideration for MU5 has been to provide the means for efficient implementation of recursive procedures (section 2.2.2) at the hardware level, and the Autocode includes this facility in a form which reflects that of the standard high-level languages. Autocode procedures may have static or dynamic namespaces and parameters which are expressions, corresponding to call-by-value parameters, or descriptors. Descriptor parameters enable reference, substitution, procedure and label parameters to be simply programmed. Procedures which yield a result may be called, as functions, in the course of evaluating an expression.

In figure 8.5 it can be seen that a procedure is preceded by a specification. This specification gives the mode of each parameter and of any result yielded by the procedure, while the procedure heading gives only the formal parameter names. Further, the specifications must be given before the first call. Thus, the compilation of procedure calls is simplified because the parameters' modes are known.

### 8.6.3 MUPL

After the MU5 software had been commissioned, and at a time when performance studies were being conducted, it was decided to transfer it to the ICL 2900. The machines were still similar enough for the CTL, and hence the MU5 Autocode and the other compilers to transfer easily, but detailed differences meant that the software coded in XPL would need to be recoded.

The more drastic step of recoding all the software in a new Manchester University Programming Language (MUPL) was taken instead, because it complemented the evaluation exercise on MU5.

Part of this evaluation exercise was concerned with the size and performance of the software. In the case of the compilers it was of interest to establish the cost of forcing all compilations through the CTL. One danger with this approach was that the high-level language translators would be as large and complex as conventional compilers, and the CTL compiler would be an equally complex addition. In fact, to take Algol as an example, its translator was 30 Kbytes, CTL was 56 Kbytes and the compiling rate was 8 000 lines/min.

Although this was not a disaster, it was felt that a few small changes would make a big difference. For example, the CTL interface was at the high-level statement level, but with its own (Autocode) precedence rules. This meant that the translators had to transform the high-level statements into CTL statements, and the CTL compiler had to then decode these statements. With hindsight it had become clear that a lower level interface having an approximate one-to-one correspondence with MU5 instructions would be better.

For the price of rewriting the compilers to target on to a new Target Machine Language (TML), and implementing the simpler TML instead of the CTL, these ideas could be put to the test. This approach, when applied to the Algol compiler mentioned above, showed a distinct improvement. Its size increased to 34 Kbytes, but the TML is only a further 12 Kbytes. The compiling rate became 10 500 lines/min. Fortran shows an even better improvement, with the size of the translator also reducing.

The change from Autocode to MUPL was a relatively small step. Although some work had been done on the much higher level language described below, it was not felt to be the right time to commit the software to this high-level language. So MUPL is really a cleaned up Autocode. The changes stem mainly from the fact that it was not required to be a representation of the CTL (or TML). Also, it was designed to include a low level machine dependent dialect (approximating to XPL) for each of the machines to which it applies. This facility is used only where complete control over the code generated is necessary, such as in test programs and some parts of the Operating System.

## 8.6.4 MUDL

As was stated above, for pragmatic reasons, a complete operating system was created for MU5 in assembly language. Furthermore, the use of Flocoder meant that it was as well structured as any high-level language implementation would be. Thus it provides the ideal vehicle for the evaluation of the efficiency of any high-level language into which it is translated.

It is in this environment that the Manchester University Design Language (MUDL) has evolved. Unlike the earlier languages, user convenience and power of expression have not been compromised for efficiency, but the efficiency has been constantly measured, and until a compiler is produced which approaches the efficiency of the handcoding, the language has only the status of being the design specification language. It was realised at an early stage that such a language was needed because the English style flowcharts were not rigorous enough. They can express very clearly the logical significance of actions and tests, but still leave too much scope for bad interpretation by the coders. So the general rule is that the designers get their ideas sorted out using English, and then firm up the specification using MUDL. As a 'temporary' expedient, translations into more efficient languages are then added.

An example of MUDL is given in figure 8.6. A full description would be inappropriate but some of its main features may be of interest.

In common with the more modern system programming languages, MUDL is a typed language, and the user can define his own composite types. The computational expressions are arbitrary operator operand sequences and operators are given equal precedence with a left to right rule determining the order of evaluation, as in the Autocode and MUPL. This has proved convenient in practice. Results or partial results can be assigned to store at any point. In fact almost any operator may be followed by '>' meaning, first the operator is applied (reversed if not commutative) to the current result and the following operand, then the new result is assigned to the following operand as well as carrying forward to the next stage of the computation. Some examples of this will be seen in figure 8.6.

The control structures of MUDL are simple and straightforward because most of the control is expressed through the flow diagrams. However, the usual facilities of 'If-Then-Else', 'For Loops' and 'While Loops' are provided.

These are intended for use in boxes where the action, although logically simple (find an entry in a list, for example) requires some conditional or repeated action.

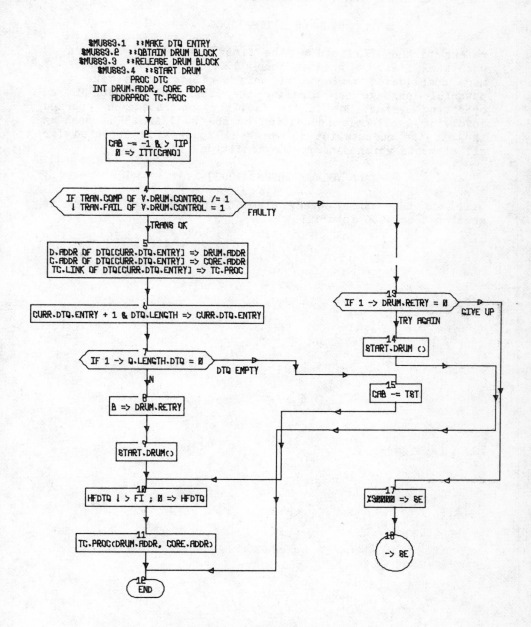

Figure 8.6 Drum Control Written in MUDL

187

It is the operand forms of MUDL which are its greatest novelty. As well as having the usual indexing facility for selecting elements in an array, elements can be selected by 'selection condition'. For example

VOL OF Z[TEMP>1000]

refers to the VOL field of the first element in the array Z when TEMP field is greater than 1000. There are a number of more complicated variants of this facility which make it a powerful language for handling the lists which occur in an operating system. One is the facility to precede an operand involving a selection condition by the word ALL. The meaning is that the computation in which it appears is repeated for all elements which satisfy the condition. Thus

ALL VOL OF Z[TEMP>1000]+>TOT

will add the VOL of every element of Z for which TEMP is greater than 1000 into TOT.

# 9  The MU5 Operating System Structure

The MU5 software comprises the Operating System, compilers for the standard languages and runtime packages to support the compiled code. It is the job of the Operating System to provide the environment in which the rest of the software and user programs will run, and to provide an interface between users and the machine. In this chapter we are concerned with the internal organisation of the Operating System. The user interface is the subject of Chapter 10.

## 9.1 INTRODUCTION

There are two contrasting approaches open to the operating system designer in deciding its internal structure, although a spectrum of compromises is possible between the two extremes. First, the design could centre around the idea of the system allocating actual machine resources such as blocks of store input/output devices, etc., directly to the user programs. In this case the environment provided by the operating system is a partition of the real machine. It has all the basic facilities of the hardware and its possible failings and complexity. Of course, the high-level language user would, to a large extent, be screened from this by the compiler and its runtime package, but not so the software writers. Hardware assistance would be required to restrict the access to the store and peripherals according to the chosen allocation. The second approach is to design an operating system which creates a virtual machine for each other piece of software, and each user program, with idealised facilities. In this case a combination of hardware and operating system software is needed to map these virtual machines on to the real hardware. Thus the choice of approach impacts the hardware design, particularly in the area of store addressing, and is an early decision that must be taken in the design of the total system. It is obvious that the resulting software structures will be quite different. For example, resource allocation can be a dominant problem in the first approach and almost non-existent in the second.

In MU5 the second approach has been followed, and there are both pragmatic and philosophical arguments to support this decision. Firstly Atlas, MU5's immediate predecessor, had pioneered the virtual machine concept with significant success. The relative ease with which the software was produced by a mere handful of people (less than ten in fact) owed much to the simplification resulting from the 'one-level store' of the virtual machine [36] and the isolation of most of the software effort from the detail of the hardware. Also, the throughput achieved by the modest configuration at the University of Manchester [37] is testimony to the cost effectiveness of the technique. In a more philosophical vein, the virtual machine concept separates out a kernel of the operating system and places it behind a well defined interface, being the specification of the virtual machine. To a large extent, programmers on each side of this interface see only this interface and their own software. This focuses and concentrates effort which can all too easily be dissipated if the horizons are too wide. The domain of a programmer should not be beyond his comprehension, which the total operating system might be. Furthermore, additional structuring and partitioning are possible within the virtual machine as a result of its relative sophistication.

It could be argued that interfaces are restricting, but this is their virtue. They must, however, be well chosen, which is where the art of large system design lies. It is important that the partitions created are logical both from the point of view of the total system and of the individual partitions, and that the interfaces form natural boundaries. It can also be argued that there is a loss of flexibility, but any design which maintains maximum flexibility has not progressed very far. The ultimate end of this attitude is a ponderous monolith as exemplified by the efforts of the computer industry. In the end these are usually partitioned arbitrarily by committee in order to apply the 'Chinese Army' approach to the implementation. Imagine a car or aeroplane produced in such a manner.

9.2 THE VIRTUAL STORE

An important part of any machine is its store, or in the case of a virtual machine, its virtual store. The virtual store of MU5 was introduced in Chapter 2 when the treatment of addresses by hardware was under discussion. It is a two-dimensional store having 16K segments each of 256 Kbytes. The format of the 32-bit address words is

| 14 | 18 |
|---|---|
| SEGNO | POS IN SEGMENT |

Obviously the Operating System must maintain tables which give the position of each segment (or its page table) in the real store. If there is a separate segment table for each virtual machine, and the addresses they contain are unique, then the segments of each virtual machine will be protected from all other virtual machines and they are said to be private. Clearly, it is also possible for the same entries to appear in several tables in which case these several virtual segments map on to the same actual store locations, and the result is a shared segment. Another form of sharing can be achieved by using the same table to map from virtual to real address for all virtual machines. In this case their virtual stores totally overlap and the segments are said to be common.

In the MU5 system the upper half of the address space, segments 8192 through 16383, is mapped through the same segment table, and is therefore common to all virtual machines. The reason for this is that many segments, such as those containing the Operating System and Compilers, need to be shared by most of the virtual machines in the system. Although this could be achieved by replicating the entries through all the segment tables, it would be less efficient than using common segments. It is not only space in the tables which is at issue, there are logical complications associated with having several virtual addresses mapping on to one real area of store which influence the overheads involved in managing the store. Also, program changing can be marginally faster when some of the store mapping registers stay the same for all programs.

For the lower half of each virtual store, there is a separate table mapping the segments, which will normally be private, but two facilities exist which allow virtual machines to share their segments. First, a segment can be sent as a message from one virtual machine to another, in which case the segment table entry is transferred to the receiving machine, rather than a copy of the segment. Second, files equate to segments, and if several virtual machines choose to access the same file simultaneously they share the same copy. More will be said about this in sections 9.6 and 9.7.

It is desirable in a segmented store to be able to associate some access control with each segment. If segments are shared or common it is essential to have this protection. Five access control bits are used in the MU5 system. A separate group of these bits is associated with each private or common segment and a shared segment has a different group for each virtual machine sharing it. In fact they are kept in segment tables as shown in figure 9.1. The first three access control bits indicate the type of access which is to be permitted, as follows

191

```
operand read access
operand write access
instruction (obey) access
```

A fourth bit, which only has relevance in the software,
controls the permission to alter any of these first three bits
and itself. A private segment normally would have the alter
permission bit set, which means that the other bits can be set
to suit the use being made of the segment. For example, a
compiler would probably compile code into a segment with
read/write/alter permission set, and at the end of compilation
change the access to read/obey only. The fifth bit, the
executive mode bit, gives the segment executive status, which
means only privileged Operating System procedures may access
it. Thus, from the point of view of protection, the MU5
Operating System is a two-state system. The multi-level
protection that would derive from having several executive
mode bits was deemed unnecessary because the Operating System
is distributed among several virtual machines instead of
across different protection levels as it is in MULTICS.

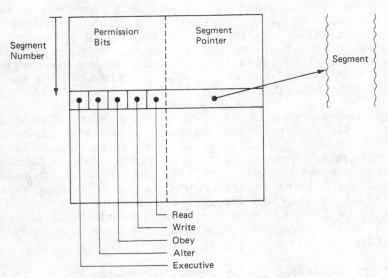

Figure 9.1 Segment Table Structure

When a virtual machine is first created for a user job, it
contains only one private segment, segment zero (the name
segment), and the common segments. Segment zero will have
read/write access only and the common segments will either
have obey/read access or executive status. There are several
ways in which further private or shared segments may be added.
For example, they can be created by use of the appropriate

command or received as messages. A typical job would have, in
addition to segment zero

       a segment of code
       a segment of arrays
       a segment for input/output control
       a segment for each open file.

The common segments contain a set of library procedures
which are regarded as an extension to the instruction set of
the virtual machine. Some will have privilege, and provide the
interface into the Operating System. All are available to
programs, written in any language, and to the statements of
the job control language. The mechanism controlling entry to
the Operating System is described in section 2.3.1.

In effect there are two forms of entry to the Operating
System. One is a voluntary entry due to a program executing a
call for an Operating System procedure. The second is an
involuntary entry resulting from the hardware noticing an
interrupt event, such as access to an undefined segment. These
'interrupt procedures' are also in the common virtual store.

## 9.3 THE IMPLEMENTATION OF THE VIRTUAL STORE

In MU5 the virtual stores are paged, and the hardware this
involves has already been described (section 6.4). This
section is concerned with the software organisation of the
paging system, but a reminder of the operation of the current
page registers (CPRs) is an appropriate starting point.

There are 32 CPRs each containing a virtual address, a real
address, the access control (or permission bits) and a use
bit. Each store access requires the CPR hardware to find the
page part of the virtual address in the associative field of a
CPR, check the access type against the permission bits, and
use the real address from the CPRs with the line bits from the
virtual address to access the store. This action is shown in
figure 9.2. Two exception conditions can arise which require
software intervention, hence they cause interrupts. First,
there is the fault condition due to the access type being
invalid, write access to a read only segment, for example.
Second, there is the more usual CPR non-equivalence interrupt
caused by the absence of the required address from the CPRs.
The software action on a fault interrupt is to cause the
corresponding virtual machine interrupt. In the case of CPR
non-equivalence there is the possibility that the required
page is already in main store, in which case the action will
be to load a CPR and re-start the program at the instruction
which caused the interrupt.

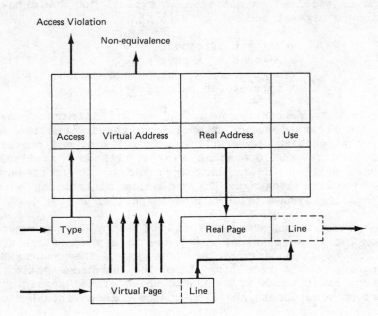

Figure 9.2 The CPR Action

In most systems this CPR loading would be done by hardware. The reason this is not so on MU5 is that MU5 is a research vehicle and the paging system was felt to be an area needing research. For the same reason, the CPRs allow the page size to be varied (in powers of 2 from 64 bytes to 256 Kbytes). In fact each CPR contains its own page size indicator, so that different page sizes might be applied to different segments, or even within the same segment, but this has never been exploited.

Three types of paging system have been implemented on MU5, and they are described separately below. If it were to be built as a production machine, one of these systems would be chosen and put into hardware. The cost of CPR loading on MU5 can average as much as 10%, but this was considered an acceptable price for the facility to conduct continuous paging experiments on a live system.

In the ICL 2900, which for reasons already stated is very similar to MU5, the paging system corresponds to the fixed page size one described in section 9.3.1. It is unlikely that this scheme would be chosen for MU5, because although the paging studies are not yet complete, there is evidence of a significant reduction in store occupancy and paging traffic in the variable page schemes.

194

## 9.3.1 Paging With Fixed Sized Pages

The emphasis in this version of the paging system was on simplicity. It is convenient to consider first how it works on a machine with only one level of main store. A fixed page size of 1 Kbyte was chosen because this resulted in a maximum of 256 pages per segment, hence the page table for a segment, which requires a 32-bit address for each page, itself fits into a page. This is significant, because the size of the backing store, which determines the total page table size, requires that the page tables are themselves paged. There is an obvious simplification if the page table for each segment can be treated as a page.

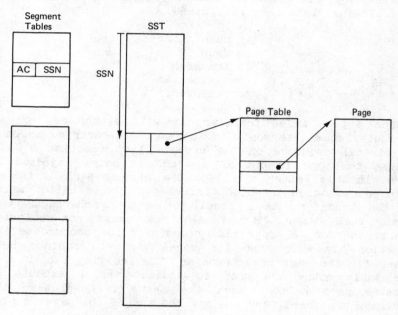

Figure 9.3 The Page Table Structure

Figure 9.3 gives the overall structure of the tables used to locate a page. Each virtual machine has its own segment table which, for each segment, indicates whether or not it exists, and gives the access control bits and system segment number (SSN). This segment table (together with the register dump and accounting information for the process) also fits into a page, which can be moved out of store when the virtual machine is inactive. As a result of segment sharing, several segment tables might have entries giving the same SSN. It is mainly this sharing of segments which makes it useful to introduce the System Segment Table (SST) as an extra level of indirection between a segment table entry and the page table for the segment. Otherwise, the same page table address could be in several segment tables, and this would create problems when the paging system moved the page table. All the information the system needs to know about a segment is kept in the SST, including a count of the number of segment table entries its SSN appears in, so that the system knows when the segment can be deleted.

The main component in an SST entry is the current page table address. The entries in this page table give the current positions of the pages. When a new segment is created it will not have any pages, they are allocated as they are accessed. Thus the page table entries have a page status component, and the following states are recognised

> in main store
> on drum
> in transfer
> not allocated
> not allowed.

When a page is in transfer, it will either be because a non-equivalence interrupt for the page has occurred in one of the virtual machines on the execute list (section 9.4), or because the page is out of use and is being rejected from store. In this latter situation the address part of the page table entry indicates which virtual machine is halted waiting for the transfer. As a result of segment sharing, it can happen that other virtual machines cause non-equivalence interrupts for a page in transfer. To accomodate this situation, in which two (or more) virtual machines become halted for the same page transfer, the individual bits of the page table entry are used to indicate which execute list processes are halted. When the transfer completes, these processes are freed, and the new address of the page is placed in the page table.

Thus the tables above allow the software to find the position and status of a page, for which a non-equivalence interrupt has occurred, and if it is in main store, load a CPR. If the page is not in main store, a transfer is initiated to bring it there, and the virtual machine causing the interrupt is halted until it arrives. It is then re-started to cause the interrupt again when, usually, the CPR will be loaded. It can happen that not only the required page but also the page table is out of main store. In this case a transfer is started to bring the page table into store, after which the virtual machine is allowed to re-start, and the second non-equivalence interrupt will cause the page to be brought in to store. Some careful thought will establish that only one step at a time can be taken towards servicing a non-equivalence interrupt. The virtual machine is then made free to re-start and possibly cause the same non-equivalence interrupt again, because the combined effects of segment sharing and program changing can alter the context. For example, in the extreme case, in the time between a virtual machine causing a non-equivalence interrupt for a drum page and being re-started, all its pages (including the last one paged in) might be removed from main store due to the actions of other higher priority virtual machines. Alternatively, in the case of shared segments, some unexpected pages might have been paged in.

The other major component of the paging system is activated when the main store becomes full and some pages and/or page tables have to be moved out (rejected). To assist this function the system needs some further tables (Core Use Tables), giving information about the individual pages in store. First, a page has to be selected for removal, and use information provided by the CPR loading algorithm is desirable. When a page is selected, three other pieces of information are needed to answer the questions

> where is its page table entry?
> where did it come from?
> has it altered?

A number of different algorithms has been explored on the MU5 system for selecting pages for rejection. The simplest system is based on a single use digit and a cyclic scan of the store. This approximates to finding the least recently used page, and it has been effective in normal running. It is less satisfactory when a single very large job fills the store, but the more usual situation is to have the active parts of several interactive jobs in store, some of which will have finished their timeslice (section 9.4).

In fact, MU5 has two levels of main store, the Local Store and the Mass Store (section 2.4), and the actual page flow was shown in figure 2.2. Pages are brought into the Local Store on demand, and when space is required they are rejected to the Mass Store. When space is required in the Mass Store they are rejected to the Drum (implemented as Fixed-head Disc in MU5). To make this extra organisation possible, the state 'in main store', in the page tables, is replaced by two states 'in Local' and 'in Mass'. Also there have to be 'Core Use Tables' for both levels of main store. A further point of detail is that there are some Operating System tables which need to be main store resident. These are kept in either Mass or Local according to their size and frequency of use. The hardware

197

allows the same sort of access to be made to either store, but direct access to the Mass Store is slow and is only used by the Operating System, for infrequently used information.

## 9.3.2 Paging with Super-pages

A degree of variation in page sizes can be added to the above scheme by allowing 'super-pages'. These are power-of-2 multiples of the basic page size on which the system operates. They can be implemented without introducing a different table structure, but a page size indication has to appear in each segment entry in the SST. Using this size information, each non-equivalence address can be properly partitioned into its page and line parts, and the appropriate sized (single, double, quadruple, etc.) page brought into store. Also, when a CPR is loaded for a page already in store, its size is given to the hardware. The core use tables must also contain page size information, and double sized pages will take two entries, quadruple ones four entries, and so on.

This scheme has been implemented on MU5 using a basic page size of 1 Kbyte with superpages of 2 and 4 Kbytes. It shows a significant improvement in CPU utilisation when superpages are used for segments which have a large active part collected into consecutive addresses. For example, the inner loop of the compilers can be organised this way.

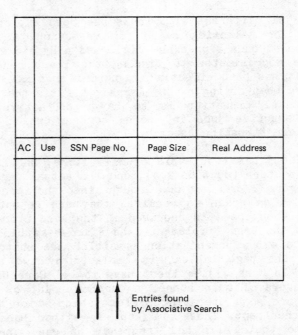

| AC | Use | SSN Page No. | Page Size | Real Address |
|----|-----|--------------|-----------|--------------|
|    |     |              |           |              |

Entries found
by Associative Search

Figure 9.4 Page Tables for Sub-pages

198

### 9.3.3 Paging with Sub-pages

If very small page sizes are to be allowed, a different approach is needed. The gain with small pages is better utilisation of space for sparsely used segments, and this is particularly relevant in the small high-speed stores. On the Drum Store and even the Mass Store, the total number of pages to be managed can become a problem, hence small pages are less attractive. Also, if the access to the store is dominated by the latency time, the balance is in favour of large pages, because this acts as a kind of look ahead for sequentially accessed information. Hence a third variant of the paging system has been implemented which uses moderate, fixed-sized pages (4 Kbytes) on the Drum, and allows smaller (binary fractions) to be used in the Mass and Local. As in the previous system, the sizes used within a segment do not change, but each segment has its own page size for Mass and Local. The Local page size may be equal to or less than the Mass page size, which may be equal to or less than the Drum page size.

A table structure similar to that of section 9.3.1 is still used to locate pages on the Drum, but a completely new structure is needed to locate the sub-pages in the Mass and Local. For each of these stores there is an additional page table, structured as shown in figure 9.4. A special Table Look Up instruction (TALU) has been provided to search these tables. In principle its operation is similar to the store-to-store orders (section 7.4), but special additional logic in the D-unit is used in its implementation in order to allow comparisons between a 32-bit operand and sequential table entries to occur once every 40 ns. The action of the CPR non-equivalence routine for this system is summarised in figure 9.5. Some points of extreme detail, such as the paging of the page tables, and the 'no space in store' condition, have been omitted. The abreviations LPT and MPT refer to the extra page tables required for the pages currently in the Local and Mass stores.

### 9.4 PROCESSOR SCHEDULING

After store control, the next most important task of the kernel of the Operating System is the allocation of the processor (or possibly processors) to the virtual machines. It should be pointed out that there might be another level of scheduling applied above this one by the job initiation modules introduced in section 9.5. They can choose to apply their own high-level scheduling rules before requesting virtual machines to run the jobs.

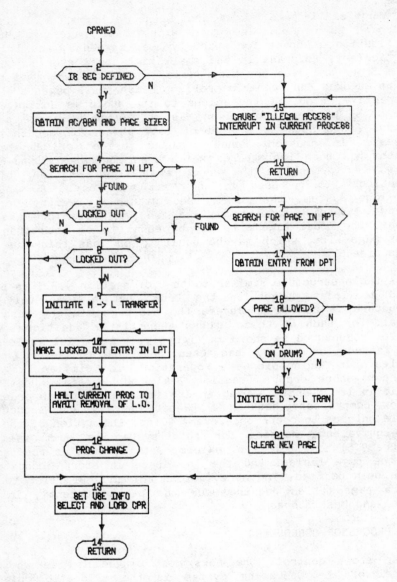

Figure 9.5 CPRNEQ Procedure for Sub-pages

Here, the problem is simply one of choosing the virtual
machine(s) to which the processor(s) are to be applied, but
account must be taken of their relative priorities and of the
fact that some contain interactive jobs, while others do not.
It is the priority number assigned to a virtual machine by its

user that determines both. The accounting system bases its charges on this priority number, which discourages users from making unreasonable choices. There are 16 priority numbers, but 0 through 7 are reserved for the system. Of the remainder 8 through 11 give the virtual machine interactive status and 12 through 15 give background status. Within each group the highest priority is given to the lowest numbers.

There are two parts to this scheduling system, and they interface through an 'execute list' which specifies 16 virtual machines, ordered according to priority. One part of the scheduling system, termed the 'low level scheduler', is concerned with allocating the processor(s) to these 16 machines, so as to maximise processor utilisation. The other 'medium level scheduler', is concerned with choosing the 16 entries on the execute list, to match theers relative priorities and interactive requirements of the virtual machines competing for the processor.

Whenever a processor is available, the basic aim of the low level scheduler is to allocate it to the highest priority virtual machine on the execute list which is free to run. Those not free to run will be halted, for a page transfer or other reason of short duration. However, the low level scheduler must guard against creating an increase in total paging traffic as a result of running more virtual machines than the main store will accommodate. It will sometimes be better to allow a processor to idle until a page transfer completes, than to run another program whose demands on space cause pages which will soon be required to be removed from main store. A full discussion of this problem cannot be included here. Briefly, the low level scheduler and the paging system between them attempt to estimate continuously the core requirement of each virtual machine. The sum of these estimates determines how many of the virtual machines on the execute list are considered as candidates for the processors before they are allowed to idle waiting for page transfers to complete.

If a virtual machine on the execute list is awaiting input, or file retrieval, both of which really mean waiting for a message, it is removed from the execute list. Another reason for removal, which applies in the interactive case, is the expiry of its 'time slice'. When entries are removed, others move up thus improving their chances of being allocated a processor. The composition of the execute list is determined by the medium level scheduler. It aims to cycle through all the interactive virtual machines, giving each one that is not waiting for a message a short burst (or 'timeslice') of active processor time. During this cycle it maintains the highest

priority background job that is free to run at the low
priority end of the execute list. At the end of the cycle, if
the proportion of processor time requested by the Computer
Operator for background work has not been obtained, the next
cycle is delayed until the background job 'catches up'. In
fact, the cycle is further complicated by the need to take
account of interactive priority. Only those virtual machines
with priority number 8 are considered every cycle. The rest
are considered every two, four or eight cycles respectively.

## 9.5 THE OPERATING SYSTEM USE OF VIRTUAL MACHINES

We have already seen that each user program is run in its own
virtual machine, and that the Operating System occupies the
upper half of each virtual machine. In addition, some parts of
the Operating System have their own virtual machines. This
structure can best be clarified by considering how it would
apply to a hypothetical machine with an arbitrarily large
number of processors connected into a common store. Imagine
that each user job in this hypothetical system is given its
own processor. Each of these processors would have access to a
common area of the store and would also have some store
dedicated to the job it is running. It would be natural for a
program requiring an Operating System facility to execute the
appropriate procedure using its own processor. In addition,
there is need to run other Operating System activities in
parallel. For example, the input for new jobs has to be read
in, and previously buffered output has to be driven out
through the output devices as they become available.
Therefore, in this hypothetical system, it is convenient to
assign a processor to each input/output device. Other
Operating System activities which are still not provided for
are the global organisational tasks; for example, job queueing
and initiation, file archiving, etc. Further processors are
allocated to each of these.

This hypothetical system is modelled in the MU5 Operating
System by applying a virtual machine to each of the above
activities assigned to a processor. To summarise its
structure, there is a small kernel of Operating System
software which implements an arbitrary set of virtual machines
which are analogous to a corresponding set of processors. The
store containing the Operating System code and its tables
appears inside every virtual machine (the common segments).
Also, in each virtual machine, there is the store private to
the job it is executing (the private segments). Any one of the
virtual machines can enter Operating System mode in order to
execute an Operating System function, on behalf of the
activity running in that machine. In addition, some virtual
machines contain no user job and they execute the Operating

202

System tasks which are not directly related to any single user job. These tasks are concerned with driving input/output peripherals and providing system wide services. The overall mapping of the MU5 Operating System into virtual machines is depicted in figure 9.6.

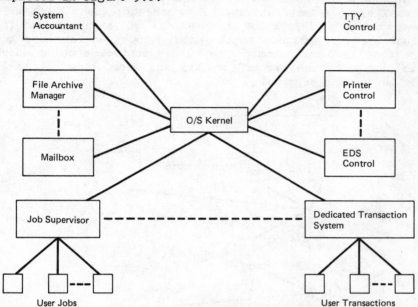

Figure 9.6 The Virtual Machines in the MU5 Operating System

This system structure applies to all members of the MU5 range. Modest configurations would probably have only one actual processor, which would be shared by all the virtual machines. Larger systems might have several processors, but not enough to assign one to each virtual machine. The largest systems might comprise several different computers, each with its own store and operating system kernel, and the rest of the virtual machines of the operating system would be distributed across these in an optimum manner. For example, the virtual machine running the file store archiving process would be in the machine that is connected to archiving devices. The actual MU5 complex at the University of Manchester (figure 2.3) is an example of a distributed system of this kind. One consequence of this distribution is that the virtual machines of the MU5 Operating System cannot rely upon shared segments as a means of communication. Instead, communication facilities between the virtual machines are provided by the message system described in the next section.

The operation of this structure when typical jobs flow through the system is illustrated in figure 9.7. Initial input

is passed from the device controllers to the JOB INITIATION
module. If the jobs are batch jobs, all their inputs are
collected by this module, and then, when the scheduling rules
allow, a new virtual machine is created to run the job, and
the inputs are passed on. A request to start an interactive
job will receive immediate attention and subsequent input will
bypass the JOB INITIATION module and go straight to the
virtual machine assigned to the job. Output generated by the
user jobs flows out through the output control modules where
it may again be subject to queueing and scheduling unless it
is to an on-line terminal.

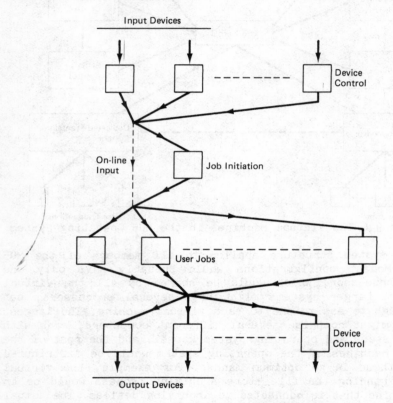

Figure 9.7 Job Flow

## 9.6 COMMUNICATION BETWEEN VIRTUAL MACHINES

Communication between the virtual machines is necessary for
several reasons. Clearly input/output has to flow through the
system from one virtual machine to another. Also, Operating
System procedures called in a user virtual machine might need
to request the services of an Operating System module running
in another virtual machine. For example, if access is

requested to a file which has been transferred on to archive media, the 'OPENFILE' procedure will require the services of the file archive manager, in order to retrieve the file. Finally, virtual machines sometimes have to synchronise, either because they are collaborating on the same job and need to keep in step or because they are in competition for a common resource.

At the time of designing the MU5 Operating System, two techniques for synchronising virtual machines (or the processes they contain) were widely known and there were various ways in which each could be adapted as a communication system. These were the semaphore system formalised by Dijkstra [38], and the event system used by a number of designers but perhaps most elegently by Bernstein, Kerr and Detlefsen [39]. Since the MU5 team at that time included Detlefsen, there was a natural tendency to move towards an event based system. The semaphore concept was only considered appropriate as a technique for synchronising access to the system tables within the kernel. For the general communication requirement it seemed too contrived. The activities in an operating system are not really analogous to railway trains moving about a network. They are more analogous to people in a large organisation each carrying out their own task, sometimes passing results and queries to other people and sometimes using shared facilities. Events seemed a more natural basis for the design. It is events such as

                    new job arrives
                    tape deck becomes available
                    card reader started by operator

that trigger many operating system activities. However, the system design never quite crystallised around the event concept, mainly because it did not lead to a satisfactory system for input/output propagation. To return to the analogy of people in an organisation, they are driven by in-trays and out-trays of messages and other more urgent(?) messages arriving by telephone. Eventually, the idea evolved of providing a message system within the Operating System, into which all the virtual machines are connected, even if they are in different computers.

In effect, this system allows any virtual machine to send a message to any other virtual machine, but the facility is provided for a virtual machine to exert some control over the messages it is to receive. This control derives from the decision that two procedures must be executed in order to achieve the transfer of a message from one virtual machine to another, and the notion of channels (see below). The sending

205

machine calls the 'SEND.MESSAGE' procedure which makes the
message available to the receiving machine. It is only taken
into the receiving machine when it calls the 'READ.MESSAGE'
procedure. It would obviously be undesirable to hold up the
sending machine until the receiving machine was ready, hence a
queue of messages is allowed to form for each machine. Some of
these may be more urgent than others. For example, if there
was a virtual machine in the system with responsibility for
queuing and initiating background jobs, it might wish operator
messages such as

'HOW MANY JOBS ARE QUEUED?'

to have priority over messages requesting the initiation of
new jobs. To avoid the need for the software in a virtual
machine to examine all waiting messages in order to find the
most urgent, they are streamed on to 'channels'. A virtual
machine has several (in fact 8) input channels, each with its
own queue of messages. The SEND.MESSAGE procedure has a
parameter giving the channel number in the destination
machine, and the READ.MESSAGE procedure also has a channel
number parameter to specify the channel from which the message
is to be read. On each channel the messages are queued in
arrival time order.

It is now evident that if channels are to be associated
with particular sorts of message, some control over the
messages that can be sent to a channel is necessary. The
mechanism is that the channels have status bits which are set
by a SET.CHANNEL.STATUS procedure and inspected by the
SEND.MESSAGE procedure. Obviously, it is not possible for the
status to refer to the logical nature of the messages to be
accepted on each channel. Instead it is used to specify which
other virtual machines may send messages to the channel. The
detail of this mechanism has been subject to much change as
the Operating System has evolved. What has been sought is a
simple but sufficient system. One obvious solution would be to
attach to each channel a list of the authorised senders, but
this is not done because of the relative high cost of handling
these variable sized lists. In this kind of system the cost of
sending messages is a critical overhead. The present system
uses only one word to indicate the status of a channel. This
provides the following states

closed        - meaning no messages will be accepted
open          - meaning all messages will be accepted
dedicated     - meaning only messages from a specified
                VM will be accepted
open to exec  - meaning only messages from VMs running
                in executive mode will be accepted

The status contains one other bit, which determines the
action to be taken when a new message is linked to a channel.
It gives the choice between the message simply being queued,
until the program running in the virtual machine chooses to
read it, and the message causing an interrupt within the
virtual machine. This, then, is the mechanism for passing
messages, but what constitutes a message?

Some messages will consist of large and variable sized
units of information, for example, a file, or a copy of a deck
of cards, or a listing to be printed. Therefore, the
SENDMESSAGE command allows a segment of the sending machine's
virtual store to contain the message. The combined effect of a
sender issuing a SENDMESSAGE command, and the recipient
issuing a READMESSAGE command, is to transfer the segment from
one virtual store to the other. This is achieved by copying
pointers from one segment table to the other and does not
involve copying the information. Unless, of course, the
sending and receiving virtual machines are in different
computers, in which case a copy is required. Usually the
sender would release his access to the segment, but it could
be retained in which case the segment would become shared,
provided only one computer was involved. In some cases the
information to be conveyed in a message is quite small, and it
would be wasteful to create and pass a segment. Thus, each
message incorporates a short header, in addition to the
segment, which is in fact optional. When a message is sent,
the header is copied into the system message queue and when it
is read the header is copied into the receiving machine's
virtual store. The message headers are used, without segments,
to propagate on-line input/output through the system, and,
with segments, to specify the action required on the segment.
This might for example be 'print it on two ply paper' or 'file
it'.

## 9.7 THE FILE SYSTEM

Since the segment of virtual store is the unit of information
that can be passed as a message, and shared between virtual
machines, it is natural to equate files with segments. A
command is therefore provided which allows a program to file
one of the segments in its virtual machine. The converse
command is also provided, by means of which an existing file
can be introduced as a segment into a virtual machine. Files
may be segments of text, code, or data. Of course, this means
that files are subject to the same size limit as segments, but
the user will not normally directly access these files
himself. A library of input/output procedures exists to map
arbitrarily large text files on to several of these basic
files.

The implementation of the above mentioned file commands requires a directory structure which restricts each user to his own set of files and relates each file name to the position of file. This directory structure is the data base on which the file commands operate. Some file systems maintain the bulk of their data base in the file store itself (as additional files). This has an obvious elegance and fits well the hierarchical nature of the directories. For example, a file can be a directory to files which themselves are directories and so on. The first implementations of the MU5 file system worked this way but it led to heavy paging traffic, even for simple file store operations, and particularly for changes such as defining a new file, which necessitate directory changes. The alternative is to keep the file system data base separate from the file store. This is the way the later implementations have been organised.

In any file system, account must be taken of the physical characteristics of the devices available for file storage. The MU5 system has four notional types of store, namely: Core, Drum, Disc and Tape. These might in practice be provided by various physical devices as follows

      Core - might be core, plated-wire or LSI store
      Drum - might be drum or fixed-head disc
      Disc - might be large moving head disc or EDS
      Tape - might be magnetic tape or EDS.

The Core and Drum stores are integrated into a 'one-level' store by means of the paging system. There will be a one-level store for each machine in the complex containing the segments of its virtual machines and any recently active files. The Disc is the first level of file backup and out of use files are moved there from the one-level stores as space is required. Similarly, when the Disc becomes full, the longest out of use files are archived to Tape. This integrated file system, in which all computers share the same overall file system, even though they have there own one-level stores, is the basis of the design of the MU5 system. It requires that the file system data base is kept on the Disc, that facilities exist to synchronise changes to this data base from different computers, and that newly created or altered files in a one-level store can be forced back to the disc if they are required by another computer.

At the time of writing, the MU5 system has not had suitable hardware to serve as the Disc, therefore each computer in the complex runs its own separate file system. A temporary mechanism is provided which allows a job in one computer to access the files in another. This is achieved by having a file

208

manager process from which files can be obtained in reply to requests sent via the message system. The file commands automatically generate these messages and service the replies once they have been told which file system is to be accessed.

The actual file system, which runs on MU5, models the full design. It has three components. These are the procedures implementing the user commands which are part of the kernel, and two processes which act as off-load manager and archive manager running in their own virtual machines. The kernel commands allow the user to create and access files in the one-level store, but they communicate with the off-load and archive managers when the requested files have been previously off-loaded or archived.

## 9.8 MACHINE INDEPENDENCE AND ADAPTABILITY

The MU5 Operating System has to run in all the computers of the complex, hence it is desirable to make it machine independent. It must also support and survive research, and must therefore be adaptable. Thus its design must anticipate change and it must be applicable to

> different hardware configurations/architectures
> different types of workload
> different user requirements and expectations.

This is not merely a question of simple tuning measures, which could be parameterised. Fundamental changes may be required to the algorithms used in several parts of the system.

The adaptability of an operating system is affected by several factors, but the most important is that the system be designed in a modular fashion. Of course, all systems are modular! It is the nature of the modules and the ways in which they interact that determine the degree of adaptability that results. For adaptability, it is essential that modules be isolated from one another, in the sense that no module assumes in its own implementation anything about the implementations of other modules. This has nothing to do with compiling modules separately, or separating them by means of a protection mechanism. It is essentially concerned with distributing the data structure of the operating system so that each module is responsible for some part of the data structure, and 'hides' it from the rest of the system.

The overall structure of the MU5 Operating System may be viewed as a hierarchy of four levels, each of which is further subdivided into modules. The four main levels in the system are

The resident system processes.
The library procedures providing basic I/O
and JCL facilities.
The basic interface procedures of the
virtual machine (command level).
The core-resident code (interrupt level).

Considering first the question of machine independence, there is no significant problem with the system processes, since they run in the virtual machines created by the rest of the system. Thus they need not be discussed further in this connection.

The basic library procedures also run in the virtual machines in normal user mode, and again there is no significant problem. Some procedures, however, access a global data structure whose form may vary according to the size and structure of the virtual store provided in the virtual machines. Therefore, the library procedures are grouped into modules which reflect this possibility.

Command level contains the implementation of the procedures which allow a process to manipulate its virtual machine environment. These conveniently fall into functional classes such as

store control commands
process control commands
communication commands.

Hence these classes are the major modules of command level. The command level and interrupt level procedures together form the system kernel which creates and supports the virtual machines in which the previous two levels of the system and the user jobs run.

At interrupt level the modules were initially chosen to correspond to those sections that would run autonomously. Thus there are modules for each class of peripheral, and for the functions of store management and processor management. In the context of machine independence, these same modules correspond with the components that might require change in moving to a different machine. In fact, such changes are mainly restricted to interrupt level since the modules here interface directly with the real machine. However, the effects of hardware differences can filter through to command level modules, for example, to enable a process to manage a non-paged, rather than a paged virtual store.

The requirement for several different versions of a module

to exist, and be maintained simultaneously, has led to the production of a much cleaner specification of the modules and their interfaces, so that any version of a module can be used with the rest of the system provided its hardware requirements are met. Given this structure, it has proved useful to introduce alternative versions of modules for reasons other than hardware differences, for example, to provide varying degrees of sophistication in areas such as scheduling.

The end result is that the total Operating System exists, in source form, as a matrix of files, in which each row contains all versions of one module of the Operating System. A particular system is built by selecting one module from each relevant row. The selection criteria are that first, one element is chosen from each row which offers a facility required in the given system, and second, the chosen element must have the required degree of sophistication and compatible hardware requirements.

As mentioned earlier, this interchangeability of modules is only realisable because of the distribution of the entire Operating System data structure among its modules. Each module has its own set of lists and tables, which are not accessed directly by any other module. Obviously the modules are not logically independent, and an event might occur in one module which requires an alteration to the data structure of another. This is provided for by 'interface procedures'. Each module may have associated with it a set of interface procedures which can be called by other modules to perform specific interfacing functions. For example, the scheduling module has interface procedures to activate and de-activate a specified process. These are called at the appropriate logical points by other modules. For example, de-activate is called by the communication commands whenever a process waits for input which is not available, and activate is called when it becomes available. The exact implementation of activate and de-activate is thus hidden within the scheduling module. Since we are not concerned with protection among modules of the system kernel, any potentially embarrassing overheads resulting from using interface procedures are avoided by the use of macro expansions rather than formal procedure calls wherever this is appropriate.

# 10  A User's View of MU5

The user sees a computing machine through its software. In the
case of MU5 this is the Manchester University Software System
(MUSS). This system is machine independent and it runs on
several machines in addition to MU5. In fact, we have already
seen that the MU5 complex contains at least one of each of the
following machines

>            MU5
>            ICL 1905E
>            PDP-11
>            MEMBRAIN 7700

and the MUSS integrates them into a single system as far as
the user is concerned. It can also run as a stand alone system
in each of these machines and some others such as ICL 2900.
The description given here applies to the MUSS in general
rather than just to the particular MU5 version.

## 10.1 PROCESSES

From the user point of view the software in the machine can be
regarded as consisting of a number of concurrent activities,
or processes, for example

>            control of the lineprinter
>            management of the system accounts
>            execution of a user job.

In principle each of these processes can be thought of as
executing within its own dedicated computer, but having some
means of communicating with the other processes. However, it
is a characteristic of many operating system activities, and
user jobs, that they require the use of a processor for only
relatively small amounts of time. The rest of the time is
spent waiting for something to happen. For example, waiting
for the lineprinter to finish printing the current line, for a
user process to supply more output for printing, or for an
on-line user to type his next line of input. Consequently, it
is possible for all of the processes to share the use of a
single processor, and the kernel of the operating system

allocates the processor to processes as required in order to provide a 'virtual machine' for each process. This structure was described in chapter 9.

An important feature of a virtual machine is that the process it contains appears to have an entire machine to itself, with complete freedom to organise itself within this machine. Thus processes need not be written in the knowledge that they will be sharing the computer with other processes. However, each process has a unique name, by means of which other processes may communicate with it, if the need arises. This is most likely in the case of system processes, and their names are chosen to relate to their function. For example the process controlling the lineprinter is called LPT and the process for starting new jobs is called JOB. For a user process, the name is assigned by the user. In addition to its name, a process also has an 'internal address' which enables the system to locate its virtual machine in order, for example, to deliver messages. The internal address consists of two integers, the System Process Number (SPN) and the Process Identifier (PID). The PID is a unique identifier for the process, whereas the SPN is the number of the virtual machine it uses, which may be reallocated when the process terminates. A system command is provided to convert between names and internal addresses, and the user interface procedures normally accept names and obtain the internal address for themselves. In the MUSS, communication between processes is achieved using the message system (section 9.6) which allows any process to send a message to any other process by specifying its internal address. A single message may convey any amount of information, up to 256 Kbytes, although in many instances it would be only one line of text. This message system also forms the only means of communication between a virtual machine and the outside world. Peripheral devices are controlled by system processes called device controllers, which communicate with other processes via the message system. Thus, information to be printed on a lineprinter must be sent as a message to LPT, the device controller in charge of the lineprinters.

10.2 SUPERVISORS

User jobs are introduced into the system by processes called supervisors. A supervisor is a process which services requests (in the form of messages) from users to start jobs. Its main function is to create and start new processes to execute these user jobs, but it can also exert some control over the execution of any process which it has created by use of the appropriate operating system procedures. There is a basic supervisor permanently resident in the system called JOB. In fact, in the MU5 complex there is a version of this supervisor

213

in each machine, each with its own unique name (JOB5E, for example is its name in the ICL 1905E). Thus a user can start a job in any machine in the complex from any terminal by addressing his input to the appropriate supervisor. In addition, any other process may act as a supervisor to provide alternatives to the basic system facilities. It was anticipated originally that this facility would be used to provide several alternative supervisors, each with its own job control language, specialised towards the needs of different user groups. In practice this has not been necessary because the basic system has proved to have sufficient flexibility for all users. The role of the basic supervisor is simply to create a virtual machine to run a process. This process then interprets its own job control commands. In fact, the job control commands take the form of calls on library procedures which are to be made within the virtual machine running the process. Differing user needs are met by the variety of procedures available. Some procedures might in practice be interpreters of other job control languages. However, even this facility has not been exploited because job control procedures, like other library procedures, can be called from programs written in the high-level languages and complicated job control sequences involving conditional and repeated actions can be written in the standard high-level languages [39].

## 10.3 THE LIBRARY

Pre-loaded into every virtual machine created by the MUSS is a set of fully compiled library procedures. These provide the process with access to all of the facilities of the system, and include

> mathematical functions
> basic input/output procedures
> compilers
> editors
> job control procedures
> JCL interpreters
> operating system interface procedures
>     ('SEND.MESSAGE', for example).

The average user would not normally have contact with the operating system interface procedures. They are used by the supervisors, the basic input/output procedures which interface the users read and print commands into the message system, and the job control procedures. The job control procedures are mainly concerned with defining the environment in which programs are to run. This usually means defining the 'documents' which form the inputs and outputs of a program.

## 10.4 INPUT/OUTPUT DOCUMENTS

Most user jobs begin as a 'document' submitted to one of the
input devices attached to the system. A document, for example,
may be a deck of cards, a reel of paper tape, or on-line input
at a terminal. The document is read by the device controller,
responsible for the input device to which it is presented, and
converted to a message in a standard internal format. It may
be routed by the user to any process in the system.

To facilitate the entry and routeing of documents, the
input device controllers recognise a rudimentary control
language. Any line of input beginning with the sequence '***'
is interpreted as a command to the device controller. The
commands are distinguished by the following character which
should be a letter (usually an 'A', 'M' or 'Z'). The commands
***A and ***M mark the start of a new document. In the first
case, the entire document up to the terminator ***Z is
buffered and then sent to the receiving process as a single
(long) message. This form of input is appropriate for use with
bulk input devices such as card readers. The command ***M
causes the subsequent input to be sent, one line at a time (as
a short message), to the destination process, and is thus more
suitable for use with interactive terminals. The input/output
library facilities used by most programs mask the difference
between these two forms of input and a program can usually be
run with either buffered or on-line input/output without it
knowing the difference.

The detail format of device controller commands is

    ***<LETTER>  PROCESS.NAME  USER.NAME  PASSWORD

where PROCESS.NAME, USER.NAME and PASSWORD follow standard
system conventions for names and specify the name of the
destination process, and the name and password of the user,
respectively. Further information may be placed on the same
line, but it is not interpreted by the device controller. This
command line is sent to the destination process either as part
of the long message, or as the first of a sequence of short
messages. Thus the destination process may make use of any
further information it contains.

The most common destination for an input document is a
supervisor such as the JOB supervisor which is described in
the following section. However, a number of other possible
destinations are useful, in particular

(1) An output device controller, in order to obtain a copy
    of the input document.

215

(2) Any user process, in order to 'connect' a terminal into an already running user process. As a consequence of this user processes may act as supervisors.

Inside a virtual machine its input/output documents are organised into streams. A process may have up to 8 input streams and 8 output streams which it can switch between at will. The basic input/output commands operate on the currently selected stream, and the 'SELECT.INPUT' 'SELECT.OUTPUT' commands allow a new current stream to be selected. When a stream ceases to be the current stream, the position of the last character processed is noted. If it is later re-selected as the current stream the input/output processing will be resumed from the point where it was left. The job control commands allow the user to associate input streams with files or (incoming) message channels, and output streams with files or outgoing messages. Depending on the 'mode' that the user assigns to an input stream, reading past the last character of the last message will either put the process into a waiting state or cause a fault interrupt. The 'mode' assigned to an output stream determines whether it is to be sent a line at a time or buffered. It also indicates whether the output is to be sent to a file, a named process, or as a reply to an input stream. In this latter case the destination will be variable. It will be to the process which sent the current message on the associated input stream. Further to this general policy of simplifying the input/output for the program in a virtual machine, a single internal code (ISO) and text format is used for all documents, regardless of source. User programs are normally designed to operate on streams, to which any type of document is assigned, at command level, before the program is entered. The main text processing procedures of the library such as editors, compilers, etc., do not require streams to be pre-defined. They have 'name' type parameters which specify either the names of files or device controllers or streams which are to be used as the input/output. Within these procedures new streams will be assigned as appropriate.

10.5 THE JOB SUPERVISOR

This is the only supervisor built into the basic system, and it provides simple facilities for the initiation of user jobs in both background and interactive mode. It interprets each message that it receives as a request to start a new user job. Messages are normally documents entered via the device controllers, but they may also be generated internally. In particular, there is a RUN.JOB command by means of which existing jobs may generate new job requests.

The form of job request allowed by the JOB supervisor is

216

```
***<A or M> JOB   USER.NAME   PASSWORD   JOB.TITLE <options>
```

where USER.NAME and PASSWORD are names, checked by the device
controller, and JOB.TITLE is the name to be assigned to the
process that will be created to run the job. The <options> are
optional parameters specifying, for example, the amount of CPU
time required for the job (T<integer>) and the priority level
at which it is to run (P<integer>). In general low numbers
mean high priority, but priorities 12-15 are scheduled as
background jobs and priorities 8-11 as interactive jobs
subject to timeslicing (section 9.4). Priorities 0-7 are
reserved for the system processes. If any of the optional
parameters are omitted, defaults are assumed which suit the
needs of typical users.

A '***A' job heading is normally used to initiate a
background job, so if the priority is not stated, P14 is
assumed. Priority 15 is 'cheaper' (section 9.4) but the
turnaround time would be longer. All the input following the
initial line up to '***Z' is passed to the created job as its
input stream zero. It should contain further job control
commands and possibly input data for the job. The alternative,
'***M', is used to initiate an interactive job, and is the
'LOG-IN' command for the system. Here the default priority is
11. After JOB has processed the ***M line and created a
process to run the user job, control of the interactive
terminal is handed to the created process, and subsequent
input is directed straight to this process, again as its input
stream zero. Output stream zero of the process is defined to
be a reply stream, hence it is automatically routed back to
the terminal.

The basic JOB supervisor exists in two variants. The
simplest one performs no 'high-level' scheduling at all. It is
intended for the smaller machines running MUSS. All jobs
submitted to it are made available for running immediately. If
at any time the system resources are insufficient to satisfy a
request to start a new job, then it is abandoned with a
message to the user or operator. The more sophisticated
version of the supervisor, capable of queueing jobs which
cannot be run immediately, schedules according to information
given by additional <options>. In either case, jobs made
available for running by a supervisor are subject to the
'medium level' and 'low level' scheduling built in to the
basic system. As described in chapter 9 the medium level
scheduler 'timeslices' the interactive jobs and allocates a
proportion of the CPU specified by the operator to the highest
priority background job free to run. If interactive jobs with
different priority numbers are competing for the CPU, ones
with lower priority numbers will receive more timeslices.

## 10.6 JOB CONTROL COMMANDS

After the initial **\*\*\*A** or M line, which causes a process to be created to run a job, commands should follow which direct the execution of the job. It was mentioned above that the system allows for the co-existence of many different job control languages, but here only the facilities available under the basic system are described. They are available without distinction to both background and interactive jobs.

Every user process begins execution in the same 'START' procedure, which first creates an output stream zero, directed at the default output device associated with the input device from which the job was submitted. For background jobs this would normally be a lineprinter (and the mode would be buffered), and for on-line jobs the user's terminal (and line by line mode). Next it reads and processes the commands on input stream zero. Each command is interpreted as a call to a library procedure, and successive commands are executed in sequence, unless one of the commands signals an error, in which case special action is taken. For background jobs, this usually involves monitoring the error and terminating the job. For an interactive job, after the error has been monitored, the faulty command is abandoned and a further command from the user is awaited.

A user at an interactive console may interrupt his job by pressing the 'BREAK' key on the console and the effect is to abandon the current command, and await a further command from the user.

Whenever the system is waiting for input from an on-line terminal, an invitation to type is printed. If a job control command is required, this prompt will be '\*\*'. At other times the usual prompt is '->', but the procedure processing the input has the option of pre-setting its own prompt message. For example, when input text for insertion into a file is expected in the NEW command, and in certain editing commands, the character that will terminate the input text is used as a prompt symbol.

### 10.6.1 Command Format

A command consists of the name of a procedure to be called, followed by its parameters, if any. Parameters are normally enclosed in brackets and separated by commas, but spaces are also acceptable as separators, and newline as the command terminator. Parameters may be omitted by typing consecutive commas, and trailing parameters may be omitted completely. In both cases, the omitted parameters are filled out as zero, which is treated a sensible default by most procedures. Examples of commands are

```
**EDIT(FILEA,FILEB)
**ALGOL(FILEC)
LIST.FILE  FILED  LPT*
```

Throughout command interpretation, non-significant spaces and blank lines are ignored. Commands may also, optionally, be preceded by '**'. This is mainly used in order to embed job control commands in program text for execution at compile time. The '**' serves as a warning to the compiler that it is a job control command, rather than further text for compilation that follows.

For the convenience of on-line users, most of the procedures in the Basic System Library have unique abbreviations of two or three letters, which may be used in place of the full procedure name. These abbreviations are listed with the summary of commands in Appendix 2.

10.6.2 Parameters

Procedures in the basic library are restricted to having only a few different parameter and result types. The main ones from the point of view of job control are

I       a single length integer

II      a 64-bit unsigned integer, which in job control contexts represents short packed character strings, such as file names, user names, etc.

S       a descriptor addressing a vector or a character string.

Private Library procedures may also be used in job control contexts provided they restrict themselves to the above parameter types.

The basic command interpreter accepts three textual forms of parameter, namely

A decimal integer (10, for example)

A hexadecimal constant, preceded by '%' (such as %10F)

A character string, which must not contain the separator symbols ',' , '!' , ')' , space or newline or begin with

H                               219

the symbol %. Non-representable characters may be inserted by writing their hexadecimal equivalent enclosed by exclamation marks.

The decimal integer form is the normal representation for parameters of type I. If it is placed in one of the other two contexts, it is interpreted as a character string of decimal digits, except for the decimal integer 0, which is always treated as the zero default. The hexadecimal form is intended as an escape mechanism and as such is a valid substitution for any parameter type. It is for this reason that strings beginning with % may not be represented. Character strings are permitted in both II and S parameter contexts. For parameters of type II, the characters are packed right-justified into a word of appropriate size; if too many characters are supplied, the required number are taken from the right hand end. The string 0 is treated specially, and is replaced by the value zero. For an S-type parameter the string is stored, and a descriptor to the string is created as the parameter.

## 10.6.3 Files

Many of the commonly used system commands (such as those for compilation and editing) operate upon files. A file is a segment of information, stored within the computer system, and identified by a filename. It may be text, compiled code or other binary information. Obviously, the commands which operate on files have filenames as parameters.

Mainly as a convenience to the on-line user, the system allows the filename parameter to be omitted in some circumstances. When this is done, a file known as the 'current file' is used automatically. The current file is a temporary file, which exists only for the lifetime of the process, and with a unique filename which cannot be confused with any of the user's filenames (in fact it is '0'). The ability to omit filename parameters and have the current file automatically assumed is useful in the common case where several successive commands operate on the same file.

At the start of a job, the current file does not exist. Certain commands allow the user to create and alter the contents of the current file. Some of these are defined in Section 10.6.4 below. Once a current file has been defined, omission of an input filename parameter automatically results in the current file being used instead.

## 10.6.4 Commands

Since job control commands are in fact simply library

procedures, it would be inappropriate to deal with them all in detail in this book. To convey the flavour of the system the commands most commonly used for manipulating files are described, and then some typical job control sequences are given in the next section. A complete list of library commands is given in Appendix 1. They should, in the main, be intelligible to readers familiar with interactive systems.

The following commands allow the user to manipulate files and set up the current file. In the headings the parameter types are shown as I, II, S. If the description needs to refer to particular parameters, P1 will denote the first P2 the second and so on.

(1) NEW(II,II)

This command is used to create a new file from the input immediately following it. Its parameters are

P1 - The Name of the permanent file to be created. If P1 is left unspecified (=0), the data input will become the current file.

P2 - A single character terminator. The input following is terminated by this character appearing at the start of a line. If the terminator is unspecified, '/' is used.

(2) OLD(II)

This command designates a copy of an existing file (name P1) to be the current file.

(3) SAVE(II)

This command preserves the current file as a permanent file (with name P1). The file also continues to be the current file.

(4) DELETE (II)

This command is used to erase a permanent file (with name P1) from the filestore.

(5) LIST.FILE(II,II,I,I)

This command lists the file specified by P1 on the device specified by P2. If the last two parameters are zero the whole file is listed, but they can be used to

221

specify a first and last line.

(6) EDIT(II,II)

This command invokes the editor to modify a text file.
This editor has the usual insertion and deletion
facilities, and positions may be specified by page and
line number or by context. A more detailed specification
of the editing facilities would not be appropriate here,
but some examples appear later.

P1 - The name of the input file to be edited. If this
is left unspecified (=0) the current file is
used.

P2 - The name of the permanent file on which the
output file is to be saved. If this is left
unspecified, the output becomes the new current
file.

10.7 EXAMPLES OF JOB CONTROL SEQUENCES

(1) A 'Null' Job

This is an example of a background job which does nothing
useful, but it illustrates the small amount of red tape
required by all jobs. The meaningful commands would be placed
before the STOP command.

```
***A JOB   USER PASS NULLJOB
STOP
***Z
```

(2) A 'Null' Algol Job

This job illustrates the structure required to compile and run
an Algol program. The actual program would be placed between
the 'BEGIN' and 'END' statements. The *END statement is needed
at the end of all programs submitted to the MUSS compilers in
order to end the compilation and switch back to command mode.
A temporary return to command mode, for example to select a
new input stream, can be made by embedding commands preceded
by '**' in the program text. If a program requires input data
it should be placed between the RUN and STOP commands. A user
program may return to command level by executing the final
end.

```
        ***A  JOB USER PASS NALG
        ALGOL
        'BEGIN'
        .
        .
        .
        'END';
        *END;
        RUN
        STOP
        ***Z
```

## (3) An Algol Job Using a File

This job illustrates two actions which would normally be used
only by on-line users. The first is the creation of a file
(FILEX) which is followed by a call on the Algol compiler to
compile the file, after which is a RUN command to run the
program.

```
        ***A JOB USER PASS  FJOB
        NEW(FILEX)
        'BEGIN'
        .
        .
        .
        'END';
        *END;
        /
        ALGOL(FILEX)
        RUN
        STOP
        ***Z
```

## (4) An Algol Job Using the Current File

The facility illustrated here would again be used by on-line
rather than background jobs, but it suffices to illustrate the
mechanism. It is similar to the previous example, except that
the file name has been omitted in the case of both the NEW and
ALGOL commands, hence the current file is used. This ceases to
exist when a job ends, unless it is saved as a permanent file
by the SAVE command also illustrated here. It should be noted
that if any command fails, those following will not be
executed. Thus if the program is faulty the file will not be
saved.

223

```
***A JOB USER PASS CFJOB
NEW
'BEGIN'
.
.
.
'END';
*END;
/
ALGOL
RUN
SAVE(FILEX)
STOP
***Z
```

## (5) Saving a Compiled Algol Program as a File

A compiled program can be saved, for subsequent running, by use of the DEFINE command thus

```
***A JOB USER PASS COMP
ALGOL FILEX
DEFINE FILEY
STOP
***Z
```

In this example a program in a file FILEX is compiled and the binary code is saved in a file FILEY. The program can subsequently be run by giving FILEY as the parameter of the RUN command. For example

```
***A JOB USER PASS RUN1
RUN FILEY
STOP
```

If the program needs data it could appear after the RUN command. If it needs input/output streams other than zero they would be defined before the RUN command. A similar mechanism allows a private library of procedures to be compiled and filed. They can subsequently be used as commands or by programs and in effect are an extension of the system library.

## (6) An Example Interactive Session

In the example given below the computer output is underlined to distinguish it from the user's input. On the actual system the distinction would be made by colour on devices which provide that facility.

224

The first command used after the log-in line is NEW, which is used to input to the current file an Algol program, for computing prime numbers. This is followed by the ALGOL command which compiles the program but finds two errors. These are corrected by editing the current file. The first edit statement copies to line 8 and 'windows' the line. The second means

                    after 'T'
                    insert 'E'
                    and window

Positions may also be selected by context but it is more convenient to use line numbers when a compiler gives them with the error reports. At the second attempt the program compiles correctly and it is entered by the RUN command. Since the program contains a call for the INI procedure which reads an integer, it prompts for data. When it is given the integer 10 it computes all prime numbers less than 10, and returns to command mode as a result of executing the final END. The program is entered again and given 100 as its data. This produces a run time error after the 22nd prime because they are stored in an array declared 0:20. At this point the current file is saved and listed, and the user logs out.


```
***M JOB MUSS SSUM DMDEMO
 DMDEMO    12.41.59. 04.11.77.
**NEW
∠'BEGIN''INTEGER'A,B,C,D,N;
∠'INTEGERARRAY' PRIMES[0:20];
∠     C:=0;
∠     N := INI;
∠     'FOR' A := 3'STEP' 1'UNTIL' N'DO'
∠     'BEGIN'
∠         D:=SQRT(A+1);
∠         'FOR'B:=2 'STP' 1'UNTIL'D 'DO'
∠            'IF' A '/' B * B = A 'THEN' 'GOTO' L1 ;
∠         OUTI(A,3);
∠         PRIMES[C] := A;
∠         NEWLINES(1);
∠         C:=Q+1;
∠L1:   'END';
∠     CAPTION ('('NO%OF%PRIMES%=%')');
∠     OUTI(C,5)
∠'END';
∠*END;
∠/
**ALGOL
MU5 ALGOL 21/10/77
```

225

```
?????1. 8      8      DELIMITER UNRECOGNISED
****1. 8      2      UNRECOGNISED
 407 BYTES INPUT
2ND PASS
****1. 13     19  Q  UNDECLARED
COMPILED SIZE IN BYTES        288
**ED
->c8w
1. 8)~↑~            'FOR'B:=2 'STP' 1'UNTIL'D 'DO'
->A'T'I'E'w
1. 8)            'FOR'B:=2 'STE~↑~P' 1'UNTIL'D 'DO'
->C13W
1. 13)~↑~           C:=Q+1;
->D'Q'I'C'
->E
 <CFILE> 12.51.49. 04.11.77. OK
**ALGOL
MU5 ALGOL 21/10/77
 408 BYTES INPUT
2ND PASS :COMPILED SIZE IN BYTES        326
 **RUN
->10
   3
   5
   7
NO OF PRIMES =       3
**RUN
->100
   3
   5
   7
  11
  13
  17
  19
  23
  29
  31
  37
  41
  43
  47
  53
  59
  61
  67
  71
  73
  79
  83
```

```
DESCRIPTOR FAULT
IN PROC/BLOCK  OUTER BLOCK  AT  1. 11
VARIABLES? **
**SAV DMPRIMES
**LF DMPRIMES &
DMPRIMES 12.53.13. 04.11.77.
1. 1  'BEGIN''INTEGER'A,B,C,D,N;
1. 2  'INTEGERARRAY' PRIMES[0:20];
1. 3      C:=0;
1. 4      N := INI;
1. 5      'FOR' A := 3'STEP' 1'UNTIL' N'DO'
1. 6      'BEGIN'
1. 7          D:=SQRT(A+1);
1. 8          'FOR'B:=2 'STEP' 1'UNTIL'D 'DO'
1. 9            'IF' A '/' B * B = A 'THEN' 'GOTO' L1 ;
1. 10          OUTI(A,3);
1. 11          PRIMES[C] := A;
1. 12          NEWLINES(1);
1. 13          C:=C+1;
1. 14  L1:  'END';
1. 15      CAPTION ('('NO%OF%PRIMES%=%')');
1. 16      OUTI(C,5)
1. 17  'END';
1. 18  *END;
1. 19  **STOP
STOP REASON    0    COST    12   TIME 12.54.38. 04.11.77.
```

# 11 Performance

The MU5 project was concerned with the design of a total system (hardware and software) for a range of machines. Only two members of this range have been built, the MU5 processor described in this book, which is a prototype of the main computing element in a 'top of the range' multicomputer system, and a 'bottom of the range' mu5. This evaluation is concerned with the larger system, although the full potential of the total system is not demonstrable because of the relatively small stores on MU5, and some discussion is included of the performance of the MU5 software on the ICL 2900. This is relevant because of the close similarity of the two systems. It is evident from the figures below that the MU5 evaluated here has not achieved its target speeds. Without wishing this to sound like an apology, because as a research project the outcome is very satisfactory, it should be remembered that the figures presented are for a first prototype. The performance of a second implementation could be much nearer the target.

## 11.1 BASIC HARDWARE SPEEDS

These have been introduced throughout this book but the summary below will set the context for what follows. Comparative figures are included for Atlas and the CDC 7600 because it is against these machines that we have chosen to evaluate the MU5 design. A throughput of 20 times Atlas was the stated target, but it was also hoped to match or better the performance of the CDC 7600 on everything except Fortran batch.

| | Main Store Access Time | Time Between Successive Fixed-pt Adds | Floating-pt Adds | Peak Inst Rate |
|---|---|---|---|---|
| Atlas | 1750 ns | 1520 ns | 2610 ns | .7 MIP |
| MU5 | 600 ns | 50 ns | 250 ns | 20 MIP |
| CDC 7600 | 220 ns | 27.5 ns | 27.5 ns | 40 MIP |

Table 11.1 Basic Performance Figures

228

Table 11.1 gives some comparative raw speeds and simple arithmetic indicates that MU5 is 3 to 30 times faster than Atlas and 2 to 9 times slower than the CDC 7600. Although access to the MU5 main store is relatively slow, its cycle time and data rate are more comparable with the CDC 7600 store, which is why parity of performance might be expected except where floating-point arithmetic dominates. The overall logical design aim has been to devise and engineer a powerful order code which exploits the technology efficiently.

## 11.2 THE POWER OF THE MU5 ORDER CODE

The results presented here are taken largely from reference [40] where the difficulties and hazards in producing such figures are more fully discussed. Intuitively it might be felt that power could be accessed by measuring, for typical tasks

(1) the size of the object code
(2) the number of instruction fetches from main store
(3) the number of operand fetches from main store

However, (2) and (3) are very dependent upon the buffering strategies involved, so a simple count of instructions obeyed is used instead. The difficulty with this is that the instructions might be very complicated, hence apparently powerful, but slow. Since none of the machines considered are microprogrammed, this effect is not pronounced, but actual elapsed times are also given as a safeguard.

Table 11.2 compares MU5 against Atlas using the results from two Algol programs, the first representing the GAMM mix [41] and the second a Quicker sort algorithm [42].

|  | Static Code Size (bits) | Number of Instructions Executed | Elapsed Run Time (s) | Average Instruction Time (ns) |
|---|---|---|---|---|
| GAMM: |  |  |  |  |
| Atlas | 8 784 | 302 080 000 | 1 027.44 | 3 400 |
| MU5 | 1 344 | 114 645 000 | 30.35 | 265 |
|  |  |  |  |  |
| Atlas:MU5 | 6.5:1 | 2.6:1 | 33.9:1 | 12.8:1 |
|  |  |  |  |  |
| QSORT: |  |  |  |  |
| Atlas | 26 880 | 163 400 000 | 504.40 | 3 090 |
| MU5 | 6 272 | 67 769 000 | 24.35 | 359 |
|  |  |  |  |  |
| Atlas:MU5 | 4.3:1 | 2.4:1 | 20.7:1 | 8.6:1 |

Table 11.2 Comparative Performance Figures for MU5 and Atlas

In these two cases it can be seen that the MU5 performance relative to Atlas is towards the extreme of the raw machine speeds. In addition it should be noted that the MU5 implementation is carrying out full array bound checking whereas the Atlas one is not. The first two columns, which approximate to the power difference of the two order codes, show the MU5 order code to be significantly better than that of Atlas.

Tables 11.3 and 11.4 compare MU5 against the CDC 7600, this time using the Curnow/Wichmann benchmark [43]. The compilers used were the May 1976 versions for MU5 (no optimisation and full array bound checking), and Algol 4.1 (level 5F compiler, 5D run time system) and FTN4.5 (level 420 compiler, 406A run time system) with full optimisation (level 5 and level 2 respectively) and no array bound checking, for the CDC 7600. It may be seen from the tables that the MU5 order code appears to be over four times as powerful for Algol, while being slightly less powerful for Fortran. The ratios of elapsed runtime when compared with the ratio of raw machine speed are in line with these figures. It is not surprising that the main 'features' of the MU5 instruction set, namely, dynamically assigned 'locals', bound checking on arrays and a recursive procedure structure, are of little advantage to Fortran programs. These figures have been confirmed for several other benchmark programs.

The figures above indicate that the aim of designing a powerful order code has to some extent been met. However, as discussed below, performance is also dependent upon the effectiveness of factors in the hardware, particularly

> the pipeline design
> the operand buffers
> the instruction buffers.

## 11.3 PIPELINE PERFORMANCE

The computer engineer's dream program is one in which the programmer refrains from using orders which write to store values which are about to be read, or which transfer control to some unexpected sequence of instructions, especially when this transfer is dependent on the state of some recently computed variable. Much of the effort in the design of the MU5 hardware went into overcoming the effects of orders such as these, and certain assumptions about their frequency of occurrence were made during the early design stages of the project. Accurate information about these frequencies was difficult to obtain since no existing computer had a similar order code. The estimated figures led to the expected overall

|  | Module 2 | Module 3 | Module 4 | Module 6 | Module 7 | Module 8 | Module 9 | Module 11 | Whole Program |
|---|---|---|---|---|---|---|---|---|---|
| **CDC 7600:** | | | | | | | | | |
| Millions of Instr. Obeyed | 1.61 | 23.0 | 16.0 | 17.9 | 21.0 | 249.0 | 182.0 | 19.1 | 529.0 |
| Elapsed Run Time (s) | 0.25 | 2.32 | 1.85 | 1.93 | 2.13 | 22.9 | 16.3 | 1.85 | 50.1 |
| Average Order Time (ns) | 155 | 101 | 115 | 108 | 102 | 92 | 89 | 96 | 95 |
| **MU5:** | | | | | | | | | |
| Millions of Instr. Obeyed | 0.68 | 6.98 | 7.08 | 9.25 | 14.9 | 35.1 | 20.9 | 15.7 | 110.0 |
| Elapsed Run Time (s) | 0.13 | 1.17 | 1.91 | 1.80 | 6.81 | 12.9 | 6.68 | 7.08 | 38.5 |
| Average Order Time (ns) | 187 | 167 | 269 | 194 | 458 | 366 | 319 | 450 | 348 |

Table 11.3 Algol Synthetic Modules

|  | Module 2 | Module 3 | Module 4 | Module 6 | Module 7 | Module 8 | Module 9 | Module 11 | Whole Program |
|---|---|---|---|---|---|---|---|---|---|
| **CDC 7600:** | | | | | | | | | |
| Millions of Instr. Obeyed | 0.46 | 4.34 | 6.78 | 4.62 | 24.0 | 29.7 | 14.2 | 15.2 | 99.1 |
| Elapsed Run Time (s) | 0.06 | 0.40 | 0.49 | 0.27 | 2.18 | 3.76 | 1.82 | 1.45 | 10.7 |
| Average Order Time (ns) | 132 | 92 | 73 | 58 | 91 | 127 | 128 | 95 | 108 |
| **MU5:** | | | | | | | | | |
| Millions of Instr. Obeyed | 0.50 | 3.81 | 7.42 | 8.41 | 14.9 | 45.9 | 16.0 | 15.8 | 113.0 |
| Elapsed Run Time (s) | 0.09 | 0.98 | 1.86 | 1.58 | 6.86 | 14.1 | 9.60 | 7.13 | 42.2 |
| Average Order Time (ns) | 185 | 256 | 251 | 188 | 461 | 307 | 599 | 451 | 374 |

Table 11.4 Fortran Synthetic Modules

performance of table 11.5, which is reproduced from reference [12]. In this table long orders are those requiring more than 16 bits for their specification (which might be orders involving long names or literals of more than 6 bits), store orders are orders of the form 'B => name', and organisational orders are the base manipulation orders such as 'NB ='. Column 2 gives the time required in excess of the basic 40 ns beat time for the execution of each type of order. Column 3 shows the expected percentage occurrences for these orders, and column 4 their net additional contribution to the execution time of an average order. It can be seen that an overall average execution time of about 120 ns was expected.

| Type of Order | Estimated Excess Time (ns) | Estimated Occurrence (%) | Net Time Added (ns) |
|---|---|---|---|
| Long | 40 | 10 | 4 |
| Store | 80 | 15 | 12 |
| Organisational | 360 | 1 | 3.6 |
| Control transfer (predicted) | 120 | 6 | 7.2 |
| Control transfer (unpredicted) | 940 | 4 | 37.6 |
| Name Store NEQ | 800 | 2 | 16 |
| Total net time added | | | 80.4 |
| Average execution time | | | 120.4 |

Table 11.5 Expected Overall Performance Table

As part of the MU5 evaluation exercise, measurements of the actual frequencies have been made for a number of programs (including the Oxford [44], London CDC [45] and Curnow/Wichmann [43] benchmarks), using a hardware System Performance Monitor (SPM). Hardware monitoring generally involves counting the occurrences of a particular type of event and recording the total obtained each time some other event, such as a clock pulse, occurs. In practice, however, many results are best recorded in the form of a histogram, showing for example, the relative number of occasions on which a given event occurs 'n' times between occurrences of some other event. Thus, as well as sixteen 32-bit counters, the SPM

232

incorporates a 512-word 16-bit store, and various modes of operation enable histograms of MU5 internal signals to be recorded. The SPM also includes a visual display unit, on which the contents of the store may be displayed [46], and histograms produced by the SPM may also be recorded in permanent form·by means of an off-line graph plotter. Figure 11.1 is an example of such a histogram, showing the distribution of the numbers of instructions obeyed between successive control transfers during the execution of one of the London CDC benchmark programs.

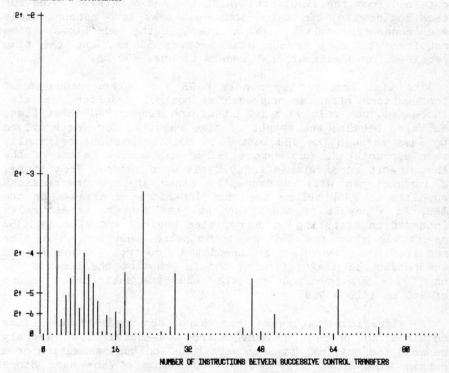

Figure 11.1 Example of an SPM Histogram

The SPM can be controlled by software in MU5 through its connection to the Exchange. In addition, signals coming into the SPM first go through validation logic, and by using a Machine Status register digit to validate the inputs, monitoring of a specific process or part of a process can be carried out. The MU5 Library contains procedures for reserving and initialising the SPM, starting and stopping monitoring (by means of the Machine Status digit), dealing with 'store full' interrupts from the SPM, reading out the store and controlling the display.

233

Measurements of the frequencies of occurrence of the order types shown in table 11.5 were made by using the contents of the appropriate parts of the PROP final function register to address the SPM store, and using the Control Register strobe to increment the corresponding SPM store location [47]. In addition, oscilloscope measurements of the execution times of various instructions have allowed both hardware and software corrections to be made to the projected performance figures. These are shown in table 11.6. Thus, whereas a 40 ns PROP beat time had been predicted, the achieved figure is 50 ns. The smaller figure was arrived at largely on the basis of results obtained from the simulator, which assumed a delay of 5 ns for each logic gate, but which could not take into account cable and connector delays. As a result, the additional time required for long orders also becomes 50 ns, and the time required for organisational orders becomes 450 ns.

The time required to supply PROP with a new sequence of instructions after an unpredicted control transfer has also increased, not only as a result of the longer PROP beat time, but also because the amount of time required for instructions to pass through the IBU Data Flow section had not originally been appreciated. Furthermore, if a jump occurs to one of the last 16-bit words within the 128-bit word fetched from store, a further gap will subsequently occur in the instructions supplied to PROP before the next 128-bit word arrives in the IBU. As a result of these factors, the average excess delay incurred in executing an unpredicted control transfer is 1350 ns rather than the 940 ns anticipated. However, the time required to execute a predicted control transfer is independent of these effects, and in practice the time of 150 ns (100 + 50) is slightly better than the anticipated figure of 160 ns (120 + 40).

A significant increase has also occurred in the time required to process a Name Store non-equivalence, largely because the original figures were based on the assumption of a single Name Store in PROP. The splitting of the Name Store into two parts requires that a search be made in the OBS Name Store whenever a PROP Name Store non-equivalence occurs, and the time required for this check is dependent on the number of instructions in the SEOP pipeline. The measured time of 1180 ns is therefore an average measured over a large number of executed instructions. The overall effectiveness of the Name Store is considered in more detail in section 11.4.

Software corrections to the original performance table have been made for both execution and compilation. The original estimates referred only to execution, and in reality there are distinct performance differences between compilation and

| Type of Order | Estimated Excess Time (ns) | Actual Excess Time (ns) | Estimated Occurrence (%) | Execution | | Compilation | |
|---|---|---|---|---|---|---|---|
| | | | | Actual Occurrence (%) | Net Time (ns) Added After Correction | Actual Occurrence (%) | Net Time (ns) Added After Correction |
| Long | 40 | 50 | 10 | 56 | 27.9 | 45.7 | 22.8 |
| Store | 80 | 100 | 15 | 6.2 | 6.2 | 9.1 | 9.1 |
| Organisational | 360 | 450 | 1 | 5.1 | 23.0 | 8.4 | 37.8 |
| Control transfer (predicted) | 120 | 100 | 6 | 8.7 | 8.7 | 8.0 | 8.0 |
| Control transfer (unpredicted) | 940 | 1350 | 4 | 4.5 | 60.7 | 10.5 | 141.8 |
| Name Store NEQ | 800 | 1180 | 2 | 3.5 | 41.3 | 11.9 | 140.4 |
| Total net time added | | | | | 167.8 | | 359.9 |
| Average instruction time | | | | | 217.8 | | 409.9 |

Table 11.6 Hardware and Software Corrected Performance Table

execution. In both phases the most noticeable differences between actual and predicted results are the increased numbers of long orders and organisational orders. Some of the increase in the number of long orders arises because the corrected figure is the number of extra beats required for the execution of orders with 16, 32 and 64-bit operands, and not just the frequency of occurrence of such orders. The frequency of occurrence of 32-bit and 64-bit literals was underestimated, however, as indeed was the frequency of control transfers using 16-bit literal operands. Although a 6-bit literal could in principle be used in many of these control transfers, the detection of these requires considerable compiler optimisation. The effects of control transfers themselves are considered in section 11.5.

Organisational orders have increased mainly as a result of changes in programming style, and in the style of compiled code, involving greater use of procedures. Entry to and exit from each procedure involves not only a control transfer but also some manipulation of the base registers. With the advantage of hindsight it would seem that the communication between the 'programmers' and 'engineers' went somewhat astray on this issue. Had the deleterious effects of these orders been properly appreciated earlier, the lock-out techniques used for other purposes in the PROP pipeline could have been extended to allow only selective inhibiting of the overlap for this type of order. Thus while a Name Base manipulation order was outstanding, for example, orders which did not require the use of the Name Base could have been allowed to proceed. For this system to have worked properly, however, extra hardware in the form of an additional adder, separate from the adder used to add name and base, would have been required to carry out the base manipulation. Alternatively, more complex procedure entry orders could have been incorporated into the instruction set, so that while the pipeline was stopped for one order, it could have executed the actions of two or more of the existing orders.

Table 11.6 by no means tells the complete story, since it does not, for example, include any reference to the effects of Compare orders or the performance of the Secondary Operand Unit. It does, however, serve to illustrate some of the problems involved, not only in designing for high performance in the first place, but also in accounting, afterwards, for all the extra nanoseconds.

The scalar product loop provides a good example of how the pipeline functions in practice. It can be coded in several ways but the best hand coded sequence is the following

```
            B = 0
            ACC = 0
       L1:  ACC *= VEC1[B]
            ACC * VEC2[B]
            B CINC LIMIT
            ACC + STACK
            IF /=, -> L1
```

Figure 11.2 shows a schematic timing diagram for two typical cycles of the loop. It is assumed that at least one cycle has already been obeyed, so that the operand LIMIT and the two descriptors VEC1 and VEC2 are all in the Name Store, and the IBU Jump Trace correctly predicts the control transfer. All instructions pass through the five stages of PROP: decode (D), addition of name and base (+), Name Store association (A), Name Store read (R) and operand alignment (S). The B orders, including Modifier Requests, use the Central Highway (H), while the ACC orders pass through Dr, the OBS Input stages (OA), the OBS Queue (Q), the OBS Output stage (OO) and Dop before reaching the ACC Input Buffer (AB). The 'ACC *=' order is shown passing through in its two phases, the first a store order writing the ACC Register content to the top-of-stack location held in the OBS Name Store, and the second loading the ACC Register with an element of VEC1. When the 'ACC +' order reaches the OBS Output stage, it is held up waiting for the updating action for the store order to be completed in OBS (O=>), since it requires the new value. This waiting time is largely overlapped with the execution of the 'ACC *' order, however. Thus the most important feature of this diagram is that the A-unit is busy for most of the time, and is not held up significantly either by the store order or by the execution in the Primary Instruction Pipeline of the statements controlling the loop. In practice a single cycle of the loop executes in slightly less than 1 μs, with the ACC Multiply occupying approximately half of this time.

## 11.4 NAME AND VECTOR STORE PERFORMANCE

Measurements of the efficiency of the Name Store have been carried out, using the SPM, for a set of 95 programs containing both Fortran and Algol jobs ranging in complexity from simple student jobs to large scientific programs. For most programs it was found that 80% ($\pm$ 5%) of operand accesses were for named variables, that no more than 120 names were used in any one program, and that in all programs 95% of name accesses were to fewer than 35% of the names used. These figures confirm the earlier Atlas results and suggest that high Name Store hit-rates should be obtained. In fact, it was found that over 96% of name accesses found their operand in one or other Name Store. Table 11.7 shows the average

237

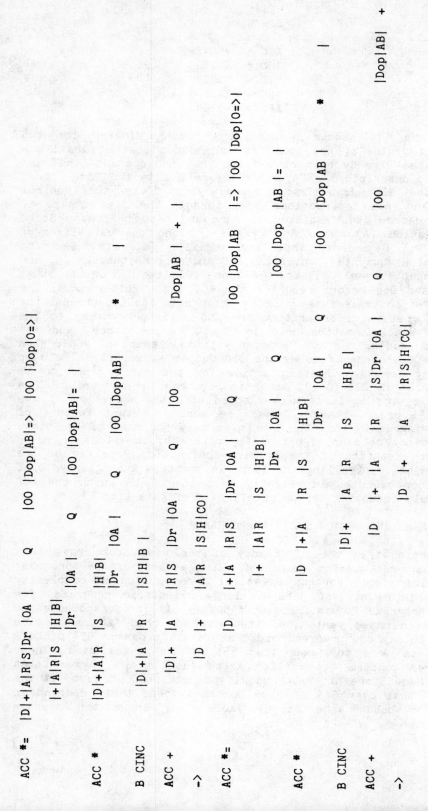

Figure 11.2 Schematic Timing Diagram of the Scalar Product Loop

hit-rates obtained, together with results for the degree of interaction between the two Name Stores. The latter presents something of a problem, since it can be seen from this table that despite the fact that 96.1% of name accesses found their operands in one or other Name Store, only 86% of these accesses found their operand in the correct Name Store. Of the remainder, 3.9% required an access via SAC to the Local Store (2.9% of PROP accesses + 1.0% of OBS accesses), while 6.1% of accesses (3.3% of PROP accesses + 2.8% of OBS accesses) required the operand to be read from the wrong Name Store, and 3.6% of accesses (1.8% + 1.8%) required their operands to be deleted from one Name Store and transferred to the other.

All Name Accesses

|  |  |
|---|---|
| In either Name Store | 96.1% |
| In correct Name Store | 86.0% |

PROP Name accesses

|  |  |
|---|---|
| NEQs | 8.0% |
| SAC.access | 2.9% |
| OBS.read | 3.3% |
| OBS.delete | 1.8% |

OBS Name accesses

|  |  |
|---|---|
| NEQs | 5.6% |
| SAC.access | 1.0% |
| PROP.read | 2.8% |
| PROP.delete | 1.8% |

Table 11.7 Name Store Hit-rates and Interactions

The performance of the Processor as a whole is affected by this comparatively high and largely unforeseen amount of interaction between the two Name Stores. The main reason for its occurrence is the way in which procedure calls are implemented. Parameters for procedures are normally passed on by stacking into the PROP Name Store, but in many cases may subsequently be used as OBS names. Conversely, it is possible for a particular word used as an OBS name in one procedure to be used in a subsequent procedure as a PROP name.

Some changes to the hardware have been made in the light of these facts. In the original design the advantage to be gained from avoiding the copying of a 64-bit word back from OBS to PROP in a case where all 64 bits were about to be overwritten (by stacking, for example) was not thought to be worth the extra complexity in the control circuits. This complexity has

239

now been introduced, and the time required to service a PROP Name Store non-equivalence in these cases reduced from over 1 µs to less than 300 ns. In terms of future machine designs it is clear that some different techniques must be adopted, either to shorten the pipeline, without loss of potential performance, or to overcome the 'ACC write back' problem, which led to the use of a split Name Store in the first place.

Because of the different purpose served by the Vector Store, its hit-rate was not expected to be as high as that of the Name Store. As we observed in Chapter 2, small groups of named variables are generally used repeatedly, while large groups of data structure elements are generally selected sequentially. However, because 128-bit words are fetched from the Main Store at a Vector Store non-equivalence, then programs using large numbers of sequentially accessed 64-bit elements could be expected to achieve a 50% hit-rate. Thus simulation studies carried out for a small number of programs during the design phase of the project indicated hit-rates in the range 58%-69%. When integer arrays (using 32-bit elements) or character strings (8-bit elements) are involved, then clearly higher hit-rates would be achieved. In fact, measurements made with the SPM using the much larger number of available benchmark programs showed considerably higher hit-rates, the highest being 97% and 85% being typical.

## 11.5 EFFECTS OF CONTROL TRANSFERS

The largest single contribution to the overall average instruction time in table 11.6 for both execution and compilation is from unpredicted control transfers (those not immediately followed down the pipeline by the correct sequence of instructions). Although their numbers have not increased significantly, for program execution, above the estimated figure, the increased time taken to obey one of these orders has had a marked effect. By comparison, the increased numbers of predicted control transfers contribute very little extra to the overall average instruction time. Furthermore, the fact that the increase in the total number of control transfers for program execution is accounted for almost entirely by predicted control transfers is indicative of a very high prediction rate in the IBU Jump Trace. This is confirmed by the figures shown in table 11.8, where the results for Algol and Fortran execution and compilation are listed separately. The first column gives the percentage of control transfers which use a literal operand and are therefore candidates for prediction by the Jump Trace. Column 2 shows the percentages of these predictable transfers which are actually predicted, and hence in column 3 the percentages of all control transfers followed by the correct sequence of instructions are shown.

240

For comparison, column 4 shows the percentages of control transfers which would be followed by correct sequences in the absence of the Jump Trace. The efficacy of the Jump Trace is shown quite dramatically by these figures. Furthermore, without the Jump Trace, the average instruction time would increase by 90 ns for Algol execution. For compilation the effects of the Jump Trace are less marked, but this is to be expected, since compilation is a data-dependent task, with many alternative processing sequences being possible. This involves the use of many multi-way jumps rather than simple loops, thus leading to the observed Jump Trace prediction rate.

|  | % Predictable Transfers | % Predictables Predicted | % Transfers Followed By Correct Sequences | |
|---|---|---|---|---|
|  |  |  | With Jump Trace | Without Jump Trace |
| **EXECUTION** |  |  |  |  |
| Algol | 87.8 | 70.3 | 66 | 17 |
| Fortran | 87.1 | 54.3 | 65 | 22 |
| **COMPILATION** |  |  |  |  |
| Algol | 85.5 | 19.1 | 41 | 27 |
| Fortran | 89.4 | 24.5 | 46 | 28 |

Table 11.8 Jump Trace Performance

Overall performance is also affected by the relative numbers of conditional and unconditional control transfers, since an unconditional transfer can be executed immediately its operand reaches the Control Register, whereas a conditional transfer may have to await the result of a previous Compare order before execution. The percentages of successful conditional, unsuccessful conditional and unconditional transfers are shown in table 11.9. The extra delay involved because of a preceding Compare order is very dependent on program context and difficult to measure accurately, and is not included in the figures shown in table 11.6. Clearly, however, the delay will be significantly different according to whether a B Compare or an X or ACC Compare order is involved. During program execution B Compare orders account, on average, for 4.55% of all orders, and can involve an extra delay of up to 150 ns. X and ACC Compare orders account on average for fewer orders (2.66%), but may

241

involve an extra delay of as much as 1 µs. This situation is one in which the pipeline approach does not help to increase instruction throughput, and it indicates a need, in a pipeline system, for the Control Point to be moved further along the pipeline towards the A-unit. For this to be successful, however, it becomes essential to supply the pipeline with the correct sequence of instructions after control transfers as frequently as possible. This necessarily involves the prediction of the outcome of a control transfer as early as possible in order to overcome store access time delays, and the Jump Trace is one technique which has been shown to achieve this requirement successfully.

|  | Successful Conditional | Unsuccessful Conditional | Unconditional | Total |
|---|---|---|---|---|
| **EXECUTION** | | | | |
| Algol | 6.0 | 2.4 | 5.6 | 14.0 |
| Fortran | 4.5 | 2.8 | 5.2 | 12.5 |
| **COMPILATION** | | | | |
| Algol | 5.5 | 5.1 | 8.4 | 19.0 |
| Fortran | 6.2 | 5.0 | 6.9 | 18.1 |

Table 11.9 Control Transfers as Percentages of All Orders

## 11.6 SOFTWARE PERFORMANCE

Some measure of the runtime performance of compilers is implicit in the above figures because they measure machine performance on high-level language programs. Other aspects of performance not included in the above are

compiling speeds
compiler/operating system sizes
interactive performance.

In order to distinguish the software influence on compiling speeds from the hardware contribution, they are given in table 11.10 as instructions obeyed (per byte of source processed and per instruction compiled). The Atlas figures, which are given for comparison, are taken from reference [48]. However, they require some interpretation. The Atlas figure of 169 instructions/byte of source is artificially low because it contains underlined delimiters achieved by use of a backspace character. The MU5 figures may be converted to times by using

242

the additional information that the average instruction rate of MU5 while compiling is 660 ns/instruction. This figure is considerably worse than the overall average mainly because compilers are 'data driven' rather than 'control driven'. That is to say, the conditional control transfers are usually dependent upon the value of data being fetched from store rather than the value of an incrementing or decrementing control variable. In addition, the compilers tend to use many short procedures and to have very short sequences of orders between control transfers. A further factor, not included in the above average, which affects the actual time for compilation is the time lost due to CPR loading. On MU5 this can be as high as 50% because of the software management of CPRs. However, a production MU5 would have hardware CPR loading thereby eliminating this effect.

|         | Inst/Byte of Source | | Inst/Compiled Instruction | |
|---------|------|-------|------|-------|
|         | MU5  | Atlas | MU5  | Atlas |
| Algol   | 227  | 169   | 720  | 1100  |
| Fortran | 116  | 355   | 1070 | 2275  |

Table 11.10 Compiling Speeds

Some compiler sizes have already been quoted in chapter 8. These are included again in table 11.11, which is a breakdown of the total software required to support interactive use of Algol and Fortran. It has been assumed throughout the design that performance, and particularly interactive performance, would be critically dependent upon the software size. The size of compiled code is one of the measures of the power of the order code discussed in section 11.2. Compiler sizes have an important bearing on the minimum size of main store on which the software system can be run, and for a given store size, the maximum number of active terminals that can be supported. However, it is really the size of the active part plus working space (or working set) of the compiler that matters, rather than its static code size.

Experiments with the MU5 software running on an ICL 2960 indicate that a 128 Kbyte store backed up by EDS is sufficient to sustain batch or light interactive use. This is supported by evidence in [49] that on MU5 the paging loss while compiling Fortran programs is less than 10% if the compiler is allowed 80 1-Kbyte pages. If peripheral activity is low, the rest of the system only requires a further 16 Kbytes. For Algol the corresponding figure is 8 Kbytes less, which might be partly due to the two-pass organisation of the compiler.

243

|                           | Total Size |
|---------------------------|-----------:|
| Bootstrap                 | 2.5 Kb     |
| Resident Kernel           | 9 Kb       |
| Paged kernel              | 9 Kb       |
| Library                   | 32 Kb      |
| Library Name Lists        | 9 Kb       |
| Algol Compiler            | 34 Kb      |
| Algol Run Time Package    | 3 Kb       |
| Fortran Compiler          | 37 Kb      |
| Fortran Run Time Package  | 12 Kb      |
| TML                       | 12 Kb      |
| Total                     | 159.5 Kb   |

Table 11.11 The Size of MUSS

For reasons already stated, the interactive performance of the MU5 software has been measured on ICL 2900 computers rather than MU5. It should be mentioned, however, that even with its limited hardware, MU5 provides an interactive computing facility to about 100 postgraduate students and staff through 25 terminals. For the evaluation of the MU5 software (MUSS) on 2900, ICL very generously made time available on machines used for the development of their own software, albeit at antisocial hours and on a variety of machine types and sites.

11.6.1 MUSS on ICL 2900

It has already been stated that the MUSS is modular, which gives rise to a range of configurations of the software to suit the size and purpose of the hardware system. The configuration used in the evaluation on 2900 was one thought to be appropriate to a general purpose timesharing system with

                    2960 Processor
                    2 Mbyte main store
                    2 EDS-200 Drives
                    normal I/O devices.

However, some of the more complicated scheduling and page turning modules were omitted to simplify the transfer of the system from MU5. Also, for the same reasons, a rather extravagent layout of main store was used, in which the system was allocated 156 Kbytes of store, even though a large fraction of this was unused. In fact, the results quoted below are for a 0.5 Mbyte system because ICL had an interest in the performance on this size of system. However, the same results

244

would have been obtained from 0.375 Mbytes if the store allocation had been tidier.

From the point of view of maintainability, it is of interest to note in passing that three separate binary versions of the system are kept on disc. Each can be re-compiled when running on either of the others. Sections can be changed and re-compiled separately without the need to compile a whole system as follows

| | |
|---|---|
| Basic Library | taking 1 min 12 s |
| Operating System | taking 4 min 47 s |
| High Level Language Library | taking 2 min 09 s |
| MUPL Compiler | taking 1 min 48 s |
| Fortran Compiler | taking 1 min 50 s |
| Algol Compiler | taking 1 min 36 s |

The load time for the system from any of the three versions is 20 s. All these times are for a 0.5 Mbyte 2960.

Since no communications processor was available on the machines used for the evaluation, interactive running had to be simulated by having a high priority process generating and absorbing the interactive message traffic. Obviously the existence of this process on the main frame system degrades its performance and hence the figures given later are on the pessimistic side. The mechanism for simulating interactive running is formalised into a library procedure 'INT.JOB.JOB' which has three parameters

    P1  -  the name of the supervisor to be used to
           initiate the interactive jobs
    P2  -  the destination file for the journal information
    P3  -  a 'substitution' symbol

The call of INT.JOB.JOB is followed by a list of data statements terminated by an '@', specifying the terminal activity to be simulated in the form

    filename       no. of terminals       no. of repeats

Each file (or 'script') is taken to be a list of commands, possibly interspersed with 'think' delays. If the symbol specified by P3 appears in a command, the terminal number is substituted. For example if '%' were the symbol in question, then a command 'DEFINEINPUT 3 FD1:%' would become

    DEFINEINPUT    3     FD1:000     for terminal 0
    DEFINEINPUT    3     FD1:001     for terminal 1
    etc.

Thus each simulated use of a particular script can have its own unique filenames. When the end of the script is reached it is repeated the requested number of times. The end result is that it is possible to simulate the effect of X terminals editing and running programs, Y terminals interactively running a big program and so on.

The performance measurements presented are based on the set of mainly Fortran programs summarised below. Most of these programs come from a benchmark used by ICL to assess their own software. F11 and F12, and two Algol programs A1 and A2, were added to show the effect of very large numbers of very small programs, such as might arise in a teaching environment. F11 and A1 were felt to reflect early beginner usage (they tabulate prime numbers) and F12 and A2, which compute solutions to the 'queens' problem, reflect the usage after a few weeks training.

|     | Source Size (lines) | (bytes) | Comp Size (bytes) | Comp | Mill Time (s) Run | Total |
|-----|--------|---------|---------|-------|--------|--------|
| F1  | 991 | 28245 | 19150 | 14.81 | 14.42 | 29.93 |
| F2  | 440 | 12035 | 7910 | 6.29 | 6.82 | 13.11 |
| F3  | 717 | 19697 | 10808 | 10.22 | 41.03 | 51.25 |
| F4  | 704 | 18715 | 11064 | 10.62 | 2.09 | 12.71 |
| F5  | 468 | 12468 | 6058 | 6.55 | 13.64 | 20.19 |
| F6  | 449 | 15437 | 12778 | 10.35 | 2.10 | 12.45 |
| F7  | 138 | 2925 | 2186 | 1.44 | 212.21 | 213.65 |
| F8  | 392 | 10477 | 8218 | 6.16 | 159.91 | 166.07 |
| F9  | 671 | 16043 | 8880 | 8.78 | 107.74 | 116.52 |
| F10 | 111 | 3154 | 2446 | 1.57 | 451.94 | 453.51 |
| F11 | 13 | 259 | 222 | 0.07 | 0.06 | 0.13 |
| F12 | 75 | 2448 | 644 | 0.53 | 1.31 | 1.84 |
| F13 | 407 | 11274 | 6096 | 5.64 | 6.29 | 11.93 |
| A1  | 14 | 341 | 340 | 0.06 | 0.07 | 0.13 |
| A2  | 17 | 3092 | 1074 | 0.66 | 1.18 | 1.84 |

Table 11.12 Job Statistics

Selections from the above group of programs have been used to generate both the batch and interactive components of the benchmark. First, in order to access batch performance, three batches of jobs were assembled and run. Their composition and the results obtained are given in table 11.13. Clearly, the first two batches are dominated by the longer jobs and show very good mill utilisation. Batch 3 involves multiple copies of the shorter jobs but the mill utilisation is still nearly 90%. This 'User Mill Utilisation' is the percentage of real time that the CPU spends executing user code. In the residual time the CPU is either executing Operating System code or waiting for disc transfers. Although the system has a multiprogramming capability, the level of multiprogramming can be set by the operator, and for the above batch tests it was set at 'one user program + system processes' only.

| | Batch 1 | Batch 2 | Batch 3 |
|---|---|---|---|
| F1 | 1 | 1 | 4 |
| F2 | 1 | 1 | 10 |
| F3 | 1 | 1 | |
| F4 | 1 | 1 | 10 |
| F5 | 1 | 1 | 10 |
| F6 | 1 | 1 | 10 |
| F7 | 1 | 1 | |
| F8 | 1 | 1 | 1 |
| F9 | 1 | 1 | |
| F10 | | 1 | |
| F11 | | | |
| F12 | | | |
| F13 | | 1 | |
| Elapsed Time | 674 | 1159 | 1010 |
| User Mill Time | 636 | 1101 | 869 |
| User Mill Util | 94.4% | 95.0% | 86.0% |

Table 11.13 Batch Job Mixes

As a first measure of interactive performance the INT.JOB.JOB facility was used to measure the rate at which various types of job could be repeatedly run before the system saturated. In table 11.14 the results obtained are compared with the batch rates. They indicate that running the jobs interactively has only marginal effect on throughput, provided all the jobs fit into main store. If this is not the case, and if all the jobs are running at the same interactive priority, then each timeslice allotted to a job requires its working set to page back. To a first approximation CPU utilisation falls to

timeslice / (timeslice + page-in time) x 100%

It is at this point that the more sophisticated paging and scheduling modules of the MUSS would have been beneficial. Clearly the above results follow a pattern, and jobs with large mill times were not run with multiple users.

Next the peak rate at which the system could support file editing activities was established. These results are summarised in table 11.15. Clearly, this rate is a function of the size of the file and the size of the edit, and to a lesser extent, the number of active terminals. All are going faster than users would type. For example, with 25 users doing 100 line edits, to the source of F1, each user would have to type 28 commands/minute to keep up with the system.

|     | Batch Time | Batch Rate | 1 User | On-line Rate 10 Users | 20 Users |
|-----|-----------|-----------|--------|-----------|----------|
| F1  | 0:34 | 1.76  | 1.76  | --.-- | --.-- |
| F2  | 0:16 | 3.75  | 3.75  | 1.38  | 0.53  |
| F3  | 0:54 | 1.11  | 1.11  | --.-- | --.-- |
| F4  | 0:15 | 4.00  | 4.00  | --.-- | --.-- |
| F5  | 0:22 | 2.73  | 2.73  | 1.70  | 0.51  |
| F6  | 0:14 | 4.29  | 4.29  | --.-- | --.-- |
| F7  | 3:43 | 0.27  | 0.27  | --.-- | --.-- |
| F8  | 2:53 | 0.35  | 0.35  | --.-- | --.-- |
| F9  | 2:03 | 0.49  | 0.49  | 0.28  | --.-- |
| F10 | 7:51 | 0.13  | 0.13  | --.-- | --.-- |
| F11 | 0:01 | 70.00 | 70.00 | 62.78 | 57.69 |
| F12 | 0:03 | 18.95 | 18.95 | --.-- | --.-- |
| F13 | 0:14 | 4.29  | 4.29  | --.-- | --.-- |
| A1  | 0:01 | 70.00 | 70.00 | --.-- | --.-- |
| A2  | 0:03 | 18.95 | 18.95 | --.-- | --.-- |

Table 11.14 Saturation Level (Jobs/min)

|               | File F12 | | File F1 | | |
|---------------|-----|------|------|------|-----|
| Lines Changed | 1   | 10   | 1    | 10   | 100 |
| 1 User        | 120 | 62.8 | 14.2 | 13.1 | 7.1 |
| 10 Users      | 120 | 62.8 | 14.2 | 13.0 | 7.0 |
| 25 Users      | 100 | 62.8 | 14.2 | 13.0 | 7.0 |

Table 11.15 Repetition Rate (Edits/min)

The main interactive assessment was based on the following 'typical' scripts.

Script A - This represents beginner usage. The script first types a new file (in fact F11) containing three errors and then continues as follows

Edit to correct one error but makes a further error.
Edit again leaving one compile and one run time error.
Compile the program to receive an error report.
Edit to correct the error but makes another.
Compile again to receive an error report.
Edit to correct all but the run time error.
Compile now OK, therefore program is run but the answer is wrong.

Edit to correct this last error.
Compile - OK.
Run - OK.
Final file is saved.

This script is filled out with think times totalling 15 min.

Script B - This is a typical program development activity.

Edit an existing file (F12) making five alterations.
Edit again making one further alteration.
Compile.
Edit making two alterations.
Compile and run.
List last 11 lines of files.
Edit making one alteration.
Compile and run.

This script is filled out with think times totalling 10 min.

Table 11.16 shows the basic characteristics of these interactive scripts, where the think times and mill times are in units of one second.

|   | Think Time | Interactions | Edits | Comps | Runs | Mill Time |
|---|---|---|---|---|---|---|
| A | 900 | 47 | 5 | 4 | 2 | 1.70 |
| B | 600 | 24 | 4 | 3 | 2 | 6.55 |

Table 11.16 Script Characteristics

It is not easy to quantify interactive performance. We decided to compute the average time a user had to wait after typing a command before being invited to type the next command. This 'response time' is given in table 11.17 as the system is progressively loaded with users of type A and B. Maximum response times occurred when the interactions required significant mill time. These maxima were never more than a small multiple of the required mill times, but obviously could be large if the demands of the users became synchronised.

It was also of interest to explore the potential of the system for running a background of batch jobs with the 40 B-type users. This interactive load requires 25% of the mill time for execution of the user code, and places a heavy load on the system functions. Nevertheless when batch B3 was run simultaneously with it, a further 45% of mill time was utilised at user level in the batch jobs.

249

|   | 1 User | 20 Users | 40 Users |
|---|--------|----------|----------|
| A | 0.11 s | 0.16 s   | 0.28 s   |
| B | 0.38 s | 0.53 s   | 0.71 s   |

Table 11.17 Average Response Times

## 11.7 BEYOND MU5

In a research sense the authors feel that the MU5 Project has been very successful. We hope that this book conveys some of the experience to the reader. The design group responsible for MU5 has now turned its attention to the design of a successor. Some of the better ideas of MU5 will be carried forward, but the evaluation phase, together with current technological developments, have stimulated many new ideas.

# Appendix 1
## Summary of the Order Code

This appendix summarises the overall pattern of the order code. Some functions in MU5 differ from the general form overleaf, which should be taken only as a statement of the general characteristics.

COMPUTATIONAL AND STORE-TO-STORE ORDERS

| cr/f | STS | B | X | AU | ADC | AFL |
|---|---|---|---|---|---|---|
| 0 | XDO = | DO = | = | = | AOD= | DUMMY | =(32) |
| 1 | XD = | D = | = (-1) | DUMMY | DUMMY | AEX= | =(64) |
| 2 | STACK | D *= | *= | X*= | AOD*= | AEX*= | *= |
| 3 | XD => | D => | => | X=> | AOD=> | AEX=> | => |
| 4 | XDB = | DB = | + | + | A+ | DUMMY | + |
| 5 | XCHK | MDR | - | - | A- | DUMMY | - |
| 6 | SMOD | MOD | * | * | A* | DUMMY | * |
| 7 | XMOD | RMOD | / | / | DUMMY | DUMMY | / |
| 8 | SLGC | BLGC | ≠ | ≠ | ≠ | DUMMY | ≠ |
| 9 | SMVB | BMVB | V | V | V | DUMMY | V |
| 10 | DUMMY | BMVE | <-ARITH | <-ARITH | <-LOG | DUMMY | <-CIRC |
| 11 | SMVE | SMVE | & | & | & | DUMMY | & |
| 12 | TALU | DUMMY | Ω | Ω | Ω | AODCOMP | Ω |
| 13 | DUMMY | BSCN | COMP | COMP | COMP | COMP | COMP |
| 14 | SCMP | BCMP | CINC | =CONVX | DUMMY | UNPACK | =CONVA |
| 15 | SUB1 | SUB2 | Ø | Ø | DUMMY | DUMMY | Ø |

| 3 | 4 | 3 | 6 |
|---|---|---|---|
| cr | f | k | n |

```
k' = 0 or  k = 0  -  LITERAL  n is 6-bit signed integer.
           k = 1  -  IR       n defines internal register.
           k = 2  -  V32      Operand is accessed directly at
           k = 3  -  V64      (NB) + unsigned n; n is scaled for V32.
           k = 4  -  S[B]     Operand is accessed via a
           k = 5  -  S[B]     descriptor at (NB) + n, using
           k = 6  -  S[0]     B or 0 as an index.
k' = 1 or  k = 7  -  K        Extended Operand.
```

| 3 | 6 | 1 | 6 |
|---|---|---|---|
| 0 | f' | k' | n |

ORGANISATIONAL ORDERS

| f' | | | | | |
|---|---|---|---|---|---|
| 0 | -> | EXIT | DUMMY | DUMMY | |
| 4 | JUMP | RETURN | DUMMY | DUMMY | |
| 8 | XC0 | XC1 | XC2 | XC3 | |
| 12 | XC4 | XC5 | XC6 | STACK LINK | |
| 16 | MS = | DL = | SPM | SET LINK | |
| 20 | XNB = | SN = | XNB + | XNB => | |
| 24 | SF = | SF + | SF = NB + | SF => | |
| 28 | NB = | NB = SF + | NB + | NB => | |
| 32 | = 0 | ≠ 0 | ≥ 0 | < 0 | -> IF, |
| 36 | ≤ 0 | > 0 | OVERFLOW | Bn | -> IF, |
| 40 | = 0 | ≠ 0 | | < 0 | set Bn IF,* |
| 44 | ≤ 0 | > 0 | OVERFLOW | Bn | set Bn IF,* |
| 48 | 0 | Bn & X | Bn~ & X | X | |
| 52 | Bn & X~ | Bn | Bn ≠ X | Bn V X | |
| 56 | Bn~ & X~ | Bn ≡ X | Bn~ | Bn~ V X | |
| 60 | X~ | Bn V X~ | Bn~ V X~ | 1 | |

*The operand specifies the way in which Bn is set as follows, where T denotes the result of the test (= 0 for NO, = 1 for YES)

| Bn = 0 | Bn & T | Bn~ & T | Bn = T |
|---|---|---|---|
| Bn & T~ | DUMMY | Bn ≠ T | Bn V T |
| Bn~ & T~ | Bn ≡ T | Bn~ | Bn~ V T |
| Bn = T~ | Bn V T~ | Bn~ V T~ | Bn = 1 |

EXTENDED OPERANDS K

```
|3  |3  |
|K  |n' |
```

|                          |                    | n' = 0 | 16-bit   signed   |
|                          |                    | n' = 1 | 32-bit   signed   |
|                          |                    | n' = 2 | 64-bit            |
| K = 0/1                  | LITERAL            | n' = 3 | 64-bit            |
|                          | (qualified by n')  |        |                   |
|                          |                    | n' = 4 | 16-bit unsigned   |
|                          |                    | n' = 5 | 32-bit unsigned   |
|                          |                    | n' = 6 | 64-bit            |
|                          |                    | n' = 7 | 64-bit            |


| K = 2 | V32  | As for k above     | n' = 0 | SF  + 16-bit Name       |
| K = 3 | V64  | (qualified by n')  | n' = 1 |  0  + 16-bit Name       |
| K = 4 | S[B] |                    | n' = 2 | NB  + 16-bit Name       |
| K = 5 | S[B] |                    | n' = 3 | XNB + 16-bit Name       |
| K = 6 | S[0] |                    | n' = 4 | UNSTACK                 |
|       |      |                    | n' = 5 | D[] - use descriptor    |
|       |      |                    |        |          in DR          |

K = 7  V-store     (access is privileged)

INTERNAL REGISTER OPERANDS

The n bits define the internal register to be used.

```
    <-16-><-16-><-16-><-16->
|0  | MS | NB  |   CO      |        |32 |          |   B    |
|1  |          |   XNB     |        |33 |          |  BOD   |
|2  |          | SN  | NB  |        |34 |    Z     |        |
|3  |          | SN  | SF  |        |35 |                   |
|4  |          |   BN      |        |36 | BOD   |   B       |
|5  |                      |        |37 |                   |
|6  |                      |        |38 |                   |
|7  |                      |        |39 |                   |


|16 |        D             |        |48 |    AEX            |
|17 |       XD             |        |49 |                   |
|18 |        |  DT         |        |50 |                   |
|19 |        |  XDT        |        |51 |                   |
|20 |        |  DOD        |        |52 |                   |
|21 |                      |        |53 |                   |
|22 |                      |        |54 |                   |
|23 |                      |        |55 |                   |
```

252

DESCRIPTOR FORMATS

Type 0  -  General Vector

```
| T |  SIZE  | |US|BC|      BOUND      |  ORIGIN (IN BYTES) |
| 2 |   3   |1 |1 |1 |                  |                     |
            |    |  |  |
            |    |  |  | -- Bound Check Inhibit
            |    |  |
            |    |  | -- Scale/do not scale according to SIZE
            |    |
            |    | -- Read only
            |
             -- Size - 1, 4, 8, 16, 32 or 64 bits
```

Type 1  -  General String

```
| T |  SIZE  |     | BOUND/LENGTH |  ORIGIN (IN BYTES) |
| 2 |   3   |  3  |      24      |         32         |
            |      |
            |      | -- Spare
            |
             -- Size - 8 bits only
```

Type 2  -  Address Vector - Format identical with Type 0

Type 3  -  Miscellaneous Sub-types

```
| T |   SUBTYPE   | BOUND/LENGTH |      ORIGIN      |
| 2 |     6      |      24      |        32        |
            |                 |
            |                 | -- Use depends on sub-type
            |
            |     0    Real Address (Executive Mode Only)
            |     1    Read/Store Direct
            |     2    Read & Mark
            |     3    Indirect
            |   4-63  Procedure Calls
```

253

# Appendix 2
# Summary of the Operating System Commands

This appendix summarises the facilities of the MUSS Basic System.

JOB CONTROL

Job Format

    ***A JOB USER PASS TITLE T<time.limit> P<priority>

    commands

    ***Z

T and P parameters are optional. For interactive jobs, ***M replaces ***A.

Command format

    **NAME (param 1, param 2, ... )

** is optional and brackets and commas can be replaced by spaces. A parameter may be a string, decimal integer, or hexadecimal constant preceded by %.

```
NEW   NEW(File, Terminator)
OLD   OLD(File)
SAV   SAVE(File)
DEL   DELETE(File)
LD    LIST.DIR()
LF    LIST.FILE(File,Destination,Start,Finish)
ALG   ALGOL(File)
FOR   FORTRAN(File)
RUN   RUN(File)
DEF   DEFINE(File, Mode)
LIB   LIB(File)
STP   STOP(Reason)
RJ    RUN.JOB(File, Supervisor, Header)
KIL   KILL(Proc)
PS    PPC.SEQ(Mode)
```

254

## INPUT/OUTPUT FACILITIES

```
AIS     ASSIGN.INPUT.STREAM(File) Str
AOS     ASSIGN.OUTPUT.STREAM(File)Str
BO      BREAK.OUTPUT(Str)
CAP     CAPTION(String)
CDE     CHANGE.DEST(Str,Dest)
CI      CURRENT.INPUT()Str
CO      CURRENT.OUTPUT()Str
DI      DEFINE.INPUT(Str, File, Mode)
DO      DEFINE.OUTPUT(Str, File, Mode, Lines, Sections)
EL      ECHO.LINE()
IB      IN.BACKSPACE(No)
IC      IN.CH() Char
ICL     IN.C.LIT() Char Literal
ICS     IN.C.STR(String Dest)
IH      IN.HEX() Hex literal
II      IN.I() Int
IIO     INIT.IO()
IL      IN.LINE() Page/Line
IM      IN.MODE() Mode
INA     IN.NAME() Char literal
IS      IN.SOURCE(Source)
IST     IN.STR(String Dest)
NL      NEWLINES(No)
NC      NEXT.CH() Char
OC      OUT.CH (Char)
ODA     OUT.DATE()
OFN     OUT.FN(File)
OHD     OUT.HDR(Header)
OHX     OUT.HEX(Hex)
OI      OUT.I(No, Field Width)
OL      OUT.LINE(Page/Line)
OM      OUT.MODE(Str) Mode
ON      OUT.NAME(Name)
OP      OUT.PROG(Seg, First Byte, Last Byte)
OR      OUT.REGS()
OSS     OUT.S.STATS(Type)
OS      OUT.STACK(Start Addr, Finish Addr)
OTI     OUT.TIME()
PR      PROMPT(String)
RI      RELEASE.INPUT(Str)
RO      RELEASE.OUTPUT(Str)
SH      SELECT.HEADER()
SI      SELECT.INPUT(Str)
SO      SELECT.OUTPUT(Str)
STE     SELECT.TEXT()
SPS     SPACES(No)
```

EDITING FACILITIES

```
ED     ED(Input, Output)
       S<pos>      SKIP   Skip to start of line
       C<pos>      COPY   Copy to start of line
       I<str>      INSERT Insert string at current position
       B<str>      BEFORE Copy up to start of string
       A<str>      AFTER  Copy up to end of string
       D<str>      DELETE Delete next occurrence of string
       W           WRITE  Print current Line
       R           RESET  Reset position
       M<file>     MERGE  Select new input file
       E           EXIT   Exit from editor
       Q           QUIT   Abandon edit
```

DOCUMENTATION FACILITIES

```
FL     FLIP(File,Level,Mode,Label,Jump,Cjump)
DR     DRAW(File,Level,Height,Width)
PIC    PIC(Input,Output,Jobtext,Width)
PL     PLOT(Input,Output)
TX     TEXT(Input,Output,Devtype)
```

VIRTUAL STORE CONTROL

```
CSE    CREATE.SEGMENT(Seg,Size,Page Size) Seg,Size
CSI    CHANGE.SIZE(Seg,Size)
INT    INTERCHANGE(Seg,Seg)
CA     CHANGE.ACCESS(Seg,Access)
RSE    RELEASE.SEGMENT(Seg)
PI     PAGE.IN(Seg,Page,Mode)
```

FILE CONTROL

```
FIL    FILE(File,Seg,Access)
OFI    OPEN.FILE(File,Seg,Access) Seg
DEL    DELETE(File)
CAT    CATALOGUE() No of Entries, Seg
ODI    OPEN.DIR(User,Pass)
RF     RENAME.FILE(File,File)
RDR    READ.DIR () User, Password
```

INTER-PROCESS COMMUNICATION

```
SCS    SET.CH.STATUS(Ch,Status,PID)
WAI    WAIT(Ch, Time)
LUP    LOOK.UP.PROCESS(Name)SPN,PID,Ch
SM     SEND.MESSAGE(Message,Dest,Ch,Seg,Access)
RM     READ.MESSAGE(Message,Source,Ch,Seg)Seg,Access,UID
```

## PROCESS CONTROL

| | |
|---|---|
| CP | CREATE.PROCESS(Proc,User,Pass,Seg Limit,CPU Limit, Seg 0,Priority,Term Ch)SPN,PID |
| SPR | SUSPEND.PROCESS(SPN,PID) |
| FP | FREE.PROCESS(SPN,PID) |
| TP | TERMINATE.PROCESS(SPN,PID,Reason) |
| KIL | KILL(Proc) |
| RST | READ.STATUS(SPN,PID) Status |
| RP | READ.PARAMETER(Param) Value |
| FI | FORCE.INT(SPN,PID,Reason) |
| STI | SET.TIMER(Time) |
| RES | RESCHEDULE(SPN,PID,Priority) |

## ERROR HANDLING

| | |
|---|---|
| STR | SET.TRAP(Trap,Addr) |
| ET | ENTER.TRAP(Trap,Reason) |
| SIT | SET.INT.TRAP(Trap,Reason) |
| SR | SET.RESTART(Addr) |
| GR | GO.RESTART() |
| TR | TRAP(Trap,Reason) |
| OUF | OUT.F(No, Message, Page/Line) |
| OUM | OUT.M(No,Message, Page/Line) |

257

REFERENCES

1. S. H. Lavington, *History of Manchester Computers*, (NCC, 1975).

2. T. Kilburn, D. Morris, J. S. Rohl and F. H. Sumner, 'A System Design Proposal', in *Information Processing 68* (North Holland, Amsterdam, 1969).

3. D. Aspinall, D. J. Kinniment and D. B. G. Edwards, 'Associative Memories in Large Computer Systems', in *Information Processing 68* (North Holland, Amsterdam, 1969).

4. J. K. Iliffe, *Basic Machine Principles*, (MacDonald, London, 1968).

5. P. J. Denning, 'Virtual Memory', *Computing Surveys*, 2, No. 3, Sept. 1970.

6. E. I. Organick, *The Multics System*, (MIT Press, Cambridge, Mass., 1972).

7. D. J. Kinniment and D. B. G. Edwards, 'Circuit Technology in a Large Computer System', *IERE Conference Proceedings* No. 25, (London, 1972).

8. D. Aspinall, D. J. Kinniment and D. B. G. Edwards, 'An Integrated Associative Memory Matrix', in *Information Processing 68* (North Holland, Amsterdam, 1969).

9. H. J. Kahn and J. W. R. May, 'The use of Logic Simulation in the design of a Large Computer System', *IERE Conference Proceedings* No. 25 (London, 1972).

10. D. J. Kinniment and J. V. Woods, 'Synchronisation and Arbitration Circuits in Digital Systems', *Proc. IEE*, 123 (1976) 961-966.

11. D. B. G. Edwards, A. E. Whitehouse, L. E. M. Warburton and I. Watson, 'The MU5 Disc System', *IEE Conference Proceedings* No. 121 (London, 1974).

258

12. R. N. Ibbett, 'The MU5 Instruction Pipeline', _Computer Journal_, 15, 1972; also in _Best Computer Papers 1973_ (Auerbach, Philadelphia, 1973).

13. 'Control Data 7600 / Cyber 70 Model 76 Computer Systems - Hardware Reference Manual' (Control Data Corp., Minnesota, 1975).

14. L. A. Taylor, 'Instruction Accessing in High Speed Computers', M.Sc. Thesis, University of Manchester, 1969.

15. F. H. Sumner, 'MU5 - An Assessment of the Design', in _Information Processing 74_ (North Holland, Amsterdam, 1974).

16. R. N. Ibbett, E. C. Phillips and D. B. G. Edwards, 'Control of the MU5 Instruction Pipeline', _IERE Conference Proceedings_ No. 25, (London, 1972).

17. G. R. Burke, 'The Design of a Central Processor Highway System', M.Sc. Thesis, University of Manchester, 1969.

18. J. Standeven, S. H. B. Lanyado and D. B. G. Edwards, 'The MU5 Secondary Operand Unit', _IERE Conference Proceedings_ No. 25 (London, 1972).

19. J. V. Woods and F. H. Sumner, 'Operand Accessing in a Pipelined Computer System', _IEE Conference Proceedings_ No. 121 (London, 1974).

20. R. N. Ibbett and M. A. Husband, 'The MU5 Name Store', _Computer Journal_, 20 (1977) 227-231.

21. W. J. Khaja, 'The Implementation of the Name Store and Associated Replacement Algorithms in the MU5 Computer', Ph.D. Thesis, University of Manchester, 1971.

22. A. E. Knowles, 'The Implementation of Virtual Storage in the MU5 Multiprocessor Computer Complex', Ph.D. Thesis, University of Manchester, 1975.

23. B. J. Parsons, 'The Design of the Store Access Control System for the MU5 Computer', M.Sc. Thesis, University of Manchester, 1971.

24. S. H. Lavington, G. Thomas and D. B. G. Edwards, 'The MU5 Multicomputer Communication System', _Trans. IEEE_, C-26 (1977) 19-28.

25. J. B. Gosling, 'Review of High-speed Addition Techniques',

Proc. IEE, 118 (1971) 29-35.

26. D. J. Kinniment and G. B. Steven, 'A Sequential State Binary Adder', Proc. IEE, 117 (1971) 1211-1218.

27. D. W. Sweeney, 'An Analysis of Floating-point Addition', IBM Systems Journal, 4 (1965) 31-42.

28. J. B. Gosling, 'Design of Large High-speed Multiplier Units', Proc. IEE, 118 (1971) 499-506.

29. S. F. Anderson, J. G. Earle, R. E. Goldschmidt and D. M. Powers, 'The IBM System/360 Model 91 Floating-point Execution Unit', IBM Journal of R and D, 11 (1971) 34-53.

30. 'Cray-1 Computer System Reference Manual (Cray Research Inc., Minneapolis, 1976).

31. P. C. Capon, R. N. Ibbett and C. R. C. B. Parker, 'The Implementation of Record Processing in MU5', IEE Conference Proceedings No. 121 (London, 1974).

32. R. A. Brooker, I. R. MacCallum, D. Morris and J. S. Rohl, 'The Compiler Compiler', Annual Review in Automatic Programming 3 (Pergamon, Oxford, 1963).

33. D. Morris, I. R. Wilson and P. C. Capon, 'A System Program Generator', Computer Journal, 13 (1970) 248-254.

34. P. C. Capon, D. Morris, J. S. Rohl, and I. R. Wilson, 'The MU5 Compiler Target Language and Autocode', Computer Journal, 15 (1972) 109-112.

35. J. Strong, J. Wegstein, A. Tritter, J. Olsztyn, O. Mock and T. Steel, 'The Problem of Programming Communications with Changing Machines'. Communications of the ACM, 1 (1958) 8.12-8.18.

36. T. Kilburn, D. J. Howarth, R. B. Payne and F. H. Sumner, 'The Manchester University Atlas Operating System - Part 1', Computer Journal, 4 (1961) 3-10.

37. D. Morris, F. H. Sumner and M. T. Wyld, 'An Appraisal of the Atlas Supervisor', Proc. ACM (1967).

38. E. W. Dijkstra, 'Cooperating Sequential Processes', in Programming Languages (Academic Press, New York, 1968).

39. A. J. Bernstein, G. D. Detlefson and R. H. Kerr, 'Process Control and Communications in a General Purpose Operating

System', A.C.M. Symposium Operating Systems Principles (Princeton University Press, 1969).

40. S. H. Lavington and A. E. Knowles, 'Assessing the Power of an Order Code', in Information Processing 77 (North Holland, Amsterdam, 1977).

41. J. Heinhold and F. L. Bauer (eds), 'Fachbegriffe der Programmier ungstechnik, Ausgearbeitet vom Fachausschutz Programmieren der Gesellschaft fur Angewandte Mathematik und Mechanik' (G.A.M.M.), (Munich, 1972).

42. R. S. Scowen, 'Qickersort, Algorithm 271', Communications of the ACM, 8 (1965) 669-670.

43. H. J. Curnow and B. A. Wichmann, 'A Synthetic Benchmark', Computer Journal, 19 (1976) 43-49.

44. C. H. Cheetham, 'Oxford University Benchmark Test' (Oxford University Report, Dec. 1969).

45. P. H. Hughes, 'University Computer Benchmark Report: Atlas/6600/1108' (University of London Atlas Computing Service Report, Aug. 1967).

46. M. A. Husband, R. N. Ibbett and R. Phillips, 'The MU5 Computer Monitoring System', Proc. European Computing Conference on Computer Performance Evaluation (London, 1976).

47. N. A. Yannacopoulos, R. N. Ibbett and R. W. Holgate, 'Performance Measurements of the MU5 Primary Instruction Pipeline', in Information Processing 77 (North Holland, Amsterdam, 1977).

48. R. A. Brooker, D. Morris and J. S. Rohl, 'Experience with the Compiler Compiler', Computer Journal, 9 (1967) 345-349.

49. R. Phillips, 'A Portable Fortran System for MUSS', M.Sc. Thesis, University of Manchester, 1978.

# INDEX